高等职业教育理实一体化系列教材·新能源汽车技术

# 新能源汽车专业英语

主　编　王万君　王丽丽　郭医军
副主编　林　法　董艳艳　唐国锋
　　　　焦安霞
参　编　陈　健　颜丙云　刘　强
　　　　王　晶　李时蕾

北京理工大学出版社
BEIJING INSTITUTE OF TECHNOLOGY PRESS

## 内容简介

本书介绍了新能源汽车的发展史以及类型，分析了纯电动汽车、混合动力电动汽车、插电式混合动力电动汽车、燃料电池电动汽车的结构原理，对新能源汽车的能量储存装置、储能系统的管理、电驱动系统、电动汽车的充电系统也做了较系统的阐述。在进行内容讲解时，作者能从读者的角度出发，论述层层递进，详略得当，概念和原理详细、精辟，使读者对知识有一个整体的认识和把握。本书内容新颖丰富、系统性强、条理清晰，是一本通俗易懂、不可多得的英文参考书籍。

本书适用于高等职业院校的新能源汽车技术、新能源汽车运用与维修等汽车类相关专业的专业英语教学，可作为应用型本科院校、中职和培训班的专业英语教材，也可供新能源汽车行业的工程技术人员和车辆工程、汽车类相关专业技术人员学习专业英语之用。

**版权专有　侵权必究**

### 图书在版编目（CIP）数据

新能源汽车专业英语 / 王万君，王丽丽，郭医军主编. —北京：北京理工大学出版社，2021.3（2021.8 重印）
ISBN 978-7-5682-9601-4

Ⅰ. ①新… Ⅱ. ①王… ②王… ③郭… Ⅲ. ①新能源－汽车工程－英语 Ⅳ. ①U469.7

中国版本图书馆 CIP 数据核字（2021）第 043003 号

| | |
|---|---|
| 出版发行 / 北京理工大学出版社有限责任公司 | |
| 社　　址 / 北京市海淀区中关村南大街 5 号 | |
| 邮　　编 / 100081 | |
| 电　　话 /（010）68914775（总编室） | |
| 　　　　　（010）82562903（教材售后服务热线） | |
| 　　　　　（010）68944723（其他图书服务热线） | |
| 网　　址 / http://www.bitpress.com.cn | |
| 经　　销 / 全国各地新华书店 | |
| 印　　刷 / 唐山富达印务有限公司 | |
| 开　　本 / 787 毫米 × 1092 毫米　1/16 | |
| 印　　张 / 15 | 责任编辑 / 武丽娟 |
| 字　　数 / 350 千字 | 文案编辑 / 武丽娟 |
| 版　　次 / 2021 年 3 月第 1 版　2021 年 8 月第 2 次印刷 | 责任校对 / 周瑞红 |
| 定　　价 / 46.00 元 | 责任印制 / 李志强 |

图书出现印装质量问题，请拨打售后服务热线，本社负责调换

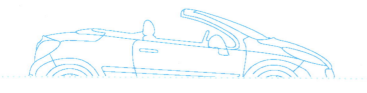

# 前言

  内燃机汽车的发展是现代工业技术最重大的成就之一。然而，高度发展的汽车工业和大量汽车的应用，在全球已经引发了严重的环境问题和能源危机。大气质量的恶化、全球变暖和石油资源的匮乏已成为人们生活中必须面对的问题。日益严格的排放和燃料效率的标准促进了安全、清洁和高效车辆的迅猛发展，以纯电动汽车、混合动力电动汽车和燃料电池电动汽车为代表的新能源汽车取得了重大进展。大力发展和推广新能源汽车，对于强化创新驱动、推进绿色低碳发展和产业升级具有重要意义。为加快培育和发展节能与新能源汽车产业，国务院印发了《节能与新能源汽车产业发展规划（2012—2020年）》，规划中明确指出新能源汽车发展目标是到2020年，纯电动汽车和插电式混合动力电动汽车生产能力达200万辆、累计产销量超过500万辆，燃料电池电动汽车、车用氢能源产业与国际同步发展。围绕实现制造强国的战略目标，国务院颁发《中国制造2025》行动纲领，其中提出将节能与新能源汽车作为大力推动的十大重点领域之一，推动自主品牌节能与新能源汽车同国际先进水平接轨。为了配合和推动我国新能源汽车技术的深入研究和人才队伍建设，我国目前迫切需要一系列与新能源汽车相关的优质参考资料和教材，本书涵盖了大部分有关新能源汽车的研究成果，使用了大量图文，论述详细，生动形象，易于读者接受。

  本书介绍了新能源汽车的发展史以及类型，分析了纯电动汽车、混合动力电动汽车、插电式混合动力电动汽车、燃料电池电动汽车的结构原理，对新能源汽车的能量储存装置、储能系统的管理、电驱动系统、电动汽车的充电系统也做了较全面系统的阐述，展示了新能源汽车技术的专业英语知识。

  全书共6章，第1章讨论了与现代运输工具相关的社会和环境问题，主要包括与现代运输工具发展相伴随的空气污染、全球变暖以及石油资源枯竭问题，还简要回顾了电动汽车、混合动力电动汽车和燃料电池电动汽车的发展历史。

  第2章介绍了新能源汽车类型，主要分析了纯电动汽车、混合动力电动汽车、插电式混合动力电动汽车、燃料电池电动汽车的结构组成、工作原理，探讨目前新能源汽车发展状况，探究未来发展趋势。

  第3、4章讨论了能量储存装置及燃料电池和储能系统的管理，电池是可替代燃油车辆开发的关键因素，电池成本和使用寿命等决定了新能源汽车的市场化进程，储能系统管理不仅要保证电池可安全可靠使用，而且要充分发挥电池的能力并延长使用寿命。

第5章讨论了电驱动系统，介绍了不同类型电动机及其基本工作原理，也集中讨论了功率电子变换器。

第6章讨论了电动汽车的充电系统、车辆和公用电网的接口技术、车辆与车辆之间的能量传递。

本书由烟台汽车工程职业学院王万君、王丽丽和郭医军担任主编，林法、董艳艳、唐国锋和焦安霞担任副主编，参与编写的还有陈健、颜丙云、刘强、王晶、李时蕾等老师。

本书在编写的过程中查阅了大量书籍、文献和资料，应用了一些网上资料和参考文献中的部分内容，在此向其作者表示深切的谢意！

由于编者水平有限，书中难免有错误与疏漏之处，恳请读者批评指正。

编　者

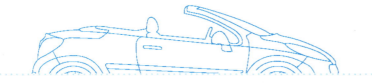 

## Chapter 1    Introduction to New Energy Vehicles　　001

  1.1  Environmental Impact　　001
      1.1.1  Air Pollution　　003
      1.1.2  Global Warming　　005
      1.1.3  Petroleum Resources　　008
  1.2  Sustainable Transportation　　012
  1.3  EV History　　015
      1.3.1  The Early Years　　015
      1.3.2  1970s　　018
      1.3.3  1980s and 1990s　　020
      1.3.4  EV Market　　023
  1.4  History of HEVs　　027
  1.5  History of Fuel Cell Vehicles　　030

## Chapter 2    New Energy Vehicle Types　　033

  2.1  Electric Vehicles　　033
      2.1.1  Configuration of Electric Vehicles　　033
      2.1.2  Conceptual Illustration of a General EV Configuration　　036
      2.1.3  System Level Diagram of an EV　　040
  2.2  Hybrid Electric Vehicles　　045
      2.2.1  Parallel Hybrid　　045
      2.2.2  Series Hybrid　　048
      2.2.3  Series-parallel Hybrid　　050
      2.2.4  Complex Hybrid　　052
  2.3  Plug-in Hybrid Electric Vehicle (PHEV)　　055
      2.3.1  Why PHEV　　055

2.3.2　Constituents of a PHEV ······ 057
 2.4　Fuel Cell Vehicles (FCVs) ······ 060

## Chapter 3　Energy Storages ······ 064

 3.1　Electrochemical Batteries ······ 066
 3.2　Battery Characterization ······ 068
 3.3　Battery Technologies ······ 072
  3.3.1　Lead-Acid Battery ······ 073
  3.3.2　Nickel-Based Batteries ······ 076
  3.3.3　Lithium-Based Batteries ······ 079
 3.4　Supercapacitors and Ultracapacitors ······ 080
 3.5　Flywheels ······ 083
 3.6　Fuel Cells ······ 087
  3.6.1　Operating Principles of Fuel Cells ······ 087
  3.6.2　Fuel Cell Technologies ······ 090

## Chapter 4　Management of Energy Storage Systems ······ 094

 4.1　Introduction ······ 094
 4.2　Battery Management ······ 096
  4.2.1　Parameter Monitoring ······ 098
  4.2.2　Calculation of SOC ······ 103
  4.2.3　Fault and Safety Protection ······ 107
  4.2.4　Charge Management ······ 109
 4.3　Battery Cell Balancing ······ 112

## Chapter 5　Electric Propulsion Systems ······ 117

 5.1　Electric Motors ······ 119
  5.1.1　Advantage of Electric Motors ······ 119
  5.1.2　Classification of Electric Motors ······ 121
 5.2　Electronic Structure ······ 129
 5.3　Electronic Converters ······ 130
  5.3.1　Components of Electronic Converters ······ 130
  5.3.2　Rectifiers ······ 132
  5.3.3　Choppers ······ 135
  5.3.4　Inverters ······ 137

## Chapter 6　Recharging Systems for Electric Vehicles ······ 140

 6.1　What Is Battery Charging ······ 141

6.2　The Various Types of Chargers ……………………………………… 143
6.3　Recharging Efficiency ……………………………………………… 151
6.4　Recharging in Complete Safety …………………………………… 153
6.5　Charging Methods ………………………………………………… 155
　　6.5.1　Constant Voltage Charge ……………………………………… 156
　　6.5.2　Constant Current Charge ……………………………………… 156
　　6.5.3　Taper Current Charge ………………………………………… 156
　　6.5.4　Pulse Charge …………………………………………………… 156
　　6.5.5　Reflex Charge ………………………………………………… 157
　　6.5.6　Float Charge …………………………………………………… 157
6.6　Termination Methods ……………………………………………… 160
　　6.6.1　Time …………………………………………………………… 160
　　6.6.2　Voltage ………………………………………………………… 161
　　6.6.3　Voltage Drop（d$V$/d$T$）………………………………………… 161
　　6.6.4　Current ………………………………………………………… 161
　　6.6.5　Temperature …………………………………………………… 161

## 第1章　新能源汽车概述 ……………………………………………… 165
1.1　环境影响 …………………………………………………………… 165
　　1.1.1　大气污染 ……………………………………………………… 165
　　1.1.2　全球变暖 ……………………………………………………… 166
　　1.1.3　石油资源 ……………………………………………………… 167
1.2　可持续发展的交通运输 …………………………………………… 169
1.3　电动汽车的发展史 ………………………………………………… 170
　　1.3.1　早期 …………………………………………………………… 170
　　1.3.2　20世纪70年代 ………………………………………………… 171
　　1.3.3　20世纪80年代和90年代 ……………………………………… 172
　　1.3.4　电动汽车的市场前景 ………………………………………… 173
1.4　混合动力电动汽车的历史 ………………………………………… 174
1.5　燃料电池电动汽车的历史 ………………………………………… 176

## 第2章　新能源汽车类型 ……………………………………………… 177
2.1　纯电动汽车 ………………………………………………………… 177
　　2.1.1　纯电动汽车结构 ……………………………………………… 177
　　2.1.2　EV结构的概念性图示 ………………………………………… 178
　　2.1.3　EV系统级原理图 ……………………………………………… 180

## 2.2 混合动力电动汽车 ·············· 182
### 2.2.1 并联式混合 ·············· 182
### 2.2.2 串联式混合 ·············· 183
### 2.2.3 混联式混合 ·············· 184
### 2.2.4 复联式混合 ·············· 185
## 2.3 插电式混合动力电动汽车 ·············· 186
### 2.3.1 为什么需要插电式混合动力电动汽车 ·············· 186
### 2.3.2 插电式混合动力电动汽车的结构 ·············· 187
## 2.4 燃料电池电动汽车 ·············· 188

# 第 3 章 能量储存装置 ·············· 190
## 3.1 电化学蓄电池组 ·············· 190
## 3.2 电池特性参数 ·············· 191
## 3.3 蓄电池技术 ·············· 193
### 3.3.1 铅酸蓄电池 ·············· 194
### 3.3.2 镍基蓄电池 ·············· 194
### 3.3.3 锂基蓄电池 ·············· 195
## 3.4 超大容量电容器和超级电容器 ·············· 196
## 3.5 飞 轮 ·············· 197
## 3.6 燃料电池 ·············· 198
### 3.6.1 燃料电池的工作原理 ·············· 198
### 3.6.2 燃料电池技术 ·············· 199

# 第 4 章 储能系统的管理 ·············· 201
## 4.1 简 介 ·············· 201
## 4.2 电池管理 ·············· 201
### 4.2.1 参数监测 ·············· 202
### 4.2.2 SOC 的计算 ·············· 205
### 4.2.3 故障和安全保护 ·············· 206
### 4.2.4 充电管理 ·············· 207
## 4.3 电池单体均衡 ·············· 208

# 第 5 章 电驱动系统 ·············· 211
## 5.1 电动机 ·············· 212
### 5.1.1 电动机应用优势 ·············· 212
### 5.1.2 电动机的分类 ·············· 212
## 5.2 电气结构 ·············· 215

5.3 功率电子变换器 ········· 216
　　5.3.1 功率电子元件 ········· 216
　　5.3.2 整流器 ········· 216
　　5.3.3 斩波器 ········· 217
　　5.3.4 逆变器 ········· 218

# 第6章　电动汽车的充电系统 ········· 219

6.1 什么是电池的充电 ········· 219
6.2 不同类型的充电器 ········· 220
6.3 充电效率 ········· 223
6.4 充电的安全问题 ········· 224
6.5 电池的充电方式 ········· 225
　　6.5.1 恒压充电 ········· 225
　　6.5.2 恒流充电 ········· 225
　　6.5.3 锥电流充电 ········· 225
　　6.5.4 脉冲充电 ········· 225
　　6.5.5 反射充电 ········· 226
　　6.5.6 浮压充电 ········· 226
6.6 充电的终止方式 ········· 226
　　6.6.1 时间 ········· 227
　　6.6.2 电压 ········· 227
　　6.6.3 电压降（dV/dT) ········· 227
　　6.6.4 电流 ········· 227
　　6.6.5 温度 ········· 228

**参考文献** ········· 229

# Chapter 1

## Introduction to New Energy Vehicles

### 1.1 Environmental Impact

**Text**（课文）

Modern society relies heavily on fossil fuel-based transportation for economic and social development freely-moving goods and people. The issues related to this trend become evident because transportation relies heavily on oil. Not only are the oil resources on Earth limited, but also the emissions from burning oil products have led to climate change, poor urban air quality and political conflict. Thus, global energy system and environmental problems have emerged, which can be attributed to a large extent on personal transportation.

Personal transportation offers people the freedom to go wherever and whenever they want. However, this freedom of choice creates a conflict, leading to growing concerns about the environment and concerns about the sustainability of human use of natural resources. The large number of automobiles in use around the world has caused and continues to cause serious problems for environment and human life. Air pollution, global warming, and the rapid depletion of the Earth's petroleum resources are now problems of paramount concern.

**New words and expressions**（单词和短语）

**1. New words**（单词）

| | |
|---|---|
| environment [ɪnˈvaɪrənmənt] | n. 环境，外界；周围，围绕；工作平台；（运行）环境 |
| fossil [ˈfɒsl] | n. 化石；僵化的事物；老顽固，食古不化的人；习语中保存的旧词<br>adj. 化石的；陈腐的，守旧的 |
| fuel [ˈfjuːəl] | n. 燃料；（为身体提供能量的）食物；（维持、增加感情的）刺激物；<br>vt. 给……加燃料，给……加油；激起； |
| conflict [kənˈflɪkt] | n. 冲突；争斗；矛盾；抵触 碰撞 vi. 不一致；矛盾；冲突 |
| paramount [ˈpærəmaʊnt] | a. 最重要的；至高无上的；卓越的；最高权力的 |

## 2. Expressions（短语）

| | |
|---|---|
| not only … but also … | 不仅……而且…… |
| oil resources | 石油资源 |
| burning oil products | 燃油制品 |
| lead to | 导致 |
| climate change | 气候改变 |
| attributed to | 归咎于 |
| natural resources | 自然资源 |
| continues to | 持续 |
| human life | 人类生存 |
| air pollution | 空气污染 |
| global warming | 全球变暖 |
| petroleum resources | 石油资源 |
| rapid depletion | 迅速递减 |

### Notes to the text（难点解析）

★1. Modern society relies heavily on fossil fuel-based transportation for economic and social development freely moving goods and people. 在现代社会，交通运输便捷地运送货物和人员，促进了经济和社会的发展，但它却极大地依赖于化石燃料。

★2. The large number of automobiles in use around the world has caused and continues to cause serious problems for environment and human life. 全世界大量汽车的应用，已经产生并正在继续引发严重的环境与人类生存问题。

### Exercises（练习）

◆1. Translate the following passages (expressions) into Chinese（英译汉）

（1）Personal transportation offers people the freedom to go wherever and whenever they want.

（2）Global energy system and environmental problems have emerged, which can be attributed to a large extent on personal transportation.

（3）fossil fuel

◆2. Translate the following passages (expressions) into English（汉译英）

（1）石油资源

（2）空气污染

（3）这种自由的选择引发了一些冲突，使人们越来越担心环境问题和自然资源的可持续使用问题。

◆3. Fill in the blanks with the suitable words according to the text

Not only are the _____ on Earth limited, but also the _____ from burning oil products have led to _____, poor urban air quality, and political conflict. Thus, global energy system and environmental problems have emerged, which can be attributed to a large extent on _____.

◆4. Directions: Answer the following questions briefly according to the text

(1) What are now problems of paramount concern?

## Reading material（阅读材料）

There are about 800 million cars in the world and about 250 million motor vehicles on the road in the United States according to the US Department of Transportation's estimate. In 2009, China overtook the United States to become the world's largest auto maker and auto market, with output and sales respectively hitting 13.79 and 13.64 million units in that year. With further urbanization, industrialization, and globalization, the trend of rapid increase in the number of personal automobiles worldwide is inevitable.

### 1.1.1 Air Pollution

## Text（课文）

At present, all vehicles rely on the combustion of hydrocarbon (HC) fuels to derive the energy necessary for their propulsion. Combustion is a reaction between the fuel and the air that releases heat and combustion products. The heat is converted to mechanical power by an engine and the combustion products are released to the atmosphere. An HC is a chemical compound with molecules made up of carbon and hydrogen atoms. Ideally, the combustion of an HC yields only carbon dioxide and water, which do not harm the environment.

Actually, the combustion of HC fuel in combustion engines is never ideal. There are other emissions from conventional fossil fuel-powered vehicles, including carbon monoxide (CO) and nitrogen oxides (NO and $NO_2$, or $NO_x$) from burning gasoline; hydrocarbons or volatile organic compounds (VOCs) from evaporated, unburned fuel; and sulfur oxide and particulate matter (soot) from burning diesel fuel. These emissions cause air pollution and ultimately affect human and animal health.

## New words and expressions（单词和短语）

### 1. New words（单词）

| combustion [kəmˈbʌstʃən] | n. 燃烧；激动；大骚动；氧化 |
| hydrocarbon (HC) [ˈhaɪdrəʊˈkɑːbən] | n. 碳氢化合物 |
| propulsion [prəˈpʌlʃn] | n. 推进；推进力 |

| gasoline [ˈgæsəliːn; ˌgæsəˈliːn] | n. 汽油 |
| --- | --- |
| reaction [rɪˈækʃən] | n. 反应；反动；保守；反进步 |
| atmosphere [ˈætməsfɪə] | n. 大气；空气；气氛；气压；气压单位；包围天体的气体；环境；（艺术的）风格，基调 |
| molecul [ˈmɔlɪkjuːl] | n. 分子 |

## 2. Expressions（短语）

| at present | 目前 |
| --- | --- |
| rely on | 依靠 |
| combustion engine | 内燃机 |
| between … and … | ……与……之间 |
| combustion products | 燃烧生成物 |
| convert to | 转换为 |
| mechanical power | 机械功率 |
| be made up | 组成 |
| carbon dioxide | 二氧化碳 |
| carbon monoxide | 一氧化碳 |
| harm the environment | 损害环境 |

### Notes to the text（难点解析）

★1. At present, all vehicles rely on the combustion of hydrocarbon (HC) fuels to derive the energy necessary for their propulsion. 目前，所有车辆依靠碳氢化合物类燃料的燃烧，以获得其驱动力所必需的能量。

★2. The heat is converted to mechanical power by an engine and the combustion products are released to the atmosphere. 热量经发动机转换为机械功率，而燃烧生成物则排入大气。

★3. There are other emissions from conventional fossil fuel-powered vehicles, including carbon monoxide (CO) and nitrogen oxides (NO and $NO_2$, or $NO_x$) from burning gasoline; hydrocarbons or volatile organic compounds (VOCs) from evaporated, unburned fuel; and sulfur oxide and particulate matter (soot) from burning diesel fuel. 以传统化石燃料为能量源的车辆还会产生其他的排放物，包括汽油燃烧产生的一氧化碳（CO）和氮氧化物（NO、$NO_2$ 和 $NO_x$）、来自蒸发和未完全燃烧气体中的碳氢化合物和挥发性有机化合物（VOCs）、柴油燃烧产生的硫氧化物和颗粒物（炭烟）等。

## Exercises（练习）

◆1. Translate the following passages (expressions) into Chinese（英译汉）

(1) combustion engine

(2) harm the environment

(3) Combustion is a reaction between the fuel and the air that releases heat and combustion products.

◆2. Translate the following passages (expressions) into English（汉译英）

(1) 机械功率

(2) 二氧化碳

(3) 热量经发动机转换为机械功率，而燃烧生成物则排入大气。

(4) 事实上，在热力发动机内碳氢化合物类燃料的燃烧绝非理想化的。

◆3. Fill in the blanks with the suitable words according to the text

An HC is a _____ compound with molecules made up of _____ and hydrogen atoms. Ideally, the combustion of an HC yields only _____ and _____, which do not harm the _____.

◆4. Directions: Answer the following questions briefly according to the text

(1) What is combustion?

(2) What will cause air pollution and ultimately affect human and animal health?

## Reading material（阅读材料）

Indeed, green plants "digest" carbon dioxide by photosynthesis. Carbon dioxide is a necessary ingredient in vegetal life. Animals do not suffer from breathing carbon dioxide unless its concentration in air is such that oxygen is almost absent.

 ### 1.1.2 Global Warming

### Text（课文）

Global warming is a result of the "greenhouse effect" induced by the presence of carbon dioxide and other gases, such as methane, in the atmosphere. These gases trap the Sun's infrared radiation reflected by the ground, thus retaining the energy in the atmosphere and increasing the temperature. An increased Earth temperature results in major ecological damages to its ecosystems and in many natural disasters that affect human populations.

Considering the ecological damages induced by global warming, the disappearance of some endangered species is a concern because this destabilizes the natural resources that feed some populations. There are also concerns about the migration of some species from warm seas to previously colder northern seas, where they can potentially destroy indigenous species and the economies that live off those species. This may be happening in the Mediterranean Sea, where barracudas from the Red Sea have been observed.

Natural disasters command our attention more than ecological disasters because of the amplitude of the damages they cause. Global warming is believed to have induced meteorological phenomena such as "El Niño," which disturbs the South Pacific region and regularly causes tornadoes, inundations, and dryness. The melting of the polar icecaps, another major result of global warming, raises the sea level and can cause the permanent inundation of coastal regions and sometimes of entire countries.

Carbon dioxide is the result of the combustion of HCs and coal. Transportation accounts for a large share (32% from 1980 to 1999) of carbon dioxide emissions. The distribution of carbon dioxide emissions is shown in Figure 1.1.

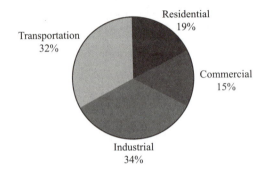

Figure 1.1　Carbon dioxide emission distribution from 1980 to 1999

## New words and expressions（单词和短语）

### 1. New words（单词）

| | |
|---|---|
| methane [ˈmeθeɪn] | n. 甲烷 |
| ecological [ˌekəˈlɔdʒɪkəl] | n. 生态学；社会生态学　a. 生态学的 |
| ecosystem [ˈiːkəuˌsɪstəm] | n. 生态系统 |
| disappearance [ˌdɪsəˈpɪərəns] | n. 看不见；消失；失踪；消散 |
| potentially [pəˈtenʃəli] | ad. 可能地；潜在地；假定地 |
| indigenous [ɪnˈdɪdʒɪnəs] | a. 土产的；天生的；固有的；内在的 |
| barracuda [ˌbærəˈkuːdə] | n. 梭子鱼 |
| amplitude [ˈæmplɪtjuːd] | n. 广阔；丰富；振幅；充分 |
| tornadoes [tɔːˈneɪdəuz] | n. 龙卷风 |
| inundation [ˌɪnʌnˈdeɪʃn] | n. 洪水；泛滥；充满；涌到 |
| dryness [ˈdraɪnɪs] | n. 干，干燥 |
| permanent [ˈpəːmənənt] | a. 长期不变的；耐久的；永久的 |

## 2. Expressions（短语）

| | |
|---|---|
| global warming | 全球变暖 |
| greenhouse effect | 温室效应 |
| natural disasters | 自然灾害 |
| ecological damage | 生态破坏 |
| polar icecap | 极地冰盖 |
| natural resources | 自然资源 |
| Mediterranean Sea | 地中海 |
| South Pacific | 南太平洋 |
| coastal regions | 沿海区域 |

### Notes to the text（难点解析）

★1. Global warming is a result of the "greenhouse effect" induced by the presence of carbon dioxide and other gases, such as methane, in the atmosphere. 全球变暖是"温室效应"的结果，而"温室效应"系由二氧化碳和其他气体（如大气中的甲烷）所引发。

★2. Carbon dioxide is the result of the combustion of HCs and coal. 二氧化碳是碳氢化合物和煤燃烧的生成物。

★3. Considering the ecological damages induced by global warming, the disappearance of some endangered species is a concern because this destabilizes the natural resources that feed some populations. 因全球变暖引发的生态破坏，某些受损害物种的消失关系到一些人口的自然资源供应的稳定性。

### Exercises（练习）

◆1. Translate the following passages (expressions) into Chinese（英译汉）

（1）global warming

（2）natural disasters

（3）The melting of the polar icecaps, another major result of global warming, raises the sea level and can cause the permanent inundation of coastal regions and sometimes of entire countries.

◆2. Translate the following passages (expressions) into English（汉译英）

（1）温室效应

（2）由于自然界灾难引起的伤害之广，使人们对自然界灾难的关注多于对生态灾害的关注。

◆3. Fill in the blanks with the suitable words according to the text

There are also concerns about the _____ of some species from warm seas to previously colder northern seas, _____ they can potentially destroy _____ species and the _____ that live off those species.

◆4. Directions：Answer the following questions briefly according to the text

What does an increased Earth temperature result in? (Or what will cause global warming?)

### Reading material (阅读材料)

The transportation sector is clearly now the major contributor to carbon dioxide emissions. It should be noted that developing countries are rapidly increasing their transportation sector, and these countries represent a very large share of the world population.

##  1.1.3 Petroleum Resources

### Text (课文)

The vast majority of fuels for transportation are liquid fuels originating from petroleum. Petroleum is a fossil fuel, resulting from the decomposition of living matters that were imprisoned millions of years ago (Ordovician, 600-400 million years ago) in geologically stable layers. This process takes millions of years to accomplish. This is what makes the Earth's resources in fossil fuels finite.

Proved reserves are "those quantities that geological and engineering information indicates with reasonable certainty can be recovered in the future from known reservoirs under existing economic and operating conditions." Therefore, they do not constitute an indicator of the Earth's total reserves. The proved reserves, as they are given in the British Petroleum 2001 estimate, are given in billion tons in Table 1.1. The R/P ratio is the number of years that the proved reserves would last if the production were to continue at its current level. This ratio is also given in Table 1.1 for each region.

Table 1.1  Proved Petroleum Reserves in 2000

| Region | Proved Reserves in 2000 in Billion Tons | R/P Ratio |
| --- | --- | --- |
| North America | 8.5 | 13.8 |
| South and Central America | 13.6 | 39 |
| Europe | 2.5 | 7.7 |
| Africa | 10 | 26.8 |
| Middle East | 92.5 | 83.2 |
| Former USSR | 9.0 | 22.7 |
| Asia Pacific | 6.0 | 15.9 |
| Total World | 142.1 | 39.9 |

The oil extracted nowadays is the easily extractable oil that lies close to the surface, in regions where the climate does not pose major problems. It is believed that far more oil lies underneath the

Earth's crust in regions such as Siberia, or the American and Canadian Arctic. In these regions, the climate and ecological concerns are major obstacles to extracting or prospecting for oil. The estimation of the total Earth's reserves is a difficult task for political and technical reasons. A 2000 estimation of the undiscovered oil resources by the US Geological Survey is given in Table 1.2.

Table 1.2 U. S. Geological Survey Estimate of Undiscovered Oil in 2000

| Region | Undiscovered Oil in 2000 in Billion Tons |
|---|---|
| North America | 19.8 |
| South and Central America | 14.9 |
| Europe | 3.0 |
| Sub-Saharan Africa and Antarctic | 9.7 |
| Middle East and North Africa | 31.2 |
| Former USSR | 15.7 |
| Asia Pacific | 4.0 |
| World (potential growth) | 98.3 (91.5) |

Although the R/P ratio does not include future discoveries, it is significant. Indeed, it is based on proved reserves, which are easily accessible to this day. The amount of future oil discoveries is hypothetical, and the newly discovered oil will not be easily accessible. The R/P ratio is also based on the hypothesis that the production will remain constant. It is obvious, however, that consumption (and therefore production) is increasing yearly to keep up with the growth of developed and developing economies. Consumption is likely to increase in gigantic proportions with the rapid development of some largely populated countries, particularly in the Asia Pacific region. Figure 1.2 shows the trend in oil consumption over the last 20 years. Oil consumption is given in thousand barrels per day (one barrel is about 8 metric tons).

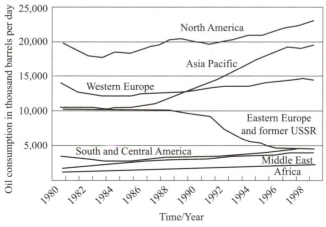

Figure 1.2 Oil consumption per region

Despite the drop in oil consumption for Eastern Europe and the former USSR, the world trend is clearly increasing, as shown in Figure 1.3. The fastest growing region is Asia Pacific, where most of the world's population lives. An explosion in oil consumption is to be expected, with a proportional increase in pollutant emissions and $CO_2$ emissions.

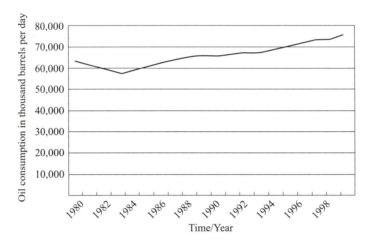

**Figure 1.3 World oil consumption**

### New words and expressions（单词和短语）

#### 1. New words（单词）

| | |
|---|---|
| geological [ˌdʒɪəˈlɔdʒɪkl] | a. 地质学的；地质的 |
| accomplish [əˈkɔmpliʃ] | vt. 达到；完成；做到；做成；使完全；使完美 |
| constitute [ˈkɔnstɪtjuːt] | vt. 组成；构成；任命；设立；制定 |
| indicator [ˈɪndɪkeɪtə] | n. 指示者；指示器 |
| estimate [ˈestɪmɪt] | v. 估计；评价；意见；判断；评定 n. 估计；评价；意见；判断 |
| extract [ɪksˈtrækt] | vt. 选录；夺取；摘取；榨取；摘录 n. 摘取物；摘录 |
| prospect [ˈprɔspekt] | n. 景色；希望；前途；展望；期望 v. 勘探；勘察；寻找 |
| significant [sɪgˈnɪfɪkənt] | a. 重大的；重要的；贵重的；有意义的；有内容的；暗示性的；有效的 |
| hypothetical [ˌhaɪpəˈθetɪkl] | a. 假设的，假想的 |
| accessible [ækˈsesəbl] | a. 易接近的；可达到的；易受影响的；易取得的；进得去的；容易弄到手的；容易轻信的 |
| gigantic [dʒaɪˈgæntɪk] | a. 巨大的；庞大的；大得惊人的 |
| particularly [pəˈtɪkjuləli] | ad. 特别，尤其；详细地；独特地 |

## 2. Expressions（短语）

| | |
|---|---|
| petroleum resources | 石油资源 |
| liquid fuel | 液态燃料 |
| originate from… | 源于…… |
| millions of years | 百万年 |
| keep up | 保持 |
| developed economy | 发达国家经济 |
| developing economy | 发展中国家经济 |
| Eastern Europe | 东欧地区 |
| the Asia Pacific region | 亚太地区 |
| oil consumption | 油消耗量 |
| $CO_2$ emissions | 二氧化碳排放量 |

## Notes to the text（难点解析）

★1. Those quantities that geological and engineering information indicates with reasonable certainty can be recovered in the future from known reservoirs under existing economic and operating conditions. 经地质和工程信息可靠地预示的储藏量，它们是在现阶段经济和运行条件下，今后由已知的储油层可被开采的储藏量。

★2. Consumption is likely to increase in gigantic proportions with the rapid development of some largely populated countries, particularly in the Asia Pacific region. 油消耗量随着某些人口大量聚居国家的迅速发展很可能呈现巨大的增长额，特别是在亚太地区。

## Exercises（练习）

◆1. Translate the following passages (expressions) into Chinese（英译汉）
（1）$CO_2$ emissions
（2）oil consumption

◆2. Translate the following passages (expressions) into English（汉译英）
（1）石油资源
（2）亚太地区
（3）石油是从地下采掘的矿物燃料，是活性物质分解的生成物。

◆3. Multiple choice questions（选择填空）
（1）Petroleum Resources are _____.
  A. limited
  B. unlimited
  C. renewable
  D. permanent

(2) The fastest growing region of the global oil consumption is _____.

A. North America Asia Pacific
B. Asia Pacific
C. Europe
D. South and Central America

◆4. Directions: Answer the following questions briefly according to the text

(1) Can you explain R/P Ratio?
(2) What makes the Earth's resources in fossil fuels finite?

### Reading material（阅读材料）

The process is roughly the following: living matters (mostly plants) die and are slowly covered by sediments. Over time, these accumulating sediments form thick layers and transform to rock. The living matters are trapped in a closed space, where they encounter high pressures and temperatures and slowly transform into either HCs or coal, depending on their nature.

## 1.2 Sustainable Transportation

### Text（课文）

The current model of the personal transportation system is not sustainable in the long run because the Earth has limited reserves of fossil fuel, which provide 97% of all transportation energy needs at the present time. To understand how sustainable transportation can be achieved, let us look at the ways energy can be derived and the ways vehicles are powered.

The energy available to us can be divided into three categories: renewable energy, fossil fuel-based non-renewable energy and nuclear energy. Renewable energy includes hydropower, solar, wind, ocean, geothermal, biomass and so on. Non-renewable energy includes coal, oil, and natural gas. Nuclear energy, though abundant, is not renewable since there are limited resources of uranium and other radioactive elements on Earth. In addition, there is concern on nuclear safety (such as the recent accident in Japan due to earthquake and tsunami) and nuclear waste processing in the long term. Biomass energy is renewable because it can be derived from wood, crops, cellulose, garbage, and landfill. Electricity and hydrogen are secondary forms of energy. They can be generated by using a variety of sources of original energy, including renewable and non-renewable energy. Gasoline, diesel, and syngas are energy carriers derived from fossil fuel.

Figure 1.4 shows the different types of sources of energy, energy carriers and vehicles. Conventional gasoline/diesel-powered vehicles rely on liquid fuel which can only be derived from fossil fuel. HEVs, though more efficient and consuming less fuel than conventional vehicles, still rely on fossil fuel as the primary energy. Therefore, both conventional cars and HEVs are not sustainable. EVs and fuel cell vehicles rely on electricity and hydrogen, respectively. Both electricity and hydrogen can be generated from renewable energy sources, therefore they are sustainable as long as only renewable energy sources are used for the purpose. PHEVs, though not totally sustainable, offer the advantages of both conventional vehicles and EVs at the same time. PHEVs can displace fossil fuel usages by using grid electricity. They are not the ultimate solution for sustainability but they build a pathway to future sustainability.

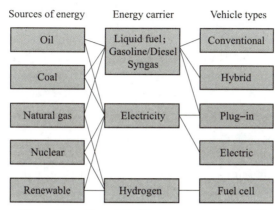

Figure 1.4  A sustainable transportation model

## New words and expressions（单词和短语）

### 1. New words（单词）

| | |
|---|---|
| category [ˈkætɪɡəri] | n. 种类；部门；类目 |
| hydropower [ˈhaɪdrəʊˌpaʊə] | n. 水力发电 |
| solar [ˈsəʊlə] | a. 太阳的，日光的；与太阳有关的；利用太阳能的 |
| geothermal [ˌdʒiːəʊˈθɜːməl] | a. 地热的；地温的 |
| biomass [ˈbaɪəʊˌmæs] | n. 生物量 |
| abundant [əˈbʌndənt] | a. 充足的；丰富的；大量的，充裕的；富有的 |
| uranium [juˈreɪniəm] | n. 铀 |
| cellulose [ˈseljuləʊs] | n. 纤维素 a. 含有纤维素的 |
| garbage [ˈɡɑːbɪdʒ] | n. 垃圾；厨房之废弃物 |
| syngas [ˈsɪnɡæs] | n. 合成气 |
| hydrogen [ˈhaɪdrɪdʒən] | n. 氢气 |

### 2. Expressions（短语）

| | |
|---|---|
| renewable energy | 可再生能源 |
| fossil fuel-based non-renewable energy | 基于化石燃料的不可再生能源 |
| nuclear energy | 核能 |
| natural gas | 天然气 |

| | |
|---|---|
| radioactive element | 放射性元素 |
| solar | 太阳能 |
| wind | 风能 |
| ocean | 海洋能 |
| coal | 煤 |
| uranium | 铀 |
| sustainable transportation | 持续发展的交通运输 |

### Notes to the text（难点解析）

★1. The energy available to us can be divided into three categories: renewable energy, fossil fuel-based non-renewable energy and nuclear energy. Renewable energy includes hydropower, solar, wind, ocean, geothermal, biomass and so on. Non-renewable energy includes coal, oil and natural gas. Nuclear energy, though abundant, is not renewable since there are limited resources of uranium and other radioactive elements on Earth. 我们能够获取的能源形式可分为三类：可再生能源、基于化石燃料的不可再生能源以及核能。可再生能源包括水力、太阳能、风能、海洋能、地热能、生物能等。不可再生能源包括煤、石油和天然气。核能虽然很丰富，但也是不可再生的，这是因为地球上的铀和其他放射性元素是有限的。

★2. PHEVs, though not totally sustainable, offer the advantages of both conventional vehicles and EVs at the same time. PHEVs can displace fossil fuel usage by using grid electricity. PHEVs虽然不是可完全持续发展的，但是同时具备了传统汽车和纯电动汽车的优点。PHEVs能够通过使用电网的电能来代替化石燃料的使用。

### Exercises（练习）

◆1. Translate the following passages (expressions) into Chinese（英译汉）

（1）Nuclear energy, though abundant, is not renewable.

（2）sustainable transportation

（3）natural gas

◆2. Translate the following passages (expressions) into English（汉译英）

（1）不可再生能源包括煤、石油和天然气。

（2）可再生能源

（3）太阳能

◆3. Fill in the blanks with the suitable words according to the text

Renewable energy includes _____, _____, _____, _____, _____, _____ and so on. Non-renewable energy includes coal, oil and natural gas. Nuclear energy, though abundant, is _____ since there are limited resources of uranium and other radioactive elements on Earth.

◆4. Directions: Answer the following questions briefly according to the text

How many categories can the energy available to us be divided into? What are they?

### Reading material (阅读材料)

Electrically-driven vehicles have many advantages and challenges. Electricity is more efficient than the combustion process in a car. Well-to-wheel studies show that, even if the electricity is generated from petroleum, the equivalent miles that can be driven by 1 gallon (3.8 L) of gasoline is 108 miles (173 km) in an electric car, compared to 33 miles (53 km) in an internal combustion engine (ICE) car. In a simpler comparison, it costs 2 cents per mile to use electricity (at US $0.12 per kW·h) but 10 cents per mile to use gasoline (at $3.30 per gallon) for a compact car.

Electricity can be generated through renewable sources, such as hydroelectric, wind, solar and biomass. On the other hand, the current electricity grid has extra capacity available at night when the usage of electricity is off-peak. It is ideal to charge electric vehicles (EVs) at night when the grid has extra energy capacity available.

## 1.3 EV History

### Text (课文)

The history of EVs is interesting. It includes the insurgence of EVs following the discovery of electricity and the means of electromechanical energy conversion and later being overtaken by gasoline-powered vehicles. Motivated by the growing concern about global pollution and the success of electric motor driven transportation in various areas, the interest is ever increasing for road EVs that can deliver the performance of ICEV counterparts.

#### 1.3.1 The Early Years

Prior to the 1830s, the means of transportation was only through steam power, because the laws of electromagnetic induction, and consequently, electric motors and generators, were yet to be discovered. Faraday demonstrated the principle of the electric motor as early as in 1820 through a wire rod carrying electric current and a magnet, but in 1831 he discovered the laws of electromagnetic induction that enabled the development and demonstration of the electric motors and generators essential for electric transportation. The history of EVs in those early years up to its peak period in the early 1900s is summarized below:

- Pre-1830—Steam-powered transportation
- 1831—Faraday's law, and shortly thereafter, invention of DC motor
- 1834—Nonrechargeable battery-powered electric car used on a short track
- 1851—Nonrechargeable 19 m/h electric car (1 mile = 1,609.344 m)
- 1859—Development of lead storage battery

- 1874—Battery-powered carriage
- Early 1870s—Electricity produced by dynamo-generators
- 1885—Gasoline-powered tricycle car
- 1900—4,200 automobiles sold, 40% steam powered, 38% electric powered, 22% gasoline powered
- 1912—34,000 EVs registered; EVs outnumber gas-powered vehicles 2-to-1
- 1920s—EVs disappear, and ICEVs become predominant

The factors that led to the disappearance of EVs after their short period of success were as follows:

1. Invention of starter motor in 1911 made gas vehicles easier to start.

2. Improvements in mass production of Henry T (gas-powered car) vehicles sold for $260 in 1925, compared to $850 in 1909. EVs were more expensive.

3. Rural areas had limited access to electricity to charge batteries, whereas gasoline could be sold in those areas.

## New words and expressions（单词和短语）

### 1. New words（单词）

| | |
|---|---|
| generator [ˈdʒenəreɪtə] | n. 发生器；发电机；发生者；创始者；生殖者 |
| summarized [ˈsʌməraɪzd] | v. 总结，概述（summarize 的过去式和过去分词） |
| predominant [prɪˈdɒmɪnənt] | a. 主要的；有势力的；占优势的；卓越的；主流的 |

### 2. Expressions（短语）

| | |
|---|---|
| electric motor | 电动机 |
| electromagnetic induction | 电磁感应 |
| top speed | 最高车速 |
| gasoline-powered vehicle | 燃油汽车 |
| DC motor | 直流电动机 |
| nonrechargeable battery-powered electric car | 不可再充电电池的电动汽车 |
| dynamo-generator | 直流发电机 |
| steam powered | 蒸汽驱动 |
| electric powered | 电驱动 |
| gasoline powered | 燃油驱动 |
| starter motor | 起动机 |
| the laws of electromagnetic induction | 电磁感应定律 |

| electric transportation | 电力交通 |
| --- | --- |
| peak period | 鼎盛时期 |

### Notes to the text（难点解析）

★1. Prior to the 1830s, the means of transportation was only through steam power, because the laws of electromagnetic induction, and consequently, electric motors and generators, were yet to be discovered. 追溯到19世纪30年代，在电磁感应定律、电动机和发电机发明之前，交通工具都是靠蒸汽驱动。

★2. Faraday demonstrated the principle of the electric motor as early as in 1820 through a wire rod carrying electric current and a magnet, but in 1831 he discovered the laws of electromagnetic induction that enabled the development and demonstration of the electric motors and generators essential for electric transportation. 早在1820年，法拉第使用一个通电的线圈和磁铁论证了电动机的原理，直到1831年，他发现了电磁感应定律，这项重大发现促进了电动机和发电机的发展，使电力交通的推广成为可能。

### Exercises（练习）

◆1. Translate the following passages (expressions) into Chinese（英译汉）

（1）gasoline-powered vehicle

（2）the laws of electromagnetic induction

（3）electric transportation

（4）Improvements in mass production of Henry T (gas-powered car) vehicles sold for \$260 in 1925, compared to \$850 in 1909. EVs were more expensive.

◆2. Translate the following passages (expressions) into English（汉译英）

（1）环境污染

（2）起动机

（3）郊区充电设施不完善，但加油很方便。

◆3. Directions：Answer the following questions briefly according to the text

Why are the histories of EVs in those early years up to their peak period in the early 1900s?

### Reading material（阅读材料）

The specifications of some of the early EVs are given below：

• 1897—French Krieger Co. EV：weight, 2,230 lb (1 lb = 0.453,592,37 kg); top speed, 15 m/h; range, 50 mile/charge

• 1900—French B. G. S. Co. EV：top speed, 40 m/h; range, 100 mile/charge

• 1915—Woods EV：top speed, 40 m/h; range, 100 mile/charge

• 1915—Lansden EV：weight, 2,460 lb; top speed, 93 mile/charge; capacity, 1 ton payload

### 1.3.2 1970s

**Text（课文）**

The scenario turned in favor of EVs in the early 1970s, as gasoline prices increased dramatically due to an energy crisis. The Arab oil embargo of 1973 increased demands for alternate energy sources, which led to immense interest in EVs. It became highly desirable to be less dependent on foreign oil as a nation. In 1975, 352 electric vans were delivered to the US Postal Service for testing. In 1976, Congress enacted Public Law 94-413, the Electric and Hybrid Vehicle Research, Development and Demonstration Act of 1976. This act authorized a federal program to promote electric and hybrid vehicle technologies and to demonstrate the commercial feasibility of EVs. The Department of Energy (DOE) standardized EV performance, which is summarized in Table 1.3.

Table 1.3  EV Performance Standardization of 1976

| Category | Personal | Commercial Use |
| --- | --- | --- |
| Acceleration 0 to 50 km/h | <15 s | <15 s |
| Gradability at 25 km/h | 10% | 10% |
| Gradability at 20 km/h | 20% | 20% |
| Forward speed for 5min | 80 km/h | 70 km/h |
| Range: Electric | 50 km, C cycle | 50 km, B cycle |
| Range: Hybrid | 200 km, C cycle | 200 km, B cycle |
| Nonelectrical energy consumption in hybrid vehicles (consumption of nonelectrical energy must be less than 75% of the total energy consumed) | <1.3 MJ/km | <9.8 MJ/km |
| Recharge time from 80% discharge | <10 h | <10 h |

The case study of a GM EV of the 1970s is as follows (System and characteristics):

Motor: separately excited DC, 34 hp (1 hp = 735.498,75 W), 2,400 r/m

Battery pack: Ni-Zn, 120 V, 735 lb

Auxiliary battery: Ni-Zn, 14 V

Motor drive: armature DC chopper using SCRs; field DC chopper using bipolar junction transistors (BJTs)

Top speed: 60 mile/h

Range: 60-80 miles

Acceleration: 0-55 mile/h in 27 s

The vehicle utilized a modified Chevy Chevette chassis and body. This EV was used mainly as a test bed for Ni-Zn batteries. Over 35,500 miles of on-road testing proved that this EV was sufficiently road worthy.

## New words and expressions（单词和短语）

### 1. New words（单词）

| | |
|---|---|
| dramatically [drəˈmætɪkəli] | ad. 从戏剧角度；戏剧性地；明显地；显著地 |
| embargo [emˈbɑːgəu] | n.（pl. embargoes）禁止；限制；阻止 vt. 禁止船舶出入港口 |
| enacted [ɪˈnæktɪd] | v. 制定（法律），通过（法案）（enact 的过去式和过去分词） |
| authorized [ˈɔːθəraɪzd] | a. 公认的；被授权的；经认可的；经核准的，授权的 |
| demonstrate [ˈdemənstreɪt] | v. 证明；示范；当众表演；表露（情绪）；阐述 |
| performance [pəˈfɔːməns] | n. 进行；执行；履行；展出；工作情况；性能规范 |
| acceleration [ækˌseləˈreɪʃən] | n. 加速；加速度；促进；加速性能 |

### 2. Expressions（短语）

| | |
|---|---|
| alternate energy sources | 替代能源 |
| Postal Service | 邮政服务业 |
| Hybrid Vehicle | 混合动力汽车 |
| Demonstration Act | 示范条例 |
| federal program | 联邦计划 |
| commercial feasibility | 商业化的可行性 |
| Department of Energy（DOE） | 美国能源部 |
| separately excited DC | 他励直流电机 |
| battery pack | 电池组 |
| auxiliary battery | 辅助蓄电池 |
| motor drive | 电机驱动 |
| armature DC chopper | 电枢直流斩波器 |
| field DC chopper | 磁场直流斩波器 |
| bipolar junction transistors（BJTs） | 双极结型晶体管 |
| energy crisis | 能源危机 |

## Notes to the text（难点解析）

★1. The scenario turned in favor of EVs in the early 1970s, as gasoline prices increased dramatically due to an energy crisis. 20 世纪 70 年代初能源危机使汽油的价格显著上升，电动

汽车受到越来越多的青睐。

★2. This act authorized a federal program to promote electric and hybrid vehicle technologies and to demonstrate the commercial feasibility of EVs. 这项条例制订了一个联邦计划，用来推进电动汽车及混合动力汽车技术的发展和阐述电动汽车商业化的可行性。

### Exercises（练习）

◆1. Translate the following passages（expressions）into Chinese（英译汉）

（1）energy crisis

（2）battery pack

（3）It became highly desirable to be less dependent on foreign oil as a nation.

◆2. Translate the following passages（expressions）into English（汉译英）

（1）电机

（2）混合动力汽车

（3）电池组

◆3. Directions：Answer the following questions briefly according to the text

Please describe the system and characteristics of a GM EV of the 1970s

### 1.3.3　1980s and 1990s

### Text（课文）

In the 1980s and the 1990s, there were tremendous developments of high-power, high-frequency semiconductor switches, along with the microprocessor revolution, which led to improved power converter design to drive the electric motors efficiently. Also in this period, factors contributed to the development of magnetic bearings used in flywheel energy storage systems, although these are not utilized in mainstream EV development projects.

In the last 2 decades, legislative mandates pushed the cause for zero-emission vehicles. Legislation passed by the California Air Resources Board in 1990 stated that by 1998, 2% of vehicles should be zero-emission vehicles（ZEV）for each automotive company selling more than 35,000 vehicles. The percentages were to increase to 5% by 2001 and to 10% by 2003. The legislation provided a tremendous impetus to develop EVs by the major automotive manufacturers. The legislation was relaxed somewhat later due to practical limitations and the inability of the manufacturers to meet the 1998 and 2001 requirements. The mandate now stands that 4% of all vehicles sold should be ZEV by 2003, and an additional 6% of the sales must be made up of ZEVs and partial ZEVs, which would require GM to sell about 14,000 EVs in California.

Motivated by the pollution concern and potential energy crisis, government agencies, federal laboratories, and the major automotive manufacturers launched a number of initiatives to push for ZEVs. The partnership for next-generation vehicles（PNGV）is such an initiative（established in 1993）, which is a partnership of federal laboratories and automotive industries to promote and develop electric and hybrid electric vehicles. The most recent initiative by the DOE and the automotive industries is the Freedom CAR initiative.

The trends in EV developments in recent years can be attributed to the followings:

- High level of activity exists at the major automotive manufacturers.
- New independent manufacturers bring vigor.
- New prototypes are even better.
- High levels of activity overseas exist.
- There are high levels of hybrid vehicle activity.
- A boom in individual ICEV to EV conversions is ongoing.

The case studies of one GM EVs of the 1990s are given below:

Saturn EV1

a. Commercially available electric vehicle made by GM in 1995.

b. Leased in California and Arizona for a total cost of about $30,000.

c. System and characteristics:

i. Motor: one, three-phase induction motors

ii. Battery pack: lead-acid batteries

iii. Motor drive: DC-to-AC inverter using IGBTs

iv. Top speed: 75 m/h

v. Range: 90 miles on highway, 70 miles in city

vi. Acceleration: 0 to 60 miles in 8.5 s

vii. Power consumption: 30 (kW·h)/(100 miles) in city, 25 (kW·h)/(100 miles) on highway

This vehicle was used as a test bed for mass production of EVs.

### New words and expressions（单词和短语）

#### 1. New words（单词）

| | |
|---|---|
| tremendous [trɪˈmendəs] | a. 巨大的；可怕的；迅速的 |
| converter [kənˈvɜːtə] | n. 变换者；[电学] 变流器；转化炉；频道变换装置 |
| mainstream [ˈmeɪnstriːm] | n. 主流 a. 主流的 |
| decade [ˈdekeɪd] | n. 十年，十年期间 |
| percentage [pəˈsentɪdʒ] | n. 百分率，部分；比率；利益 |
| additional [əˈdɪʃənəl] | a. 额外的；补充的；附加的；添加的，追加的 |
| initiative [ɪˈnɪʃɪətɪv] | n. 初步；创始；创制权；优先权 a. 开始的；创始的；初步的 |
| partnership [ˈpɑːtnəʃɪp] | n. 合伙；合作；合股；合伙企业；合伙人身份 |
| prototype [ˈprəʊtətaɪp] | n. 原型；标准；典范；样板 |
| individual [ˌɪndɪˈvɪdjuəl] | a. 个别的；单独的 n. 个体；私营企业、小型企业 |

## 2. Expressions（短语）

| | |
|---|---|
| high-power | 大功率 |
| high-frequency | 高频 |
| semiconductor switch | 半导体开关 |
| microprocessor revolution | 微处理器技术 |
| magnetic bearing | 磁轴承 |
| flywheel energy storage system | 飞轮储能系统 |
| zero-emission vehicle | 零排放车辆（ZEV） |
| California Air Resources Board | 美国加州空气资源委员会 |
| practical limitation | 实用性的限制 |
| government agency | 政府机关 |
| federal laboratory | 联邦实验室 |
| hybrid electric vehicle | 混合动力汽车 |
| DOE | 美国能源部 |
| ICEV | 内燃机汽车 |
| power consumption | 功率消耗 |
| three-phase induction motor | 三相感应电机 |
| battery pack-lead-acid | 铅酸蓄电池 |
| IGBT（insulated gate bipolar transistor） | 绝缘栅双极型晶体管 |

### Notes to the text（难点解析）

★1. The mandate now stands that 4% of all vehicles sold should be ZEV by 2003. 要求到2003年，4%为零排放车辆。

★2. A boom in individual ICEV to EV conversions is ongoing. 私营企业和小型企业也开始从生产内燃机汽车转变到生产电动汽车。

### Exercises（练习）

◆1. Translate the following passages（expressions）into Chinese（英译汉）

（1）zero-emission vehicles

（2）three-phase induction motor

（3）Motivated by the pollution concern and potential energy crisis, government agencies, federal laboratories, and the major automotive manufacturers launched a number of initiatives to push for ZEVs.

◆2. Translate the following passages (expressions) into English (汉译英)
(1) 大型汽车制造商开发热情高涨。
(2) 新成立的制造商为电动汽车的发展带来活力。
(3) 新标准更适合其发展。
(4) 私营企业和小型企业也开始从生产内燃机汽车转变到生产电动汽车。

◆3. Fill in the blanks with the suitable words according to the text

In the 1980s and the 1990s, there were tremendous developments of _____, high-frequency _____, along with the microprocessor revolution, which led to improved power converter design to drive the electric motors _____.

## Reading material (阅读材料)

GM Impact 3 (1993 completed):
a. Based on 1990 Impact displayed at the Los Angeles auto show
b. Two-passenger, two-door coupe, street legal and safe
c. Initially, 12 built for testing; 50 built by 1995 to be evaluated by 1,000 potential customers
d. System and characteristics:
i. Motor: one, three-phase induction motors; 137 hp; 12,000 r/m
ii. Battery pack: lead-acid (26), 12 V batteries connected in series (312 V), 869 lb
iii. Motor drive: DC-to-AC inverter using insulated gate bipolar transistors (IGBTs)
iv. Top speed: 75 m/h
v. Range: 90 miles on highway
vi. Acceleration: 0 to 60 miles in 8.5 s
vii. Vehicle weight: 2,900 lb
This vehicle was used as a test bed for mass production of EVs.

 ### 1.3.4  EV Market

### Text (课文)

We normally discuss the use of EVs for passengers and public transportation but tend to forget about their use as off-road vehicles in specialty applications, where range is not an issue. EVs have penetrated the market of off-road vehicles successfully over the years for clean air as well as for cost advantages. Examples of such applications are airport vehicles for passenger and ground support; recreational vehicles as in golf carts and for theme parks, plant operation vehicles like forklifts and loader trucks; vehicles for disabled persons; utility vehicles for ground transportation in closed but large compounds, etc.

The major impediments for mass acceptance of EVs by the general public are the limited EV range and the lack of EV infrastructure. The solution of the range problem may come from extensive researches and development efforts in batteries, fuel cells, and other alternative energy storage devices. An alternative approach is to create awareness among people on the problems of global warming and the advantages of EVs, while considering the fact that most people drive less than 50 miles a day, a requirement that can be easily met by today's technology.

The appropriate infrastructure must also be in place for EVs to become more popular. The issues related to infrastructure are as follows:

- Battery charging facilities: residential and public charging facilities and stations
- Standardization of EV plugs, cords, outlets, and safety issues
- Sales and distribution
- Service and technical support
- Parts supply

The current initial cost of an EV is also a big disadvantage for the EV market. The replacement of the batteries, even for HEVs, is quite expensive, added to which is the limited life problem of these batteries. The cost of EVs will come down as volume goes up, but in the meantime, subsidies and incentives from the government can create momentum.

The increasing use of EVs will improve the job prospects of electrical engineers. The new jobs related to EVs will be in the following areas:

- Power electronics and motor drives: Design and development of the electrical systems of an EV
- Power generation: Increased utility demand due to EV usage
- EV infrastructure: Design and development of battery charging stations and of hydrogen generation, storage and distribution systems

## New words and expressions（单词和短语）

### 1. New words（单词）

| | |
|---|---|
| passenger [ˈpæsɪndʒə] | n. 乘客，旅客；过路人；徒步旅行者 |
| impediment [ɪmˈpedɪmənt] | n. 口吃；妨碍（物）；阻碍；身体障碍 |
| infrastructure [ˈɪnfrəˌstrʌktʃə] | n. 基础（结构）；基础设施 |
| extensive [ɪksˈtensɪv] | a. 广阔的；广泛的；广博的；粗放的 |
| appropriate [əˈprəʊprieɪt] | a. 适合的；专属的；特有的；固有的；正当的 |
| residential [ˌrezɪˈdenʃəl] | a. 住所的；适宜居住的；与居住有关的 |
| volume [ˈvɒljuːm] | n. 书本；容积；卷；册；体积；音量 |
| subsidy [ˈsʌbsədi] | n. 补贴，津贴，补助金；鼓励 |
| incentives [ɪnˈsentɪvz] | n. 激励某人做某事的事物（incentive 的复数形式）；刺激；诱因；动机；奖励 |

### 2. Expressions（短语）

| | |
|---|---|
| off-road vehicles | 非道路车辆市场 |

| | |
|---|---|
| ground support | 地面支持 |
| golf cart | 高尔夫手推车 |
| general public | 公众 |
| limited EV range | 有限的 EV 续驶里程 |
| battery | 蓄电池 |
| energy storage device | 能源存储装置 |
| battery charging facility | 电池充电设施 |
| sales and distribution | 出售和分配规范 |
| service and technical support | 服务和技术支持 |
| parts supply | 零部件供应 |
| job prospect | 就业前景 |
| disabled person | 残疾人 |
| electrical engineer | 电子工程师 |
| battery charging station | 充电站 |

## Notes to the text（难点解析）

★1. EVs have penetrated the market of off-road vehicles successfully over the years for clean air as well as for cost advantages. 电动汽车使用清洁技术，且在使用中花费小，所以近几年来，它成功地进入非道路车辆市场。

★2. The increasing use of EVs will improve the job prospects of electrical engineers. 电动汽车的广泛应用会改善电子工程师的就业前景。

## Exercises（练习）

◆1. Translate the following passages (expressions) into Chinese（英译汉）

（1）The appropriate infrastructure must also be in place for EVs to become more popular.

（2）But in the meantime, subsidies and incentives from the government can create momentum.

（3）The current initial cost of an EV is also a big disadvantage for the EV market. The replacement of the batteries, even for HEVs, is quite expensive, added to which is the limited life problem of these batteries.

◆2. Translate the following passages (expressions) into English（汉译英）

（1）充电设施——住宅区充电站和公共充电站

（2）电动汽车插头、软线、插座等安全问题的相关标准

◆3. Multiple choice questions（选择填空）

The new jobs related to EVs will be in the _____ areas.

A. design and development of the electrical systems of an EV

B. power generation

C. EV infrastructure

D. design and development of battery charging stations

◆4. Fill in the blanks with the suitable words according to the text

The solution of the range problem may come from extensive researches and development efforts in _____, _____, and other alternative energy storage devices. An alternative approach is to create awareness among people on the problems of _____ and the _____ of EVs, while considering the fact that most people drive less than 50 miles a day, a requirement that can be easily met by _____.

◆5. Directions: Answer the following questions briefly according to the text

(1) How to solve the range problem of EV?

(2) What are the appropriate infrastructure must also be in place for EVs?

### Reading material（阅读材料）

Unfortunately, the EV market collapsed in the late 1990s. What caused the EV industry to fail? The reasons were mixed, depending on how one looks at it, but the followings were the main contributors to the collapse of EVs in the 1990s:

Limitations of EVs: These concerned the limited range (most EVs provided 60 – 100 miles, compared to 300 or more miles from gasoline-powered vehicles); long charging time (eight or more hours); high cost (40% more expensive than gasoline cars); and limited cargo space in many of the EVs available.

Cheap gasoline: The operating cost (fuel cost) of cars is insignificant in comparison to the investment that an EV owner makes in buying an EV.

Consumers: Consumers believed that large sports utility vehicles (SUVs) and pickup trucks were safer to drive and convenient for many other functions, such as towing. Therefore, consumers preferred large SUVs instead of smaller efficient vehicles (partly due to the low gasoline prices).

Car companies: Automobile manufacturers spent billions of dollars in researches, development, and deployment of EVs, but the market did not respond very well. They were losing money in selling EVs at that time. Maintenance and servicing of EVs were additional burdens on the car dealerships. Liability was a major concern, though there was no evidence that EVs were less safe than gasoline vehicles.

Gas companies: EVs were seen as a threat to gas companies and the oil industry. Lobbying by the car and gasoline companies of the federal government and the California government to drop the mandate was one of the key factors leading to the disappearance of EVs in the 1990s.

Government: The CARB switched at the last minute from a mandate for EVs to hydrogen vehicles.

Battery technology: Lead acid batteries were used in most EVs in the 1990s. The batteries were large and heavy, and needed a long time to charge.

Infrastructure: There was limited infrastructure for recharging batteries.

## 1.4 History of HEVs

**Text（课文）**

Surprisingly, the concept of an HEV is almost as old as the automobile itself. The primary purpose, however, was not so much to lower the fuel consumption but rather to assist the IC engine to provide an acceptable level of performance. Indeed, in the early days, IC engine engineering was less advanced than electric motor engineering.

Early hybrid vehicles were built in order to assist the weak IC engines of that time or to improve the range of EVs. They made use of the basic electric technologies that were then available. In spite of the great creativity that featured in their design, these early hybrid vehicles could no longer compete with the greatly improved gasoline engines that came into use after World War I. The gasoline engine made tremendous improvements in terms of power density, the engines became smaller and more efficient, and there was no longer a need to assist them with electric motors. The supplementary cost of having an electric motor and the hazards associated with the lead–acid batteries were key factors in the disappearance of hybrid vehicles from the market after World War I.

However, the greatest problem that these early designs had to cope with was the difficulty of controlling the electric machine. Power electronics did not become available until the mid–1960s and early electric motors were controlled by mechanical switches and resistors. They had a limited operating range incompatible with efficient operation. Only with great difficulty could they be made compatible with the operation of a hybrid vehicle.

Dr. Victor Wouk is recognized as the modern investigator of the HEV movement. In 1975, along with his colleagues, he built a parallel hybrid version of a Buick Skylark. The engine was a Mazda rotary engine, coupled to a manual transmission. It was assisted by a 15 hp separately excited DC machine, located in front of the transmission. Eight 12 V automotive batteries were used for energy storage. A top speed of 80 m/h (129 km/h) was achieved with acceleration from 0 to 60 m/h in 16 s.

The series hybrid design was revived by Dr. Ernest H. Wakefield in 1967, when working for Linear Alpha Inc. A small engine coupled to an AC generator, with an output of 3 kW, was used to keep a battery pack charged. However, the experiments were quickly stopped because of technical problems. Other approaches studied during the 1970s and the early 1980s used range extenders, similar in concept to the French Vendovelli and Priestly 1899 design. These range extenders were intended to improve the range of EVs that never reached the market. Other prototypes of hybrid vehicles were built by the Electric Auto Corporation in 1982 and by the Briggs & Stratton Corporation in 1980. These were both parallel hybrid vehicles.

Despite the two oil crises of 1973 and 1977, and despite growing environmental concerns, no HEV made it to the market. The researchers' focus was drawn by the EV, of which many prototypes were built during the 1980s. The lack of interest in HEVs during this period may be attributed to the lack of practical power electronics, modern electric motor, and battery technologies. The 1980s

witnessed a reduction in conventional IC engine-powered vehicle sizes, the introduction of catalytic converters, and the generalization of fuel injection.

The HEV concept drew great interest during the 1990s when it became clear that EVs would never achieve the objective of saving energy. The Ford Motor Corporation initiated the Ford Hybrid Electric Vehicle Challenge, which drew efforts from universities to develop hybrid versions of production automobiles.

Automobile manufacturers around the world built prototypes that achieved tremendous improvements in fuel economy over their IC engine-powered counterparts. The most significant effort in the development and commercialization of HEVs was made by Japanese manufacturers. In 1997, Toyota released the Prius sedan in Japan. Honda also released its Insight and Civic Hybrid. These vehicles are now available throughout the world. They achieve excellent figures of fuel consumption. Toyota's Prius and Honda's Insight vehicles have historical value in that they are the first hybrid vehicles commercialized in the modern era to respond to the problem of personal vehicle fuel consumption.

### New words and expressions（单词和短语）

**1. New words（单词）**

|  |  |
| --- | --- |
| surprisingly [səˈpraɪzɪŋli] | ad. 惊人地；令人羡慕地；使人惊讶地；出人意外地 |
| resistor [rɪˈzɪstə] | n. 电阻器，电阻 |
| prototype [ˈprəʊtətaɪp] | n. 原型；标准；典范；样板 |
| concept [ˈkɒnsept] | n. 观念，概念 |
| assist [əˈsɪst] | v. 参加，出席；协助（做一部分工作）<br>n. 帮助；辅助机械专置 |
| investigator [ɪnˈvestɪɡeɪtə(r)] | n. 研究者；调查者；侦查员 |
| incompatible [ˌɪnkəmˈpætəbl] | n. 互不相容的人或事物<br>adj. 不相容的；矛盾的；不能同时成立的 |
| revive [rɪˈvaɪv] | vt. 使复兴；使苏醒；回想起；重演，重播<br>vi. 复兴；复活；苏醒；恢复精神 |
| catalytic [ˌkætəˈlɪtɪk] | n. 催化剂；刺激因素<br>adj. 接触反应的；起催化作用的 |
| supplementary [ˌsʌplɪˈmentri] | n. 补充者；增补物<br>adj. 补充的；追加的 |
| couple [ˈkʌpl] | n. 对；夫妇；数个<br>vt. 结合；连接；连合<br>vi. 结合；成婚 |

| | | |
|---|---|---|
| acceleration [əkˌseləˈreɪʃn] | n. | 加速，促进；[物]加速度；跳级 |
| generalization [ˌdʒenrəlaɪˈzeɪʃn] | n. | 概括；普遍化；一般化 |
| injection [ɪnˈdʒekʃn] | n. | 注射；注射剂；充血；射入轨道 |
| release [rɪˈliːs] | n. | 释放；发布；新发行的东西；排放；解脱 |
| | v. | 释放；放开；发泄；免除；松开；使不紧张 |
| sedan [sɪˈdæn] | n. | 轿车；轿子 |

### 2. Expressions（短语）

| | |
|---|---|
| as old as… | 和……一样年代悠久 |
| fuel consumption | 燃油的消耗量 |
| hybrid vehicle | 混合动力电动汽车 |
| parallel hybrid vehicle | 并联式混合动力电动汽车 |
| series hybrid vehicle | 串联式混合动力电动汽车 |
| electric technology | 电动汽车应用技术 |
| mechanical switch | 机械开关 |
| Mazda rotary engine | 马自达旋转式发动机 |
| manual transmission | 手动变速器 |
| power electronics | 电力电子技术 |
| modern electric motor | 现代电动机 |
| battery technology | 蓄电池应用技术 |
| fuel injection | 燃料喷射 |
| AC generator | 交流发电机 |

### Notes to the text（难点解析）

★1. Indeed, in the early days, IC engine engineering was less advanced than electric motor engineering. 事实上，早期内燃机工程技术的进步不及电机工程技术。

★2. The gasoline engine made tremendous improvements in terms of power density, the engines became smaller and more efficient, and there was no longer a need to assist them with electric motors. 就功率密度而言，汽油发动机取得了惊人的进步，发动机变得更小、更有效，并且不再需要电动机予以辅助。

### Exercises（练习）

◆1. Translate the following passages (expressions) into Chinese（英译汉）

(1) The HEV concept drew great interest during the 1990s when it became clear that EVs

would never achieve the objective of saving energy.

(2) Toyota's Prius and Honda's Insight vehicles have historical value in that they are the first hybrid vehicles commercialized in the modern era to respond to the problem of personal vehicle fuel consumption.

◆2. Translate the following passages (expressions) into English (汉译英)

(1) 油耗

(2) 混合动力汽车

(3) 功率密度

(4) 全世界汽车制造业生产的混合动力电动汽车原型取得了巨大的进步，它们在燃油经济性方面超过了对应的内燃机汽车。

◆3. Fill in the blanks with the suitable words according to the text

The _____ cost of having an electric motor and the hazards _____ with the lead-acid batteries were key factors in the _____ of hybrid vehicles from the market after World War I.

◆4. Directions: Answer the following questions briefly according to the text

Can you describe briefly the history of HEVs?

### Reading material (阅读材料)

Efforts in Europe are represented by the French Renault Next, a small parallel hybrid vehicle using a 750 $cm^3$ spark-ignited engine and two electric motors. This prototype achieved 29.4 km/L (70 m/g) with the maximum speed and acceleration performance comparable to conventional vehicles. Volkswagen also built a prototype, the Chico. The base was a small EV, with a nickel-metal hydride battery pack and a three-phase induction motor. A small two-cylinder gasoline engine was used to recharge the batteries and provide additional power for high-speed cruising.

## 1.5　History of Fuel Cell Vehicles

### Text (课文)

As early as 1839, Sir William Grove (often referred to as the "Father of the Fuel Cell") discovered that it may be possible to generate electricity by reversing the electrolysis of water. It was not until 1889 that two researchers, Charles Langer and Ludwig Mond, coined the term "fuel cell" as they were trying to engineer the first practical fuel cell using air and coal gas. Although further attempts were made in the early 1900s to develop fuel cells that could convert coal or carbon into electricity, the advent of IC engine temporarily quashed any hopes of further development of the fledgling technology.

Francis Bacon developed what was perhaps the first successful fuel cell device in 1932, with a hydrogen-oxygen cell using alkaline electrolytes and nickel electrodes—inexpensive alternatives to the catalysts used by Mond and Langer. Due to a substantial number of technical hurdles, it was not until 1959 that Bacon and the company first demonstrated a practical 5 kW fuel cell system. Harry

Karl Ihrig presented his now-famous 20-hp fuel-cell-powered tractor that same year.

Historically, the first vehicle equipped with a fuel cell was an Austin A40 modified by Karl Kordesch, in 1970, with an alkaline fuel-cell. This vehicle was equipped with a 25 ($N \cdot m^3$) pressurized hydrogen tank installed on the roof, which ensured 300 km of autonomy; this prototype operated for three years without any particular problems.

In spite of these first encouraging results, the following prototypes were equipped with "acid polymer" or "PEM" cells, whose development corresponds to the most important research tasks of the late 1980s. The most dynamic manufacturer by far in this development, in the early 1990s was, and still remains, Daimler-Benz, now Daimler-Chrysler. Since then, the vast majority of the world's manufacturers have engaged on the same pathway.

In more recent decades, a number of manufacturers—including major automakers—and various federal agencies have supported ongoing researches into the development of fuel cell technology for use in fuel cell vehicles and other applications. Hydrogen production, storage, and distribution are the biggest challenges. Truly, fuel-cell-powered vehicles still have a long way to go to enter the market.

### New words and expressions（单词和短语）

#### 1. New words（单词）

| | |
|---|---|
| quash [kwɒʃ] | vt. 撤销；镇压；宣布无效；捣碎 |
| alkaline [ˈælkəlaɪn] | adj. 碱性的；含碱的 |
| electrolysis [ɪˌlekˈtrɒləsɪs] | n. 电解 |

#### 2. Expressions（短语）

| | |
|---|---|
| fuel cell vehicle | 燃料电池电动汽车 |
| alkaline fuel-cell | 碱性燃料电池 |
| acid polymer | 酸性聚合物电池 |
| Daimler-Benz | 戴姆勒-奔驰公司 |
| in more recent decades | 近几十年来 |

### Notes to the text（难点解析）

★1. Hydrogen production, storage, and distribution are the biggest challenges. 氢的生成、储存和配置是当前面临的最大挑战。

★2. Truly, fuel-cell-powered vehicles still have a long way to go to enter the market. 事实上，燃料电池电动汽车进入市场仍然需要经历相当长的过程。

## Exercises(练习)

◆1. Translate the following passages (expressions) into Chinese(英译汉)

(1) fuel cell

(2) in more recent decades

(3) Although further attempts were made in the early 1900s to develop fuel cells that could convert coal or carbon into electricity, the advent of IC engine temporarily quashed any hopes of further development of the fledgling technology.

◆2. Translate the following passages (expressions) into English(汉译英)

1932年Francis Bacon成功研制了也许是第一台燃料电池装置。

◆3. Directions: Answer the following questions briefly according to the text

Please introduce the "Father of the Fuel Cell"

## Reading material(阅读材料)

National Aeronautics and Space Administration (NASA) also began building compact electric generators for use on space missions in the late 1950s. NASA soon came to fund hundreds of research contracts involving fuel cell technology. Fuel cells now have a proven role in the space program, after supplying electricity for several space missions.

# Chapter 2

## New Energy Vehicle Types

## 2.1 Electric Vehicles

### 2.1.1 Configuration of Electric Vehicles

**Text** (课文)

Unlike a conventional vehicle driven by an ICE, an electric vehicle (EV) is propelled by electricity which is stored in an energy storage system (ESS), such as batteries, ultracapacitors, or flywheels. Electric vehicles are also referred to as pure EV or battery EV (BEV) in case the main energy storage is a battery pack. The configuration of a BEV is shown in Figure 2.1.

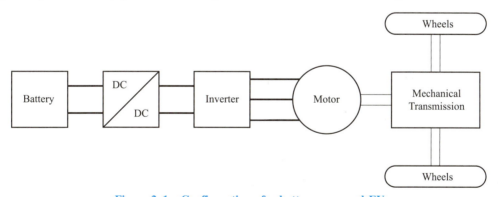

Figure 2.1  Configuration of a battery-powered EV

The battery-powered electric vehicle is comprised of a battery for energy storage, an electric motor, and an inverter. The battery is charged through a charger which can be either carried on-board or fitted at the charging point. The inverter is responsible for the direction and amount of power flow to/from the electric motor such that the vehicle speed and moving direction can be controlled. It has to be noted that during the braking process, the battery is charged by regenerative energy. The DC/DC converter is used to match the battery pack voltage and that of the DC bus of the inverter and can be optional. The mechanical transmission shown here is a generic term for gears and speed reduction. In contrast to conventional vehicles, EVs and other advanced vehicles do not have the need for automatic transmission as the case in conventional vehicles.

The limited travel range of BEVs (without recharging) prompted the research and development of fuel cell electric vehicles (FCEV). The fuel cell-powered electric vehicles have almost the same configuration as a BEV as shown in Figure 2.2, except for the energy source. Hydrogen fuel is required and stored on board. The FCEV represents a true zero-emission vehicle for a long term. The Honda FCX was the first FCEV to be certified for use in the US.

The traction motors used in electric vehicles are usually classified into DC motors, induction motors or permanent magnet motors. Disadvantages of DC motors have forced EV researchers to turn their attention to AC motors. The maintenance-free and low-cost induction motors have attracted many EV developers. However, the problems of size and weight for high-speed operation exist in the meantime. High power density offers a major advantage by permanent magnet motors, which is attractive for EV propulsion solution in spite of the high cost of the motors.

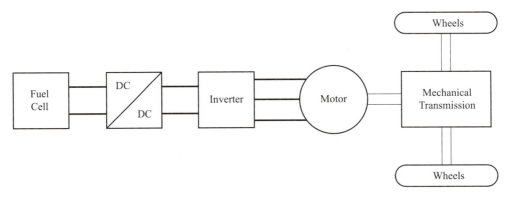

Figure 2.2　Configuration of FCEV

## New words and expressions（单词和短语）

### 1. New words（单词）

| | |
|---|---|
| configuration [kənˌfɪɡəˈreɪʃn] | n. 布局；结构；构造；格局；形状；（计算机的）配置 |
| inverter [ɪnˈvɜːtə] | n. 变换（压、流、频）器；倒换（倒相、反演、反相）器；逆变器；换流器；电流换向器；变换电路；转换开关；变换电路，转换开关； |
| gear [ɡɪə] | n. 排挡；齿轮；传动装置；挡；（某种活动的）设备，用具，衣服 |
| conventional [kənˈvenʃənl] | adj. 符合习俗的，传统的；常见的；惯例的 |
| propel [prəˈpel] | vt. 推进；驱使，激励；驱策 |
| flywheel [ˈflaɪwiːl] | n. [机] 飞轮，惯性轮；调速轮 |
| optional [ˈɒpʃənl] | adj. 可选择的，随意的 |

| | |
|---|---|
| mechanical [məˈkænɪkl] | adj. 机械的；力学的；呆板的；无意识的；手工操作的 |
| transmission [trænzˈmɪʃn] | n. 传动装置，[机] 变速器；传递；传送；播送 |
| automatic [ˌɔːtəˈmætɪk] | n. 自动机械；自动手枪<br>adj. 自动的；无意识的；必然的 |
| density [ˈdensəti] | n. 密度 |

**2. Expressions（短语）**

| | |
|---|---|
| energy storage system (ESS) | 储能系统 |
| be comprised of… | 由……组成 |
| energy storage | 电池 |
| electric motor | 电动机 |
| carried onboard | 随车自带的 |
| regenerative energy | 再生能量 |
| DC bus of the inverter | 变频器的直流母线 |
| speed reduction | 减速器 |
| automatic transmission | 自动变速器 |
| fuel cell electric vehicle (FCEV) | 燃料电池汽车 |
| zero-emission vehicle | 零排放车辆 |
| traction motor | 牵引电动机 |
| induction motor | 交流异步电动机，感应电动机 |
| AC motor | 交流电动机 |
| maintenance-free | 免维护 |
| ultracapacitor | 超级电容 |
| permanent magnet motor | 永磁电动机 |
| DC motor | 直流电动机 |
| generic term | 通用名称 |

## Notes to the text（难点解析）

★1. The inverter is responsible for the direction and amount of power flow to/from the electric motor such that the vehicle speed and moving direction can be controlled. 逆变器负责控制流入或者流出电动机的功率流方向和大小以达到控制汽车的速度和运动方向。

★2. High power density offers a major advantage by permanent magnet motors, which is attractive for EV propulsion solution in spite of the high cost of the motors. 高功率密度是永磁电动

机的一个主要优势,尽管电动机的成本高,但是在解决电动汽车的推进问题时还是很有吸引力的。

### Exercises(练习)

◆1. Translate the following passages(expressions)into Chinese(英译汉)

(1) The battery-powered electric vehicle is comprised of a battery for energy storage, an electric motor, and an inverter.

(2) The FCEV represents a true zero-emission vehicle for a long term.

(3) DC motors

(4) induction motors

(5) permanent magnet motors

◆2. Translate the following passages(expressions)into English(汉译英)

(1) 机械变速器

(2) 零排放

(3) 高功率密度是永磁电动机的一个主要优势。

◆3. Fill in the blanks with the suitable words according to the text

The battery-powered electric vehicle is comprised of _____, _____, and _____.

◆4. Directions:Answer the following questions briefly according to the text

(1) What are the advantages of the AC motors?

(2) What are the disadvantages of the AC motors?

### Reading material(阅读材料)

The EV has many advantages over the conventional internal combustion engine vehicle (ICEV), such as absence of emissions, high efficiency, independence from petroleum, and quiet and smooth operation. The operational and fundamental principles in EVs and ICEVs are similar. There are, however, some differences between ICEVs and EVs, such as the use of a gasoline tank versus batteries; ICE versus electric motor, and different transmission requirements.

## 2.1.2　Conceptual Illustration of a General EV Configuration

### Text(课文)

A modern electric drive train is conceptually illustrated in Figure 2.3. The drive train consists of three major subsystems: electric propulsion, energy source, and auxiliary. The electric propulsion subsystem is comprised of the vehicle controller, the electronic power electronic converter, the electric motor, mechanical transmission, and driving wheels. The energy source subsystem involves the energy source, the energy management unit, and the energy refueling unit. The auxiliary subsystem consists of the power steering unit, the hotel climate control unit, and the auxiliary power supply.

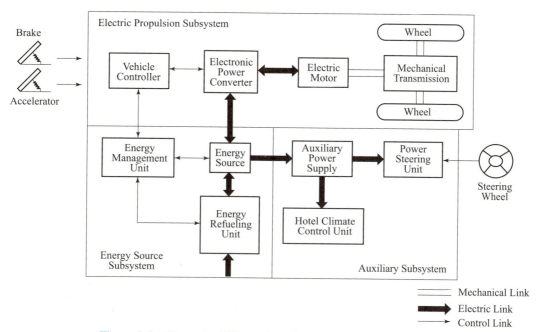

Figure 2.3 Conceptual illustration of a general EV configuration

Based on the control inputs from the accelerator and brake pedals, the vehicle controller provides proper control signals to the electronic power converter, which functions to regulate the power flow between the electric motor and energy source. The backward power flow is due to the regenerative braking of the EV and this regenerated energy can be restored into the energy source, provided the energy source is receptive. Most EV batteries as well as ultracapacitors and flywheels readily possess the ability to accept regenerative energy. The energy management unit cooperates with the vehicle controller to control the regenerative braking and its energy recovery. It also works with the energy refueling unit to control the refueling unit and to monitor the usability of the energy source. The auxiliary power supply provides the necessary power with different voltage levels for all the EV auxiliaries, especially the hotel climate control and power steering units.

There are a variety of possible EV configurations due to the variations in electric propulsion characteristics and energy sources, as shown in Figure 2.4.

a. Figure 2.4 (a) shows the configuration of the first alternative, in which an electric propulsion replaces the IC engine of a conventional vehicle drive train. It consists of an electric motor, a clutch, a gearbox, and a differential.

b. With an electric motor that has a constant power in a long speed range, a fixed gearing can replace the multispeed gearbox and reduce the need for a clutch. This configuration not only reduces the size and weight of the mechanical transmission, it also simplifies the drive train control because gear shifting is not needed.

c. Similar to the drive train in (b), the electric motor, the fixed gearing, and the differential can be further integrated into a single assembly while both axles point at both driving wheels. The whole drive train is further simplified and compacted.

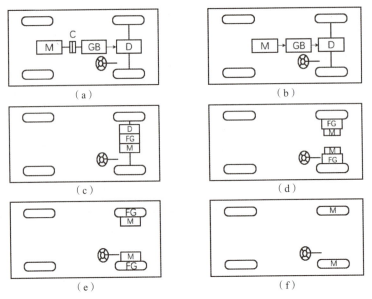

C: Clutch  D: Differential  FG: Fixed Gearing  GB: Gearbox  M: Electric Motor

**Figure 2.4  Possible EV configuration**

(a) conventional driveline with multigear transmission and clutch; (b) single-gear transmission without need of a clutch;

(c) integrated fixed gearing and differential; (d) two separate motors and fixed gearing with their driveshaft;

(e) direct drive with two separate motors and fixed gearing; (f) two separate in-wheel motor drives

d. In Figure 2.4 (d), the mechanical differential is replaced by using two traction motors. Each of them drives one side wheel and operates at a different speed when the vehicle is running along a curved path.

e. In order to further simplify the drive train, the traction motor can be placed inside a wheel. This arrangement is the so-called in-wheel drive. A thin planetary gear set may be employed to reduce the motor speed and enhance the motor torque. The thin planetary gear set offers the advantage of a high-speed reduction ratio as well as an inline arrangement of the input and output shaft.

f. By fully abandoning any mechanical gearing between the electric motor and the driving wheel, the out-rotor of a low-speed electric motor in the in-wheel drive can be directly connected to the driving wheel. The speed control of the electric motor is equivalent to the control of the wheel speed and hence the vehicle speed. However, this arrangement requires the electric motor to have a higher torque to start and accelerate the vehicle.

### New words and expressions (单词和短语)

#### 1. New words (单词)

conceptual [kənˈseptʃuəl]　　　　　　adj. 概念上的

illustration [ˌɪləˈstreɪʃn]　　　　　　n. 说明；插图；例证；图解

| | | |
|---|---|---|
| propulsion [prəˈpʌlʃn] | n. 推进；推进力 | |
| refueling [ˌriːˈfjuːəlɪŋ] | v.（尤指给飞机）补充燃料；（交通工具）添加燃料；n. 加燃料 | |
| pedals [ˈpedlz] | n. 踏板；脚踏；方向舵脚蹬（pedal 的复数） | |
| accelerator [əkˈseləreɪtə(r)] | n. 加速踏板；催化剂；[机]加速装置 | |
| subsystem [səbˈsɪstəm] | n. 子系统；子系统；次系统；分系统；副系统 | |
| auxiliary [ɔːɡˈzɪliəri] | adj. 辅助的；备用的<br>n. 助动词；辅助工；辅助人员 | |
| regenerative [rɪˈdʒenərətɪv] | adj.（能力或过程）再生的，再造的 | |
| recovery [rɪˈkʌvəri] | n. 恢复；痊愈；改善；回升；复苏；取回；收回；复得 | |
| clutch [klʌtʃ] | n.（汽车等起换挡功能的）离合器踏板；（尤指发动机和排挡的）离合器；一群（人或动物）；一批（物品） | |
| gearbox [ˈɡɪəbɒks] | n. 变速器；齿轮箱 | |
| differential [ˌdɪfəˈrenʃl] | n. 差别；差额；差价；（尤指同行业不同工种的）工资级差；（汽车）差动齿轮，分速器，差速器行星齿轮 | |
| simplified [ˈsɪmplɪfaɪd] | v. 使简化；使简易 | |
| compacted [kəmˈpæktɪd] | v. 把……紧压在一起（或压实） | |

## 2. Expressions（短语）

| | |
|---|---|
| power electronic converter | 电力电子变换器 |
| electric drive train | 电力驱动系 |
| consist of | 组成 |
| mechanical transmission | 机械传动装置 |
| energy management unit | 能量管理单元 |
| energy refueling unit | 能量的燃料供给单元 |
| power steering unit | 动力转向单元 |
| hotel climate control unit | 车内气候控制单元 |
| auxiliary supply unit | 辅助电源 |
| brake pedal | 制动踏板 |
| fixed gearing | 固定挡的齿轮传动装置 |
| curved path | 弯曲路径 |
| electric motor | 电动机 |

### Notes to the text（难点解析）

★1. Based on the control inputs from the accelerator and brake pedals, the vehicle controller provides proper control signals to the electronic power converter, which functions to regulate the power flow between the electric motor and energy source. 基于来自加速和制动踏板的控制输入，车辆控制器向电力电子变换器给出正确的控制信号，变换器行使控制电动机与能源之间的功率流的功能。

### Exercises（练习）

◆1. Translate the following passages (expressions) into Chinese（英译汉）

（1）It consists of an electric motor, a clutch, a gearbox and a differential.

（2）With an electric motor that has a constant power in a long speed range, a fixed gearing can replace the multispeed gearbox and reduce the need for a clutch.

（3）conventional vehicle drive train

（4）the power steering unit

◆2. Translate the following passages (expressions) into English（汉译英）

（1）电力电子变换器

（2）车内气候控制单元

（3）为进一步简化驱动系，牵引电动机可安置在车轮内。

◆3. Directions: Answer the following questions briefly according to the text

（1）What does the drive train consist of and how do they work?

（2）What are the possible EV configurations?

### Reading material（阅读材料）

The clutch and gearbox may be replaced by an automatic transmission. The clutch is used to connect or disconnect the power of the electric motor from the driven wheels. The gearbox provides a set of gear ratios to modify the speed-power (torque) profile to match the load requirement. The differential is a mechanical device (usually a set of planetary gears), which enables the wheels of both sides to be driven at different speeds when the vehicle runs along a curved path.

## 2.1.3　System Level Diagram of an EV

### Text（课文）

The complete EV consists of not only the electric drive and power electronics for propulsion, but also other subsystems to make the whole system work. In Figure 2.5, one needs a battery (or a fuel cell) to provide the electrical energy. This is shown by the block on the left which provides power to drive the electric motor. The motor is part of the EV power-train, labeled as EVPT on the right. For each of these items, battery or EVPT, there is a controller. The battery controller can control the charging or discharging, and similarly the EVPT controller will control the speed or torque of the motor by controlling the power electronics. It should be realized that even though the blocks in the diagram are shown to be at quite different positions, in reality they could be physically very close. The reason is due to packaging and also, by positioning them nearby, it is possible to reduce the high-current and high-voltage cable lengths. Similarly, although the controllers named the FC controller (for Fuel Cell controller or battery controller) and the EVPT controller are shown separately to indicate separate functionality, in reality they could be part of the same physical box and could even share the same microprocessors to achieve their functions. These aspects are subtle design issues involving cost and packaging. In addition, there is a box shown as the "Interface." This is the controller box that receives signals and also power, both high voltage for propulsion and low voltage for certain specific devices which operate at low voltage, and then through the "Interface" function channelizes them to the EVPT motor or the high-voltage battery. Again, these function separation blocks may be merged when physically integrating the system.

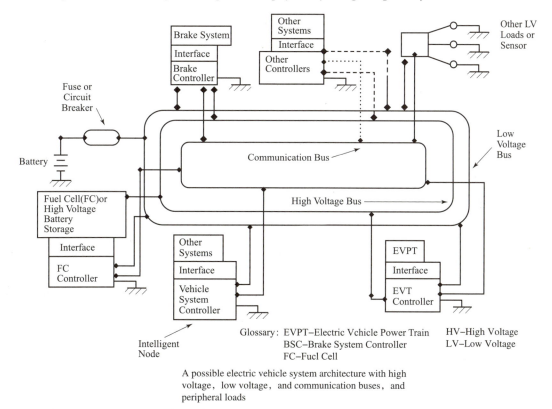

A possible electric vehicle system architecture with high voltage, low voltage, and communication buses, and peripheral loads

**Figure 2.5 System-level diagram of an EV**

In addition to the above blocks, there are various other blocks, for example, the vehicle controller, which can receive signals on the velocity of the vehicle, driver pedal position, and so on, and make a decision whether additional torque is needed from the motor or not, based on that information it can send the signal to the EVPT controller with the appropriate torque request. Similarly the brake controller can receive signals corresponding to brake pedal position, vehicle velocity, and so on, and decide how much brake force is needed. It can also receive signals like the battery's state of charge and can figure out whether the opportunity of regenerative braking is present. If it is possible, it can then send signals to the EVPT controller to carry this out. All this illustrates the importance of continuous flow of information and signals between various control blocks and corresponding decision-making in each subsystem.

Information transmission between various blocks is normally done through a controller area network (CAN) bus. This is basically a type of computer network where a single wire can contain multiple information or communication signals multiplexed together. Some sort of protocol has to be used when multiple signals are to be shared. In other words, there is some sort of priority-based signal flow when trying to share the same physical medium. For relatively slow signals, for example, to turn the door lock switch, one can afford to wait, whereas for very important functions like braking and steering, which are safety functions, the signals need to be transmitted immediately. There are some newer protocols which can allow such activities. In addition, for safety-critical functions, it may be necessary to have additional hardware-based backup communication mechanisms, so as to avoid failures.

## New words and expressions （单词和短语）

### 1. New words （单词）

|  |  |
| --- | --- |
| diagram [ˈdaɪəɡræm] | n. 简图；图解；图表；示意图 |
| powertrain [ˈpaʊəˌtreɪn] | n. 动力传动部件 |
| controller [kənˈtrəʊlə(r)] | n. （尤指大型机构或部门的）管理者，控制者，指挥者；（机器的）控制器，调节器；（公司的）财务总管 |
| charging [ˈtʃɑːdʒɪŋ] | v. 充电 |
| discharging [dɪsˈtʃɑːdʒɪŋ] | v. 放电 |
| torque [tɔːk] | n. （使机器等旋转的）转矩 |
| microprocessor [ˌmaɪkrəʊˈprəʊsesə(r)] | n. 微处理器 |
| protocol [ˈprəʊtəkɒl] | n. 礼仪；外交礼节；条约草案；议定书；（协议或条约的）附件；（数据传递的）协议，规程，规约 |
| braking [ˈbreɪkɪŋ] | v. 用闸减速；制动<br>brake 的现在分词 |
| steering [ˈstɪərɪŋ] | n. （车辆等的）转向装置<br>v. 驾驶（船、汽车等）；掌控转向盘；行驶；操纵；控制 |
| block [blɒk] | n. 块；街区；大厦；障碍物<br>vt. 阻止；阻塞；限制；封盖<br>adj. 成批的，大块的；交通堵塞的 |

| subtle [ˈsʌtl] | adj. 微妙的；精细的；敏感的；狡猾的；稀薄的 |
| --- | --- |
| interface [ˈɪntəfeɪs] | n. 界面；＜计＞接口；交界面<br>v.（使通过界面或接口）接合，连接；[计算机]使联系<br>vi. 相互作用（或影响）；交流，交谈 |
| merge [mɜːdʒ] | vt. 合并；使合并；吞没<br>vi. 合并；融合 |
| velocity [vəˈlɒsəti] | n. [物] 速度 |
| signal [ˈsɪɡnəl] | n. 信号；暗号；导火线<br>vt. 标志；用信号通知；表示<br>adj. 显著的；作为信号的<br>vi. 发信号 |
| multiplex [ˈmʌltɪpleks] | n. [测] 多倍仪；多重通道<br>vi. [通信] 多路传输；多工<br>vt. [通信] 多路传输<br>adj. 多样的，多元的；[通信] 多路传输的 |
| medium [ˈmiːdɪəm] | n. 方法；媒体；媒介；中间物；溶剂；灵媒；中庸<br>adj. 中间的，中等的；半生熟的；（投球）中速的 |
| transmit [trænzˈmɪt] | vt. 传输；传播；发射；传达；遗传<br>vi. 传输；发射信号 |

2. Expressions（短语）

| electric drive | 电驱动 |
| --- | --- |
| power electronic | 电力电子器件 |
| vehicle controller | 整车控制器 |
| velocity of the vehicle | 汽车车速 |
| driver pedal position | 驾驶员踏板位置 |
| communication signals multiplexed | 多路复用通信信号 |
| controller urea network（CAN） | 控制器局域网 |
| priority-based signal flow | 优先级的信号流 |

### Notes to the text（难点解析）

★1. In addition, there is a box shown as the "Interface." This is the controller box that receives signals and also power, both high voltage for propulsion and low voltage for certain specific devices which operate at low voltage, and then through the "Interface" function channelizes them to

043

the EVPT motor or the high-voltage battery. 另外，还有一个盒子叫"接口"。这是一个接收信号和功率的控制器盒，既包括驱动需要的高压，也包括某些在低压下工作的特定设备所需要的低压。通过这个接口的功能，将这些信号传递到 EVPT 电动机或高压电池。

★2. It can also receive signals like the battery's state of charge and can figure out whether the opportunity of regenerative braking is present. 整车控制器也能接收蓄电池荷电状态信号，判断是否能够进行再生制动。

★3. All this illustrates the importance of continuous flow of information and signals between various control blocks and corresponding decision-making in each subsystem.

所有这些表明，各种控制器模块和进行相应动作的子系统之间连续信息流和信号非常重要。

### Exercises（练习）

◆1. Translate the following passages (expressions) into Chinese（英译汉）

（1）It should be realized that even though the blocks in the diagram are shown to be at quite different positions, in reality they could be physically very close.

（2）And similarly the EVPT controller will control the speed or torque of the motor by controlling the power electronics.

（3）The motor is part of the EV power-train, labeled as EVPT on the right.

◆2. Translate the following passages (expressions) into English（汉译英）

（1）汽车车速

（2）电力电子器件

（3）一辆完整的纯电动汽车不仅包括驱动需要的电驱动零部件和电力电子器件，也包括其他一些使整个系统有效工作的子系统。

◆3. Directions：Answer the following questions briefly according to the text

How does EV work？

### Reading material（阅读材料）

From a technical viewpoint, the EV has another benefit. In the ICE, which is a reciprocating engine, the torque produced is pulsating in nature. The flywheel helps smooth the torque which would otherwise cause vibration. In the EV, the motor can create a very smooth torque and, in fact, it is possible to do away with the flywheel, thus saving material and manufacturing cost, in addition to reducing weight. And finally, the efficiency of an ICE (gasoline to shaft torque) is very low. The engine itself has about 30%–37% efficiency for a gasoline and about 40% for a diesel engine, but by the time the power arrives at the wheel the efficiency is just 5%–10%. On the other hand, the efficiency of the electric motor is very high, on the order of 90%. The battery and power electronics to drive the motor also have high efficiency. If each of these components has an efficiency on the order of 90%, by the time the battery energy leaves the motor shaft, the overall efficiency will be something like 70%. This is still substantially higher than that in the ICE.

## 2.2　Hybrid Electric Vehicles

### Text（课文）

There are two or more power sources in a hybrid electric vehicle (HEV). Normally an ICE is combined with a battery, an electric motor, and/or an electric generator in the most common types of hybrid electric vehicles. Hybrid electric vehicles can be classified into four different types according to how the power-train components are arranged: series, parallel, series-parallel and complex hybrid.

#### 2.2.1　Parallel Hybrid

In a parallel HEV, an electric motor and an ICE are connected to the transmission through a mechanical coupling device, such as separate clutches, so that the vehicle can either be driven by the ICE, or by the electric motor, or by both. The power requirements of the motor in a parallel HEV are lower than that of an EV with similar size. The configuration of the parallel HEV is shown in Figure 2.6.

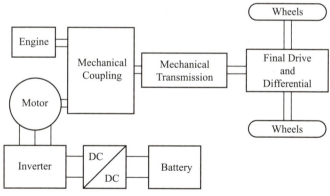

**Figure 2.6　Configuration of a parallel HEV**

The parallel HEV has the following advantages. First, a parallel HEV needs only two propulsion components, ICE and an electric motor. The motor can be operated as a generator and vice versa. Second, the engine and the motor can be rated at reduced power levels for short-distance trips. For long-distance trips, the engine may be designed for maximum power, while the motor/generator may still be rated to half the maximum power. However, the mechanical structure and power-train control is complex due to the necessity of power coupling for the ICE and the motor. It is also this complexity that gives more freedom for the power-train control to optimize fuel economy and vehicle performance.

The mechanical coupling is realized through the use of pulleys, gears, clutches, or a common shaft for the engine and motor. Mechanical coupling between motor and ICE can be configured to share a common transmission, or use separate transmissions or even separate axles. The mechanical transmission is also no longer restrained by the traditional automatic transmissions. For example, planetary gear sets have been introduced in parallel hybrids in place of the traditional CVT. The flexibility of configurations in parallel HEV offers the maximum advantage for fuel economy optimization in hybrid electric vehicles.

## New words and expressions（单词和短语）

### 1. New words（单词）

|  |  |
| --- | --- |
| engine [ˈendʒɪn] | n. 发动机；引擎；火车头；机车；有……型发动机的；有……个引擎的 |
| motor [ˈməʊtə(r)] | n. 电动机；发动机；马达；汽车 |
| pulley [ˈpʊli] | n. 滑轮；滑轮组；滑车 |
| gear [ɡɪə] | n. 排挡；齿轮；传动装置；挡；（某种活动的）设备，用具，衣服 |
| clutch [klʌtʃ] | n. 离合器 |
| shaft [ʃɑːft] | n.（电梯的）升降机井；通风井；竖井；井筒；（箭、高尔夫球杆等的）杆；（锤等的）柄；（机器的）轴 |
| transmission [trænzˈmɪʃn] | n. 变速器 |
| parallel [ˈpærəlel] | n. 平行线；对比<br>adj. 平行的；类似的，相同的<br>vt. 使……与……平行 |
| complexity [kəmˈpleksəti] | n. 复杂，复杂性；复杂错综的事物 |
| optimize [ˈɒptɪmaɪz] | vt. 使最优化，使完善<br>vi. 优化；持乐观态度 |
| flexibility [ˌfleksəˈbɪləti] | n. 灵活性；弹性；适应性 |

### 2. Expressions（短语）

|  |  |
| --- | --- |
| electric motor | 电动机 |
| hybrid electric vehicle | 混合动力电动汽车 |
| traditional CVT | 传统的无级变速器（CVT） |
| electric generator | 发电机 |
| parallel hybrid | 并联式混合 |
| mechanical coupling device | 机械耦合装置 |
| separate clutch | 离合器 |
| propulsion component | 推进组件 |

| | |
|---|---|
| planetary gear sets | 行星轮系 |
| separate axle | 传动轴 |

## Notes to the text（难点解析）

★1. Hybrid electric vehicles can be classified into four different types according to how the power-train components are arranged: series, parallel, series-parallel and complex hybrid. 根据动力总成系统组件的配置情况，混合动力电动汽车可以分为四种不同的类型：串联式、并联式、混联式以及复联式混合动力电动汽车。

★2. However, the mechanical structure and power-train control is complex due to the necessity of power coupling for the ICE and the motor. It is also this complexity that gives more freedom for the power-train control to optimize fuel economy and vehicle performance. 然而，电动机与发动机功率耦合会导致机械结构与动力总成控制较为复杂。但同时正是这种复杂性，使动力总成控制更加灵活，以优化燃油经济性与车辆动力性能。

## Exercises（练习）

◆1. Translate the following passages (expressions) into Chinese（英译汉）

（1）For long-distance trips, the engine may be designed for maximum power, while the motor/generator may still be rated to half the maximum power.

（2）The flexibility of configurations in parallel HEV offers the maximum advantage for fuel economy optimization in hybrid electric vehicles.

（3）parallel hybrid

（4）planetary gear sets

◆2. Translate the following passages (expressions) into English（汉译英）

（1）并联式混合动力电动汽车的电动机功率需求低于同样大小的纯电动汽车。

（2）电动机

（3）发电机

（4）图 a

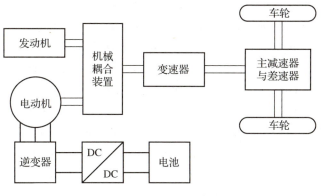

图 a  并联式混合动力电动汽车的结构

### Reading material（阅读材料）

The parallel hybrid needs only two propulsion devices, the ICE and the electric motor, which can be used in the following modes:

1) Motor-alone mode: When the battery has sufficient energy, and the vehicle power demand is low, the engine is turned off. And the vehicle is powered by the motor and battery only.

2) Combined power mode: At high power demand, the engine is turned on and the motor also supplies power to the wheels.

3) Engine-alone mode: During highway cruising and at moderately high power demands, the engine provides all the power needed to drive the vehicle. The motor remains idle. This is mostly due to the fact that the battery SOC is already at a high level but the power demand of the vehicle prevents the engine from turning off, or it may not be efficient to turn the engine off.

4) Power split mode: When the engine is on, but the vehicle power demand is low and the battery SOC is also low, a portion of the engine power is converted to electricity by the motor to charge the battery.

5) Stationary charging mode: The battery is charged by running the motor as a generator and driven by the engine, without the vehicle being driven.

6) Regenerative braking mode: The electric motor is operated as a generator to convert the vehicle's kinetic energy into electric energy and store it in the battery. Note that, in regenerative mode, it is in principle possible to run the engine as well, and provide additional current to charge the battery more quickly (while the propulsion motor is in generator mode) and command its torque accordingly, that is, to match the total battery power input. In this case, the engine and motor controllers have to be properly coordinated.

### 2.2.2　Series Hybrid

### Text（课文）

The configuration of a series HEV as shown in Figure 2.7 is simpler than that of a parallel HEV. Only the electric motor provides all the propulsion power. An ICE on board drives a generator which can charge the battery when the state of charge (SOC) of the battery drops below a certain level. Beyond the ICE and the generator the propulsion system is the same as in an EV. The series HEV has advantages including flexibility of location of engine-generator set and simplicity of drive-train, but meanwhile, due to its intrinsic structure, the series HEV needs more propulsion components (i.e., ICE, generator and motor). The fact that no mechanical link exists between the engine and mechanical transmission can have the engine operate in its most efficient region by adjusting its speed and torque. The electric motor has to be designed for the maximum power required by the vehicle. For long-distance missions, the three propulsion components need to be sized for maximum power.

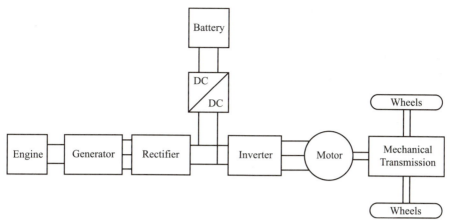

Figure 2.7　Configuration of a series HEV

### New words and expressions（单词和短语）

#### 1. New words（单词）

| | |
|---|---|
| simplicity [sɪmˈplɪsəti] | n. 简单（性）；容易（性）；质朴；淳朴；简单（或质朴、朴素）之处 |
| intrinsic [ɪnˈtrɪnzɪk] | adj. 固有的；内在的；本身的 |
| component [kəmˈpəʊnənt] | adj. 组成的；构成的<br>n. 组成部分；成分；组件，元件 |

#### 2. Expressions（短语）

| | |
|---|---|
| state of charge (SOC) | 电池的荷电状态 |
| series HEV | 串联式混合动力汽车 |
| maximum power | 最大功率 |
| the propulsion power | 驱进动力 |

### Notes to the text（难点解析）

★1. An ICE on board drives a generator which can charge the battery when the state of charge (SOC) of the battery drops below a certain level. 当电池的荷电状态（SOC）下降到低于设定值时，车载发动机会驱动发电机对电池进行充电。

★2. The fact that no mechanical link exists between the engine and mechanical transmission can have the engine operate in its most efficient region by adjusting its speed and torque. 在发动机和机械传动之间不存在机械连接，可通过调整发动机速度和转矩使其工作在最大效率区。

### Exercises（练习）

◆1. Translate the following passages (expressions) into Chinese（英译汉）

（1）Only the electric motor provides all the propulsion power.

(2) The electric motor has to be designed for the maximum power required by the vehicle.

◆2. Translate the following passages (expressions) into English (汉译英)

(1) 串联式混合动力电动汽车

(2) 最大功率

◆3. Directions: Answer the following questions briefly according to the text

Please draw the configuration of a series HEV.

### Reading material (阅读材料)

Based on the vehicle operating conditions, the propulsion components on a series HEV can operate with different combinations:

1) Battery alone: When the battery has sufficient energy, and the vehicle power demand is low, the I/G set is turned off, and the vehicle is powered by the battery only.

2) Combined power: At high power demands, the I/G set is turned on and the battery also supplies power to the electric motor.

3) Engine alone: During highway cruising and at moderately high power demands, the I/G set is turned on. The battery is neither charged nor discharged. This is mostly due to the fact that the battery's state of charge (SOC) is already at a high level but the power demand of the vehicle prevents the engine from turning off, or it may not be efficient to turn the engine off.

4) Power split: When the I/G is turned on, the vehicle power demand is below the I/G optimum power, and the battery SOC is low, then a portion of the I/G power is used to charge the battery.

5) Stationary charging: The battery is charged from the I/G power without the vehicle being driven.

6) Regenerative braking: The electric motor is operated as a generator to convert the vehicle's kinetic energy into electric energy and charge the battery.

### 2.2.3 Series-parallel Hybrid

### Text (课文)

Considering the advantages of both series and parallel configurations, manufacturers and researchers have developed series-parallel hybrid electric vehicles. These HEVs can operate by either using electric motor alone or with the assistance of the ICE. The configuration of the series-parallel HEV is shown in Figure 2.8. In this configuration, power of the ICE and the electric motor is coupled to drive the vehicle in parallel operation, while power flow from engine to generator and then to the electric motor can be considered series.

There are many choices to design the "mode selection" device. The simplest one is clutches to select which shaft is connected to the ICE, i.e., to connect either the final drive or the electric generator to the ICE. Another choice is to have a power split device such as a planetary gear train to split the ICE power to the drive shaft and the electric generator.

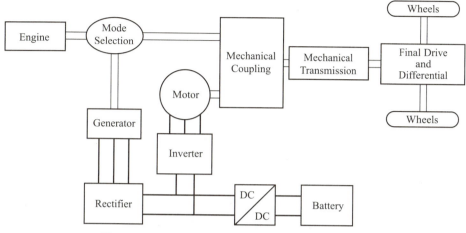

Figure 2.8　Configuration of a series-parallel HEV

The battery can be charged by the power of the generator. The electric motor can also supply power to the front wheels in parallel with the ICE. A control unit is in charge of driving mode selection. When short bursts of power are needed, the ICE and the electric motor together provide the power required by the vehicle demand.

The Toyota Prius, shown in Figure 2.9, is a typical series-parallel HEV where a small series element is placed in addition to the primarily parallel HEV. In Toyota Prius, the battery remains charged in prolonged waiting periods such as traffic lights or in traffic jam. According to the report from the United States Environmental Protection Agency, the 2008 Prius is the most fuel-efficient car sold in the US.

Figure 2.9　Toyota Prius

### New words and expressions（单词和短语）

#### 1. New words（单词）

| | |
|---|---|
| series-parallel hybrid | 混联式混合 |
| mode selection | 模式选择 |
| driving mode | 驱动模式 |

| Toyota Prius | 丰田普锐斯 |
| United States Environmental Protection Agency | 美国环境保护局 |

### Notes to the text（难点解析）

★1. In this configuration, power of the ICE and the electric motor is coupled to drive the vehicle in parallel operation, while power flow from engine to generator and then to the electric motor can be considered series. 在此结构中，内燃机和电动机的功率耦合驱动汽车运行在并联模式下，但是功率由发动机到发电机再到电动机的过程可以看作是串联的。

★2. Another choice is to have a power split device such as a planetary gear-train to split the ICE power to the drive shaft and the electric generator. 另外一种选择是采用一种功率分流装置（例如行星齿轮组）将发动机的输出功率分流到传动轴和发电机。

### Exercises（练习）

◆1. Translate the following passages (expressions) into Chinese（英译汉）
（1）The battery can be charged by the power of the generator.
（2）traffic lights
（3）a planetary gear-train
◆2. Directions: Answer the following questions briefly according to the text
Please draw the configuration of the series-parallel HEV.

### Reading material（阅读材料）

Prius is a Latin word meaning "to go before." When the Prius was first released, it was selected as the world's best-engineered passenger car for 2002. The car was chosen because it is the first hybrid vehicle that seats four to five people plus their luggage, and is one of the most economical and environmentally friendly vehicles available. Then in 2004, the second-generation Prius won the prestigious Motor Trend Car of the Year Award and Best-engineered Vehicle of 2004.

## 2.2.4 Complex Hybrid

### Text（课文）

There exist other configurations of HEVs which cannot be classified into the above three types. An example is shown in Figure 2.10 which has dual-axle four-wheel drive capability with multiple electric machines and an ICE. It is very much similar to the series-parallel hybrid system. However, the main difference is that the electric motor connected to the power split/combine device in the complex hybrid allows for bidirectional power flow, while the generator in the series-parallel hybrid only permits unidirectional power flow. This bidirectional power flow results in the three propulsion power (due to the ICE and two electric motors) operating modes that are impossible in the series-parallel hybrid. Another difference is that usually the series-parallel hybrid is propelled through front wheels by an engine and/or an electric motor. However, in the complex hybrid, the front-wheel axle and rear-wheel axle are separately driven by a hybrid power-train and an electric motor, respectively. In normal operation mode, the power from ICE is split to propel the front axle and to drive the electric motor (as a generator) to charge the battery. When the load request is low, the battery supplies power to the front electric motor to drive the front axle and it is unnecessary to use both the ICE and rear electric motor. If the vehicle is running at heavy load (e. g. acceleration), both the engine and front electric motor provide power to drive the front axle and meanwhile the rear electric motor propels the rear wheels. Both the front and rear electric motors become generators to charge the battery in the regenerative mode (braking or deceleration). Another dual-axle complex hybrid system differs from the previous one in terms of function exchange between front and rear wheels, i. e. , icons of front and rear wheels exchange their positions. Other variations also exist, e. g. the Toyota Highlander, which employs three electric motors and an ICE to maximize the fuel economy of the vehicle, as well as to improve the vehicle driveability. Unfortunately, the complex hybrid suffers from the high complexity and cost, which is similar to the series-parallel hybrid.

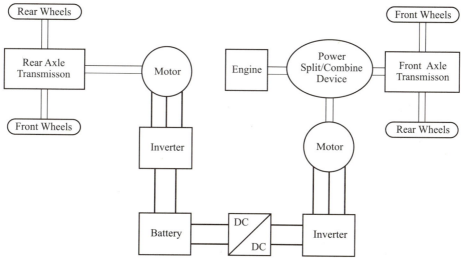

Figure 2.10　Configuration of a complex HEV

## New words and expressions（单词和短语）

### 1. New words（单词）

| split [splɪt] | v. 分流；分裂，使分裂（成不同的派别）；分开，使分开（成为几个部分）；分担；分摊；分享 |
|---|---|
| acceleration [əkˌseləˈreɪʃn] | n. 加速；加快；（车辆）加速能力，加速的幅度；加速度 |
| bidirectional [ˌbaɪdɪˈrekʃənl] | adj. 双向的；双向作用的 |

| | |
|---|---|
| unidirectional [ˌjuːnɪdɪˈrekʃənl] | adj. 单向的；单向性的 |
| propel [prəˈpel] | vt. 推进；驱使；激励；驱策 |

### 2. Expressions（短语）

| | |
|---|---|
| dual-axle four-wheel drive | 双轴四轮驱动 |
| complex hybrid | 复联式混合 |
| power flow | 功率流 |
| propulsion power operating mode | 推进动力运行模式 |
| heavy load | 大负载 |
| regenerative mode | 再生模式 |
| dual-axle complex hybrid system | 双轴复联式混合动力系统 |
| Toyota Highlander | 丰田汉兰达 |
| normal operation mode | 一般的运行模式 |
| power split/combine | 功率分流或汇合 |

### Notes to the text（难点解析）

★1. However, the main difference is that the electric motor connected to the power split/combine device in the complex hybrid allows for bidirectional power flow, while the generator in the series-parallel hybrid only permits unidirectional power flow. 然而主要的区别在于，复联式混合动力汽车中连接到功率分流或汇合装置的电动机允许双向功率流，而混联式混合动力的发电机只允许单向功率流。

★2. However, in the complex hybrid, the front-wheel axle and rear-wheel axle are separately driven by a hybrid power-train and an electric motor, respectively. 然而在复联式混合动力电动汽车中，前轮和后轮分别由混合动力总成系统和一个电动机来驱动。

### Exercises（练习）

◆1. Translate the following passages (expressions) into Chinese（英译汉）

(1) Both the front and rear electric motors become generators to charge the battery in the regenerative mode (braking or deceleration).

(2) When the load request is low, the battery supplies power to the front electric motor to drive the front axle.

(3) complex hybrid

◆2. Translate the following passages (expressions) into English（汉译英）

(1) 再生模式

(2) 一般运行模式

(3) 双轴复联式混合动力电动汽车

◆3. Directions: Answer the following questions briefly according to the text

Please draw the configuration of the complex hybrid HEV.

### Reading material (阅读材料)

Toyota produced the world's first mass-marketed modern HEV in 1997, the Prius. The worldwide sales of the Prius exceeded 1 million units in 2009. It uses a planetary gear set to realize continuous variable transmission (CVT). Therefore, conventional transmission is not needed in this system. The engine is connected to the carrier of the planetary gear while the generator is connected to the sun gear. The ring gear is coupled to the final drive, as is the electric motor. The planetary gear set also acts as a power/torque split device. During normal operations, the ring gear speed is determined by the vehicle speed, while the generator speed can be controlled such that the engine speed is in its optimum efficiency range. The 6.5 (A·h), 21 kW nickel metal hydride battery pack is charged by the generator during coasting and by the propulsion motor (in generation mode) during regenerative braking. The engine is shut off during low-speed driving.

The same technology has been used in the Camry hybrid, the Highlander hybrid, and the Lexus brand hybrids. However, the Highlander and the Lexus brand hybrids add a third motor at the rear wheel. The drive performance, such as for acceleration and braking, can thus be further improved.

## 2.3 Plug-in Hybrid Electric Vehicle (PHEV)

### 2.3.1 Why PHEV

#### Text (课文)

The PHEV, as the name suggests, differs from an HEV only by the fact that it allows one to plug in a cable running from the vehicle to a household utility wall socket at home or elsewhere to charge the vehicle's battery. To extend the flexibility of the system, it is also possible in principle to use the engine and/or the battery system in the vehicle to generate AC power and feed it back to the utility grid. Since plug-in allows a fair amount of external utility system energy to drive the vehicle, it is helpful to use a larger battery than in a regular HEV. A larger battery is not a required part of the PHEV, but having one definitely benefits fuel economy and also increases the range of the vehicle when fully charged. In an HEV, using a much larger battery may not necessarily be the optimal choice in terms of design, since the ICE is always capable of kicking in, when the battery needs to be charged. People sometimes think that a large battery is mandatory for a PHEV, which may not be the ease. How large the battery can be depends on the packaging space available in the vehicle. If the battery size is small, the benefits from the PHEV will be merely incremental, whereas if it is too big it can be very expensive and will take longer to recharge from the utility system. Note also that the household utility system may have some limitations on how much current it can sustain in charging a battery system, hence some safeguards are necessary for the plug-in. Since the cost of utility energy at present is much lower than the price of gasoline, it makes sense to use the PHEV, where possible.

## New words and expressions（单词和短语）

### 1. New words（单词）

|  |  |
| --- | --- |
| cable [ˈkeɪbl] | n. 缆绳；电缆；海底电报<br>vt. 打电报 |
| socket [ˈsɒkɪt] | n. 插座；窝，穴；牙槽<br>vt. 给……配插座 |
| principle [ˈprɪnsəpl] | n. 原理，原则；主义，道义；本质，本义；根源，源泉 |
| utility [juːˈtɪləti] | n. 实用；效用；公共设施；功用<br>adj. 实用的；通用的；有多种用途的 |
| incremental [ˌɪnkrɪˈmentəl] | adj.（定额）增长的；逐渐的，逐步的；递增的 |
| mandatory [ˈmændətəri] | n. 受托者（等于 mandatary）<br>adj. 强制的；托管的；命令的 |

### 2. Expressions（短语）

|  |  |
| --- | --- |
| plug-in hybrid electric vehicle（PHEV） | 插电式混合动力电动汽车 |
| as the name suggests | 顾名思义 |
| feed it back to | 反哺 |
| utility grid | 公用电网 |

## Notes to the text（难点解析）

★1. In a HEV, using a much larger battery may not necessarily be the optimal choice in terms of design, since the ICE is always capable of kicking in, when the battery needs to be charged. 在 HEV 上，当蓄电池需要充电时，由于内燃机总能够介入，因此从设计来看，使用更大的蓄电池不一定是最佳的选择。

★2. Note also that the household utility system may have some limitations on how much current it can sustain in charging a battery system, hence some safeguards are necessary for the plug-in. 我们也应当注意，居民用电系统在为蓄电池系统充电时，其提供的电流大小有限制，因此有必要为插电方式设计保护装置。

## Exercises(练习)

◆1. Translate the following passages (expressions) into Chinese(英译汉)

(1) How large the battery can be depends on the packaging space available in the vehicle.

(2) plug-in hybrid electric vehicle

◆2. Translate the following passages (expressions) into English(汉译英)

(1) 如果电池较小,那么PHEV的成本较低;反之,电池较大,成本就会很高,也需要花很长的时间利用电网充电。

(2) 原则上,PHEV能够利用发动机和/或蓄电池系统产生交流电,反哺公用电网。

◆3. Directions: Answer the following questions briefly according to the text

What are the differences between HEV and PHEV?

## Reading material(阅读材料)

PHEVs are hybrid electric vehicles that can draw and store energy from an electric grid (or a renewable energy source), to eventually propel the vehicle.

This simple functional change allows a PHEV to displace petroleum with multisource electrical energy, including renewable energy resources, such as wind and solar energy. Such a change has critical beneficial impacts on the overall transportation sector petroleum consumption, total emissions, as well as on the performance and makeup of the electrical grid. PHEVs are seen as one of the most promising means to improve the near-term sustainability of the transportation as well as stationary energy sectors. Surveys have shown that there exists a considerable market for PHEVs. Renault and Daimler-Chrysler have produced limited production PHEVs. General Motors and Ford Motor Co. have developed and displayed PHEV concept vehicles.

###  2.3.2 Constituents of a PHEV

## Text(课文)

A PHEV now has an extra connecting socket in the vehicle, from where a lead can be pulled out and plugged into the wall utility outlet. Obviously, when the vehicle is connected to a utility outlet, its propulsion motor is not needed and neither is the ICE as far as turning the wheels is concerned. However, the vehicle may still need to use auxiliary loads (normally low-voltage loads at 12V), the air-conditioner (can be low voltage as well), or the healer and some lights. Hence it is appropriate to deliver those loads at low voltage. If fast charging of the battery is necessary, it will also be appropriate to run the ICE and use the propulsion motor as a generator, or have a separate generator for this purpose. Depending on the scheme used, changes in the gear-train system are called for. Even though the whole process of interconnection between the utility and the PHEV system is simple in principle, there are quite a few considerations to be taken into account, as it will be obvious from the possible architecture for such a vehicle shown in Figure 2.11.

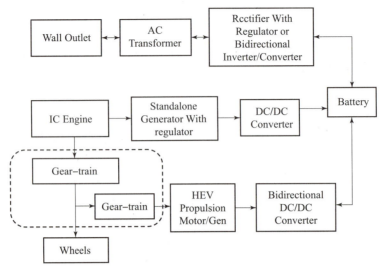

Figure 2.11  A possible architecture for the plug-in hybrid vehicle and home outlet interface

From Figure 2.11, it is apparent that in order to charge the battery, one path goes directly from the wall outlet to the battery, through a transformer isolation and a rectifier or DC/DC converter combination. This situation is directly involved with the plug-in part of the system. The bottom part of the figure shows that the charging process is done by either driving a standalone alternator, or using the propulsion motor itself run as a generator, ultimately charging the battery. Of course, it is understood that, when plugged in, the vehicle is stationary and the wheels are not moving. Even though the process indicated in the bottom part of Figure 2.11 is not involved directly with the plug-in, an overall power management process has to coordinate both the plug-in and the ICE, since there may be a situation when fast charging becomes necessary, and both the plug-in and the ICE (in generation mode) need to run concurrently. Finally, note the inclusion of a bidirectional converter in the plug-in part of the figure. This covers the possibility that in future the utility regulations may allow power to be fed back into the utility grid from the vehicle, assuming it has enough power to do so. This issue is not an immediate consideration within the automotive industry at present. However, the possibility may in fact help use the vehicle as an emergency generator to light a home in case there is a utility power failure.

Fundamentally the only difference between the HEV and the PHEV is related to the upper part of Figure 2.11, where the wall outlet is used to charge the battery. The size of the battery may be substantially different. In addition, as indicated above, the plug-in system has to be properly coordinated with the rest of the charging process and the overall power management in the vehicular system.

### New words and expressions（单词和短语）

**1. New words（单词）**

outlet ['aʊtlet]　　　　　　　　　　n. 出口，排放孔；[电] 电源插座；销路；发泄的方法；批发商店

| | |
|---|---|
| considerations [kənˌsɪdə'reɪʃnz] | n. 考虑；注意事项（consideration 的复数形式）；体贴 |
| constituent [kən'stɪtʃuənt] | n. 成分；选民；委托人<br>adj. 构成的；选举的；有任命（或选举）权的；立宪的； |
| architecture ['ɑːkɪtektʃə(r)] | n. 建筑学；建筑风格；建筑式样；架构 |
| apparent [ə'pærənt] | adj. 显然的；表面上的 |
| rectifier ['rektɪˌfaɪə] | n. [电]整流器；改正者，矫正者 |
| alternator ['ɔːltəneɪtə(r)] | n. [电]交流发电机 |
| stationary ['steɪʃənri] | n. 不动的人；驻军<br>adj. 固定的；静止的；定居的；常备军的 |
| concurrently [kən'kʌrəntli] | adv. 兼；同时发生地 |
| coordinate [kəʊ'ɔːdɪneɪt] | v. 调节，配合；使动作协调；（衣服、家具等）搭配；与……形成共价键<br>adj. 同等的，并列的；配位的；坐标的 |
| substantially [səb'stænʃəli] | adv. 非常；大大地；基本上；大体上；总的来说 |

### 2. Expressions（短语）

| | |
|---|---|
| utility outlet | 电源插座 |
| auxiliary load | 辅助负载 |
| air-conditioner | 空调 |
| bidirectional converter | 双向变换器 |
| utility grid | 电网 |
| emergency generator | 应急发电机 |
| wall outlet | 壁装电源插座 |
| utility power failure | 电力设施故障 |

### Notes to the text（难点解析）

★1. Obviously, when the vehicle is connected to a utility outlet, its propulsion motor is not needed and neither is the ICE. 显然，当汽车与电源插座相连时，它的驱动电动机和内燃机就不再需要了。

★2. If fast charging of the battery is necessary, it will also be appropriate to run the ICE and use the propulsion motor as a generator, or have a separate generator for this purpose. 如果电池的快速充电是必需的，则应恰当运行内燃机，且驱动电动机被用作发电机，或利用一个独立的发电机来达到这一目的。

### Exercises（练习）

◆1. Translate the following passages (expressions) into Chinese（英译汉）

(1) Fundamentally the only difference between the HEV and the PHEV is related to the upper part of Figure 2.11, where the wall outlet is used to charge the battery.

(2) However, the possibility may in fact help use the vehicle as an emergency generator to light a home in case there is a utility power failure.

◆2. Translate the following passages (expressions) into English（汉译英）

(1) 辅助负载

(2) 空调

(3) 电源插座

### Reading material（阅读材料）

PHEVs are sometimes called range-extended electric vehicles or extended range electric vehicles. They always have on-board gasoline or diesel that can be used to drive the vehicle for an extended distance, when the on-board battery energy is depleted and furthermore, these vehicles can provide high fuel economy during the extended driving range. The large battery pack can accept more regenerative braking energy and provide more flexibility for engine optimization during the extended driving range. The Chevy Volt is equipped with a full-sized electric motor so that pure electric driving can be realized for all kinds of driving conditions.

## 2.4 Fuel Cell Vehicles (FCVs)

### Constituents and Some Issues of a FCV

### Text（课文）

The same figure which was used for the EV applies here. It can be seen from Figure 2.2 that the high-voltage source is already labeled as either a battery or fuel cell. The constituent elements are therefore, identical to the EV.

One of the problems with the fuel cell is that it is a unidirectional device, that is, it can deliver power output, but unlike a battery or an ultracapacitor, it can not receive any power back. Obviously then, the fuel cell has to be ruled out for any regenerative efforts in a vehicle. This implies that a battery or an ultracapacitor has to be introduced in order to gain a regenerative capability. It is not just for regenerative braking that a storage battery or an ultracapacitor is necessary: such storage elements also serve as mechanism by which the fuel cell can be started. This is important for both series and parallel hybrid vehicles. The battery or ultracapacitor has to be designed to meet such a starting current capability for at least half a minute, if not longer. In addition, based on the typical drive cycle of the vehicle, an assessment has to be made about the regenerative needs of the vehicle during braking and the size of the battery or uhracapacitor should be large enough for the worst case scenario.

The second problem with the fuel cell is its sensitivity in terms of the individual cell voltage. This gives an indication of the health of the fuel cell condition. If the cell voltages show a difference, that can indicate a problem. Fuel cells generally can not handle large transients, hence a battery often helps reduce the size of fuel cell needed and protects it during large transients in the dynamic process.

The fuel cell, not the cell per se but rather the whole module, along with all the peripheral devices like a compressor, water disposal mechanism, and warming system, together lead to a relatively low overall system efficiency.

## New words and expressions（单词和短语）

### 1. New words（单词）

| | |
|---|---|
| identical [aɪˈdentɪkl] | n. 完全相同的事物<br>adj. 同一的；完全相同的 |
| regenerative [rɪˈdʒenərətɪv] | adj.（能力或过程）再生的，再造的 |
| sensitivity [ˌsensəˈtɪvəti] | n. 体贴；体恤；体察；敏锐的感觉；悟性；容易生气；易被惹恼；敏感 |
| mechanism [ˈmekənɪzəm] | n. 机制；原理；途径；进程；机械装置；技巧 |
| assessment [əˈsesmənt] | n. 评定；估价 |
| transient [ˈtrænziənt] | n. 瞬变现象；过往旅客；候鸟<br>adj. 短暂的；路过的 |
| peripheral [pəˈrɪfərəl] | adj. 外围的；次要的；（神经）末梢区域的<br>n. 外部设备 |
| disposal [dɪˈspəʊzl] | n. 处理；支配；清理；安排 |

### 2. Expressions（短语）

| | |
|---|---|
| fuel cell vehicle（FCV） | 燃料电池电动汽车 |
| dynamic process | 动态过程 |
| peripheral device | 外围设备 |
| water disposal mechanism | 水分处理机构 |
| high-voltage source | 高压源 |
| cell voltage | 电池电压 |

## Notes to the text（难点解析）

★1. One of the problems with the fuel cell is that it is a unidirectional device, that is, it can deliver power output, but unlike a battery or an ultracapacitor, it can not receive any power back. 燃料电池的一个问题是，它是一种单向设备，也就是说，它能输出能量，与蓄电池或超级电容器不同，它不能回收能量。

★2. Fuel cells generally can not handle large transients, hence a battery often helps reduce the size of fuel cell needed and protects it during large transients in the dynamic process. 燃料电池不能承受大的瞬变，因此蓄电池有助于减小燃料电池的尺寸，在动态过程中保护它不会剧变。

## Exercises（练习）

◆1. Translate the following passages (expressions) into Chinese（英译汉）

（1）The battery or ultracapacitor has to be designed to meet such a starting current capability for at least half a minute, if not longer.

（2）The second problem with the fuel cell is its sensitivity in terms of the individual cell voltage.

（3）high-voltage source

★2. Translate the following passages (expressions) into English（汉译英）

（1）外围设备

（2）水分处理机构

（3）很显然，在汽车上它不能实现再生制动。

## Reading material（阅读材料）

The criteria that manufacturers had to take into account to choose the fuel cell most adapted to the light vehicle are numerous; the main ones are the following:

1）technology for which the cost projections are the lowest and in any event of the same order of magnitude as the current cost of the thermal engine;

2）specific mass and volume equivalent to those of a thermal engine;

3）low enough operating temperature to authorize an acceptable start-up time (from 1 to 2 minutes) but high enough to allow a residual heat evacuation mode compatible with the volume available;

4）technology compatible with correct operation in the traditional temperature range ($-30$℃ to $+40$℃);

5）operation with air as a combustive and insensitivity to gases and pollutants included in the air.

Taking these criteria into account led virtually all manufacturers to make the choice of the technology known as PEM. The Canadian manufacturer, Ballard Power Systems, currently equips the majority of the prototypes comprising PEM systems. Nevertheless, whilst the fuel cell is the main component of this new technology, the fuel is at the center of the debate on this subject. If the final fuel is hydrogen, which all agree is the fuel of the future, this gas is not distributed today on the road. Consequently, two major approaches currently clash:

1) whatever the primary fuel selected, hydrogen is manufactured in-station and distributed to users in a form that is to be specified (gas under pressure, liquid, absorbed);

2) the vehicle carries a hydrocarbon fuel (hydrocarbon or alcohol) and transforms it on-board (reforming) into hydrogen, as and when it is needed.

# Chapter 3
## Energy Storages

### Text（课文）

"Energy storages" are defined as devices that store energy, deliver energy outside (discharge), and accept energy from outside (charge). There are several types of energy storages that have been proposed for EV and HEV applications. These energy storages, so far, mainly include chemical batteries, ultracapacitors or supercapacitors, and ultra-high-speed flywheels. The fuel cell is a type of energy converter.

There are a number of requirements for energy storages applied in an automotive application, such as specific energy, specific power, efficiency, the maintenance requirement, management, costs, environmental adaptation and friendliness, and safety. For application on an EV, specific energy is the first consideration since it limits the vehicle range. On the other hand, for HEV applications, specific energy becomes less important and specific power is the first consideration, because all the energy is from the energy source and sufficient power is needed to ensure vehicle performance, particularly during acceleration, hill climbing, and regenerative braking. Of course, other requirements should be fully considered in the vehicle drive-train development.

### New words and expressions（单词和短语）

#### 1. New words（单词）

| | |
|---|---|
| converter [kənˈvɜːtə(r)] | n. （使）转变的人（或物）；转换器；整流器；变频器；转换程序；变焦镜 |
| range [reɪndʒ] | n. 范围；幅度；排；山脉<br>vi. （在……内）变动；平行，列为一行；延伸；漫游；射程达到 |
| application [ˌæplɪˈkeɪʃn] | n. 应用；申请；应用程序；敷用；（对事物、学习等）投入 |
| requirement [rɪˈkwaɪəmənt] | n. 要求；必要条件；必需品 |
| efficiency [ɪˈfɪʃnsi] | n 效率；效能；功效 |
| deliver [dɪˈlɪvə(r)] | vt. 交付；发表；递送；释放；给予（打击）；给……接生<br>vi. 实现；传送；履行；投递 |

| | |
|---|---|
| storage [ˈstɔːrɪdʒ] | n. 存储；仓库；贮藏所 |
| consideration [kənˌsɪdəˈreɪʃn] | n. 考虑；原因；关心；报酬 |
| acceleration [əkˌseləˈreɪʃn] | n. 加速，促进；[物]加速度；跳级 |
| adaptation [ˌædæpˈteɪʃn] | n. 适应；改编；改编本，改写本 |

### 2. Expressions（短语）

| | |
|---|---|
| chemical batteries | 化学蓄电池组 |
| specific energy | 比能量 |
| specific power | 比功率 |
| regenerative braking | 再生制动 |
| maintenance requirement | 维护要求 |
| drive-train | 驱动系统 |

### Notes to the text（难点解析）

★1. "Energy storages" are defined as devices that store energy, deliver energy outside (discharge), and accept energy from outside (charge). "能量储存"定义为储存能量、向外传送能量（放电）和从外部接收能量（充电）的装置。

★2. For application on an EV, specific energy is the first consideration since it limits the vehicle range. 就电动汽车的应用而言，比能量是首要的技术条件，因为它约束了车辆的行程。

### Exercises（练习）

◆1. Translate the following passages (expressions) into Chinese（英译汉）
(1) The fuel cell is a type of energy converter.
(2) specific energy
(3) drive-train

◆2. Translate the following passages (expressions) into English（汉译英）
(1) 比功率
(2) 再生制动

◆3. Directions：Answer the following questions briefly according to the text
Could you tell us several requirements for energy storages applied in an automotive application?

### Reading material（阅读材料）

The hybridization of energy storage involves combining two or more energy storages together so that the advantages of each can be brought out and the disadvantages can be compensated by others. For instance, the hybridization of a chemical battery with an ultracapacitor can overcome problems such as the low specific power of chemical batteries and low specific energy of ultracapacitors, thus achieving high specific energy and high specific power. Basically, the hybridized energy storage consists of two basic energy storages, one with high specific energy and the other with high specific power.

## 3.1 Electrochemical Batteries

**Text（课文）**

Electrochemical batteries, more commonly referred to as "batteries," are electrochemical devices that convert electrical energy into potential chemical energy during charging, and convert chemical energy into electric energy during discharging. A battery is composed of several cells stacked together. A cell is an independent and complete unit that possesses all the electrochemical properties. Basically, a battery cell consists of three primary elements: two electrodes (positive and negative), immersed into electrolyte as shown in Figure 3.1.

Battery manufacturers usually specify the battery with coulometric capacity (ampere-hours), which is defined as the number of ampere-hours gained when discharging the battery from a fully charged state until the terminal voltage drops to its cut-off voltage, as shown in Figure 3.2. It should be noted that the same battery usually has a different number of ampere-hours at different discharging current rates. Generally, the capacity will become smaller with a large discharge current rate, as shown in Figure 3.3. Battery manufacturers usually specify a battery with a number of ampere-hours along with a current rate. For example, a battery labeled as 100 (A·h) at C/5 rate has a 100 (A·h) capacity at a 5h discharge rate (discharging current = 100/5 = 20 A).

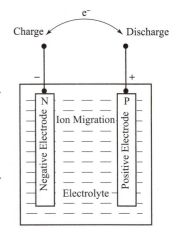

Figure 3.1  A typical electrochemical battery cell

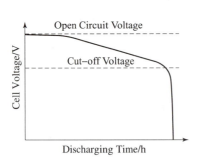

Figure 3.2  Cut-off voltage of a typical battery

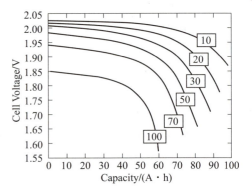

Figure 3.3  Discharge characteristics of a lead-acid battery

## New words and expressions（单词和短语）

### 1. New words（单词）

| | |
|---|---|
| electrochemical [ɪˌlektrəʊˈkemɪkəl] | adj. ［物化］电化学的；［物化］电气化学的 |
| electrode [ɪˈlektrəʊd] | n. ［电］电极；电焊条 |
| electrolyte [ɪˈlektrəlaɪt] | n. 电解液，电解质；电解 |
| terminal [ˈtɜːmɪnl] | n. 航空站；终点站；终端机；线接头；末端；晚期病人 adj. 晚期的；无可挽回的；末端的；终点的；期末的 |
| manufacturer [ˌmænjuˈfæktʃərə(r)] | n. 制造商；［经］厂商 |
| label [ˈleɪbl] | v. 贴标签于；把……归类，给……扣帽子；用示踪剂使（物质等）示踪 n. 标签；商标；绰号；唱片公司；词目标注 |

### 2. Expressions（短语）

| | |
|---|---|
| electrical energy | 电能 |
| chemical energy | 化学能 |
| cut-off voltage | 终止电压 |
| a fully charged state | 全荷电状态 |
| discharging current rate | 电流放电率 |
| be referred to as | 被称为 |
| discharging current | 放电电流 |

## Notes to the text（难点解析）

★1. Generally, the capacity will become smaller with a large discharge current rate. 一般，在高电流放电率的情况下，容量将变得较小。

★2. It should be noted that the same battery usually has a different number of ampere-hours at different discharging current rates. 应该注意，同样的蓄电池在不同的电流放电率下，通常具有不同的安时数。

## Exercises（练习）

◆1. Translate the following passages (expressions) into Chinese（英译汉）

（1）A cell is an independent and complete unit that possesses all the electrochemical properties.

（2）electrical energy

（3）chemical energy

◆2. Translate the following passages (expressions) into English（汉译英）

（1）终止电压

(2) 电流放电率

(3) 在充电时，它将电能变换为潜在的化学能。

## 3.2　Battery Characterization

### Text（课文）

Capacity (C)

The battery capacity specifies the amount of electric charge a battery can supply before it is fully discharged. The SI unit of battery capacity is the coulomb. A more general unit for battery capacity is ampere-hour (A·h), with 1 (A·h) = 3,600 C. For example, a battery of 20 (A·h) can supply 1 A current for 20 hours or 2 A for 10 hours, or in theory 20 A for 1 hour. But in general the battery capacity is dependent on discharge rate.

There are two ways of indicating battery discharge rate: $C$ rate is the rate in amperes, while $nC$ rate will discharge a battery in $1/n$ hours. For example, a rate of $C/2$ will discharge a battery in 2 hours, and a rate of $5C$ will discharge a battery in 0.2 hours. For a 2 (A·h) battery, the $C/5$ rate is 400 mA while its $5C$ rate is 10 A.

Energy Stored (E)

The energy stored in a battery is dependent on battery voltage and the amount of charge stored within. The watt hour or (W·h) is the SI unit for energy stored. Assume a constant voltage (CV) for the battery. Then E (W·h) = V × C, where V is the voltage and C is the capacity in (A·h). The capacity of the battery changes with the discharge rate, and the associated discharging current affects the voltage value. The energy scored is thus not a constant quantity and is a function of two variables, namely, the voltage and capacity of the battery.

State of Charge (SOC)

A key parameter in the electric vehicle is the SOC of the battery. The SOC is a measure of the residual capacity of a battery. Typically, the battery SOC is maintained between 20% and 95%.

A common mistake that people may make about a battery's charge is that when a battery "goes dead," the voltage goes from 12 to 0V (for a 12V battery). In reality a battery's voltage varies between 12.6 V with a SOC of 100% to approximately 10.5 V with a SOC of near 0. It is advised that the SOC should not fall below 40% which corresponds to a voltage of 11.9 V. All batteries have an SOC percentile vs voltage curve which can be either looked up from the manufacturer's data or determined experimentally. An example of an SOC percentile vs voltage curve of a lead acid battery is shown in Figure 3.4. Note that for a lithium-ion battery, the curve may be much flatten especially for the mid-SOC range of 40%–80%.

Depth of Discharge (DOD)

The depth of discharge (DOD) is the percentage of battery capacity to which the battery is discharged.

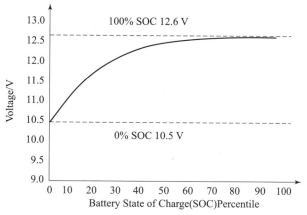

Figure 3.4  SOC percentile vs voltage curve for a 12V battery

Generally, a battery is prevented from having a low DOD. The withdrawal of at least 80% of battery capacity is regarded as a deep discharge. One important precaution is that the charge in a battery should never be discharged down to zero voltage, otherwise the battery may be permanently damaged. So, in this case, a cutoff voltage is defined for the battery voltage so that the voltage at the battery terminals will never drop below this cutoff voltage. This point is referenced as 100% DOD.

Specific Energy

Specific energy means how much electrical energy can be stored per unit mass of battery. The SI unit for this quantity is watt hour per kilogram. Knowing the energy stored and specific energy of the battery, the mass of the battery can be easily obtained by dividing the energy by specific energy. Again, the specific energy is not a constant parameter since the energy stored varies with discharge rate. A comparison of the specific energy of various energy sources (typical numbers) is given in Table 3.1.

Table 3.1  Specific energy of different energy sources

| Energy Source | Specific Energy /[(W·h)·kg$^{-1}$] | Energy | Specific Energy /[(W·h)·kg$^{-1}$] |
|---|---|---|---|
| Gasoline | 12,500 | Nickel Metal Hydride Battery | 50 |
| Natural Gas | 9,350 | Lithium Polymer Battery | 200 |
| Methanol | 6,050 | Lithium Ion Battery | 120 |
| Hydrogen | 33,000 | Flywheel (Carbon Fiber) | 30 |
| Coal | 8,200 | Ultracapacitor | 3.3 |
| Lead Acid Battery | 35 | | |

Energy Density

Energy density means how much electrical energy can be stored per cubic meter of battery volume. It is computed by dividing the energy stored in the battery by the battery volume. The SI unit for energy density is watt hour per cubic meter.

Specific Power and Power Density

Specific power means how much power can be supplied per kilogram of the battery. Note that this quantity is dependent on the load served by the battery and is thus highly variable and anomalous. The SI unit of specific power is watt per kilogram. Specific power is the ability of the battery to supply energy. Higher specific power indicates that it can give and take energy quickly. Volume specific power is also called power density or volume power density, indicating the amount of power (time rate of energy transfer) per unit volume of the battery. If a battery has high specific energy but low specific power, this means that the battery stores a lot of energy, but gives it out slowly. A Ragone plot is used to depict the relationship between specific power and specific energy of a certain battery.

Number of Deep Cycles and Battery Life

EV/HEV batteries can undergo a few hundred deep cycles to as low as 80% DOD of the battery. Different battery types and design result in different numbers of deep cycles. Also, the usage pattern will affect the number of deep cycles a battery can sustain before malfunction. The United States Advanced Battery Consortium (USABC) has a mid-term target of 600 deep cycles for EV batteries. This specification is very important since it affects battery life time in terms of deep-cycle number. So, generally, we should reduce the chances of DOD in the control strategy for EVs and HEVs in order to limit the operating cost of the vehicles.

### New words and expressions（单词和短语）

#### 1. New words（单词）

| | |
|---|---|
| capacity [kəˈpæsəti] | n. 能力；容量；资格，地位；生产力 |
| variable [ˈveəriəbl] | n. [数] 变量；可变物，可变因素<br>adj. 变量的；可变的；易变的，多变的；变异的，[生物] 畸变的 |
| quantity [ˈkwɒntəti] | n. 量，数量；大量；总量 |
| maintain [meɪnˈteɪn] | vt. 维持；继续；维修；主张；供养 |
| approximately [əˈprɒksɪmətli] | adv. 大约，近似地；近于 |
| depth [depθ] | n. [海洋] 深度；深奥 |
| percentage [pəˈsentɪdʒ] | n. 百分比；百分率，百分数 |
| withdrawal [wɪðˈdrɔːəl；wɪθˈdrɔːəl] | n. 撤退，收回；提款；取消；退股 |
| precaution [prɪˈkɔːʃn] | n. 预防，警惕；预防措施<br>vt. 警惕；预先警告 |
| cubic [ˈkjuːbɪk] | adj. 立方体的，立方的 |
| anomalous [əˈnɒmələs] | adj. 异常的；不规则的；不恰当的 |

| | |
|---|---|
| volume [ˈvɒljuːm] | n. 量；体积；卷；音量；大量；册<br>adj. 大量的<br>vt. 把……收集成卷 |
| plot [plɒt] | n. 情节；图表；阴谋；（专用的）小块土地<br>vt. 密谋；绘图；划分；标绘<br>vi. 密谋；策划；绘制 |
| depict [dɪˈpɪkt] | vt. 描述；描画 |
| undergo [ˌʌndəˈɡəʊ] | vt. 经历，经受，忍受 |
| sustain [səˈsteɪn] | vt. 维持；支撑；承担；忍受；供养；证实 |
| malfunction [ˌmælˈfʌŋkʃn] | n. 故障，失灵<br>v. 发生故障，不起作用 |
| target [ˈtɑːɡɪt] | n. 目标，指标；（攻击的）对象；靶子<br>v. 把……作为目标；面向，对准（某群体） |

## 2. Expressions（短语）

| | |
|---|---|
| discharge rate | 放电率 |
| be dependent on | 取决于 |
| the SI unit | 国际制单位 |
| residual capacity | 剩余电量 |
| deep discharge | 深度放电 |
| be referenced as | 被参考为 |
| specific energy | 比能量 |
| constant parameter | 固定值 |
| electrical energy | 电能 |
| energy density | 能量密度 |
| specific power | 比功率 |
| deep cycle | 深度循环 |
| result in | 导致，结果是 |
| control strategy | 控制策略 |

### Notes to the text（难点解析）

★1. One important precaution is that the charge in a battery should never be discharged down to zero voltage, otherwise the battery may be permanently damaged. 特别需要注意的是，电池电

压不能降到 0 V，否则电池将会永久性损坏。

★2. If a battery has high specific energy but low specific power, this means that the battery stores a lot of energy, but gives it out slowly. 如果电池有高的比能量和低的比功率，则意味着电池储存了很多能量，但是能量放出的速度很慢。

### Exercises（练习）

◆1. Translate the following passages (expressions) into Chinese（英译汉）

（1）Higher specific power indicates that it can give and take energy quickly.

（2）In reality a battery's voltage varies between 12.6 V with a SOC of 100% to approximately 10.5 V with a SOC of near 0.

（3）deep cycle

（4）energy density

（5）SOC

（6）DOD

◆2. Translate the following passages (expressions) into English（汉译英）

（1）控制策略

（2）比能量

（3）剩余电量

（4）国际单位

◆3. Directions: Answer the following questions briefly according to the text.

What is SOC? What is DOD?

### Reading material（阅读材料）

#### Ampere-hour (or Charge) Efficiency

Ampere-hour efficiency is the ratio between the electric charge given out during discharging a battery and the electric charge needed for the battery to return to the previous charge level. In practice, these two values will never be equal, limiting the efficiency to 100%. In fact, the typical values of charge efficiency range from 65% to 90%. The efficiency depends on various factors such as the battery type, temperature, and rate of charge.

## 3.3 Battery Technologies

### Text（课文）

The viable EV and HEV batteries consist of the lead-acid battery, nickel-based batteries such as nickel/iron, nickel/cadmium, and nickel-metal hydride (Ni-MH) batteries, and lithium-based batteries such as lithium-polymer (Li-P) and lithium-ion (Li-I) batteries.

###  3.3.1 Lead-Acid Battery

The lead-acid battery has been a successful commercial product for over a century and is still widely used as the electrical energy storage in the automotive field and other applications. Its advantages are its low cost, mature technology, and relatively high-power capability. These advantages are attractive for application in HEVs, where high power is the first consideration. The materials involved (lead, lead oxide, and sulfuric acid) are rather low cost when compared with their more advanced counterparts. Lead-acid batteries also have several disadvantages. The energy density is low, mostly because of the high molecular weight of lead. The temperature characteristics are poor. Below $10^0 C$, specific power and specific energy are greatly reduced. This aspect severely limits the application of lead-acid batteries for the traction of vehicles operated in cold climates.

The presence of highly corrosive sulfuric acid is a potential safety hazard for vehicle occupants. The hydrogen released by the self-discharge reactions is another potential danger, since this gas is extremely flammable even in tiny concentrations. The hydrogen emission is also a problem for hermetically sealed batteries. Indeed, in order to provide a good level of protection against acid spills, it is necessary to seal the battery, thus trapping the parasitic gases in the casing. As a result, pressure may build up in the battery, causing swelling and mechanical constraints on the casing and sealing. The lead in the electrodes is an environmental problem because of its toxicity. The emission of lead consecutive to the use of lead-acid batteries may occur during the fabrication of the batteries, in the case of vehicle wreck (spill of electrolyte through cracks), or during their disposal at the end of battery life.

Different lead-acid batteries with improved performance are being developed for EVs and HEVs. Improvements of the sealed lead-acid batteries in specific energy over 40 (W·h)/kg, with the possibility of rapid charge, have been attained. Advanced lead-acid batteries have been developed to remedy their disadvantages. The specific energy has been increased through the reduction of inactive materials such as the casing, current collector, separators, and so on. The lifetime has been increased by over 50%—at the expense of cost, however. The safety issue has been improved, with electrochemical processes designed to absorb the parasitic releases of hydrogen and oxygen.

### New words and expressions（单词和短语）

#### 1. New words（单词）

| | | |
|---|---|---|
| viable [ˈvaɪəbl] | | adj. 可行的；能养活的；能生育的 |
| commercial [kəˈmɜːʃl] | | n. 商业广告<br>adj. 商业的；营利的；靠广告收入的 |
| advantage [ədˈvɑːntɪdʒ] | | n. 优势；利益；有利条件<br>vt. 有利于；使处于优势 |

| | | |
|---|---|---|
| application [ˌæplɪˈkeɪʃn] | | n. 应用；申请；应用程序；敷用；（对事物、学习等）投入 |
| consideration [kənˌsɪdəˈreɪʃn] | | n. 考虑；原因；关心；报酬 |
| counterpart [ˈkaʊntəpɑːt] | | n. 副本；配对物；极相似的人或物 |
| molecular [məˈlekjələ(r)] | | adj. 分子的；由分子组成的 |
| aspect [ˈæspekt] | | n. 方面；方向；形势；外貌 |
| severely [sɪˈvɪəli] | | adv. 严重地；严格地，严厉地；纯朴地 |
| traction [ˈtrækʃn] | | n. 牵引；[机][车辆] 牵引力 |
| presence [ˈprezns] | | n. 存在；出席；参加；风度；仪态 |
| corrosive [kəˈrəʊsɪv] | | n. 腐蚀物<br>adj. 腐蚀的；侵蚀性的 |
| occupant [ˈɒkjəpənt] | | n. 居住者；占有者 |
| reaction [rɪˈækʃn] | | n. 反应，感应；反动，复古；反作用 |
| flammable [ˈflæməbl] | | n. 易燃物<br>adj. 易燃的；可燃的；可燃性的 |
| concentration [ˌkɒnsnˈtreɪʃn] | | n. 浓度；集中；浓缩；专心；集合 |
| hydrogen [ˈhaɪdrədʒən] | | n. [化学] 氢 |
| emission [ɪˈmɪʃn] | | n. （光、热等的）发射，散发；喷射；发行 |
| acid [ˈæsɪd] | | n. 酸<br>adj. 酸的；讽刺的；刻薄的 |
| electrode [ɪˈlektrəʊd] | | n. [电] 电极；电焊条 |
| toxicity [tɒkˈsɪsəti] | | n. [毒物] 毒性 |
| disposal [dɪˈspəʊzl] | | n. 处理；支配；清理；安排 |
| fabrication [ˌfæbrɪˈkeɪʃn] | | n. 制造，建造；装配；伪造物 |
| consecutive [kənˈsekjətɪv] | | adj. 连贯的；连续不断的 |
| wreck [rek] | | n. 破坏；失事；残骸；失去健康的人<br>vt. 破坏；使失事；拆毁 |
| parasitic [ˌpærəˈsɪtɪk] | | adj. 寄生的（等于 parasitical） |
| remedy [ˈremədi] | | v. 补救，纠正，改进；治疗<br>n. 补救；疗法；解决办法；（硬币的）公差 |

## 2. Expressions（短语）

| | |
|---|---|
| consist of… | 由……构成 |
| low cost | 低成本 |
| mature technology | 成熟的技术 |
| sulfuric acid | 硫酸 |
| in cold climates | 在冷气候下 |
| safety hazard | 安全隐患 |
| build up | 增加，加强 |

### Notes to the text（难点解析）

★1. This aspect severely limits the application of lead-acid batteries for the traction of vehicles operated in cold climates. 这一状况严格地限制了铅酸蓄电池在冷气候下的车辆牵引中的应用。

★2. The specific energy has been increased through the reduction of inactive materials such as the casing, current collector, separators, and so on. 由于减少了不活泼物质，例如壳体、集电极和隔膜等，比能量已经提高。

### Exercises（练习）

◆1. Translate the following passages (expressions) into Chinese（英译汉）

(1) Its advantages are its low cost, mature technology, and relatively high-power capability.

(2) The presence of highly corrosive sulfuric acid is a potential safety hazard for vehicle occupants.

(3) self-discharge

(4) lead-acid batteries

◆2. Translate the following passages (expressions) into English（汉译英）

(1) 安全隐患

(2) 在冷气候下

(3) 因铅具有毒性，电极上的铅涉及环境问题。

◆3. Directions：Answer the following questions briefly according to the text

Let's discuss the advantages and disadvantages of the lead-acid batteries.

### Reading material（阅读材料）

Lead-acid batteries had ever been the most popular choice of batteries for EVs. Lead-acid batteries can be designed to be high powered and are inexpensive, safe, and reliable. A recycling infrastructure is in place for them. However, low specific energy, poor cold temperature performance, and short calendar and cycle life are among the obstacles to their use in EVs and HEVs.

The lead-acid battery has a history that dates to the middle of the 19th century, and it is currently a mature technology. The first lead-acid battery was produced as early as in 1859. In the early 1980s, over 100,000,000 lead-acid batteries were produced per year. The long existence of the lead-acid battery is due to the following:

Relatively low cost

Easy availability of raw materials (lead, sulfur)

Ease of manufacture

Favorable electromechanical characteristics

### 3.3.2 Nickel-Based Batteries

**Text** (课文)

Nickel is a lighter metal than lead and has very good electrochemical properties desirable for battery applications. There are four different nickel-based battery technologies: nickel-iron, nickel-zinc, nickel-cadmium, and Ni-MH.

Ni-MH battery

The Ni-MH battery has been on the market since 1992. Its characteristics are similar to those of the nickel/cadmium battery. The principal difference between them is the use of hydrogen, absorbed in a metal hydride, for the active negative electrode material in place of cadmium. Because of superior specific energy to Ni-Cd and since it is free from toxicity or carcinogenicity, such as cadmium, the Ni-MH battery is superseding the Ni-Cd battery.

At present, Ni-MH battery technology has a nominal voltage of 1.2V and attains a specific energy of 65 (W·h)/kg and a specific power of 200 W/kg. A key component of the Ni-MH battery is the hydrogen storage metal alloy, which should be formulated to obtain a material that is stable over a large number of cycles.

Because the Ni-MH battery is still under continual development, its advantages based on present technology are summarized as follows: it has the highest specific energy [70-95(W·h)/kg] and highest specific power (200-300W/kg) of nickel-based batteries; environmental friendliness (cadmium free); a flat discharge profile (smaller voltage drop); and rapid recharge capability. However, this battery still suffers from its high initial cost. It may also have a memory effect and be exothermic during charging.

The Ni-MH battery has been considered as an important near-term choice for EV and HEV applications. A number of battery manufacturers, such as GM Ovonic, GP, GS, Panasonic, SAFT, VARTA, and YUASA, have actively engaged in the development of this battery technology, especially for powering EVs and HEVs. Since 1993, Ovonic has installed its Ni-MH battery in the Solectric GT Force EV for testing and demonstration. A 19-kW·h battery has delivered over 65(W·h)/kg, 134 km/h, acceleration from zero to 80 km/h in 14s, and a city driving range of 206 km. Toyota and Honda have used the Ni-MH battery in their HEVs—Prius and Insight, respectively.

## New words and expressions（单词和短语）

### 1. New words（单词）

| | |
|---|---|
| characteristic [ˌkærəktəˈrɪstɪk] | n. 特征；特性；特色<br>adj. 典型的；特有的；表示特性的 |
| absorb [əbˈzɔːb; əbˈsɔːb] | vt. 吸收；吸引；承受；理解；使……全神贯注 |
| principal [ˈprɪnsəpl] | adj. 主要的；资本的<br>n. 首长；校长；资本；当事人 |
| hydrogen [ˈhaɪdrədʒən] | n. [化学]氢 |
| superior [suːˈpɪərɪə(r)] | n. 上级，长官；优胜者，高手；长者<br>adj. 上级的；优秀的，出众的；高傲的 |
| supersede [ˌsuːpəˈsiːd] | vt. 取代，代替；紧接着……而到来<br>vi. 推迟行动 |
| alloy [ˈælɔɪ] | v. 把……铸成合金；使……减低成色<br>n. 合金 |
| formulate [ˈfɔːmjuleɪt] | vt. 规划；用公式表示；明确地表达 |
| continual [kənˈtɪnjuəl] | adj. 持续不断的；频繁的 |
| summarize [ˈsʌməraɪz] | vt. 总结；概述<br>vi. 做总结；做概括 |
| profile [ˈprəʊfaɪl] | n. 侧面；轮廓；外形；剖面；简况<br>vt. 描……的轮廓；扼要描述 |
| exothermic [ˌeksəʊˈθɜːmɪk] | adj. 发热的；放出热量的；[热]放热的 |
| demonstration [ˌdemənˈstreɪʃn] | n. 示范；证明；示威游行 |

### 2. Expressions（短语）

| | |
|---|---|
| metal hydride | 金属氢化物 |
| in place of | 代替 |
| be similar to… | 与……相似 |
| key component | 关键组成 |
| metal alloy | 金属合金 |
| suffer from | 忍受，遭受 |
| memory effect | 记忆效应 |

| | |
|---|---|
| near-term | 近期 |
| driving range | 行程范围 |

### Notes to the text（难点解析）

★1. Because of superior specific energy to Ni-Cd and since it is free from toxicity or carcinogenicity, such as cadmium, the Ni-MH battery is superseding the Ni-Cd battery.

当与镍-镉蓄电池相比较时，因其占优的比能量，及其免除于毒性或致癌性的性能，Ni-MH 蓄电池正在取代镍-镉蓄电池。

★2. A key component of the Ni-MH battery is the hydrogen storage metal alloy, which should be formulated to obtain a material that is stable over a large number of cycles. 这类 Ni-MH 蓄电池的关键组成是贮氢合金，它被配制以获得在大量循环中稳定反应的物质。

### Exercises（练习）

◆1. Translate the following passages（expressions）into Chinese（英译汉）

（1）However, this battery still suffers from its high initial cost. It may also have a memory effect and be exothermic during charging.

（2）environmental friendliness

（3）metal hydride

★2. Translate the following passages（expressions）into English（汉译英）

（1）记忆效应

（2）行程范围

（3）Ni-MH 蓄电池正在取代镍-镉蓄电池。

★3. Directions：Answer the following questions briefly according to the text

What are the advantages of Ni-MH batteries?

### Reading material（阅读材料）

The operating voltage of Ni-MH is almost the same as that of Ni-Cd, with flat discharge characteristics. The capacity of the Ni-MH is significantly higher than that of Ni-Cd, with specific energy ranging from 60 to 80（W·h）/kg. The specific power of Ni-MH batteries can be as high as 250 W/kg.

The Ni-MH batteries have penetrated the market in recent years at an exceptional rate. The Chrysler electric minivan "Epic" uses a Ni-MH battery pack, which gives a range of 150 km. Ni-MH battery packs are being used in Toyota HEV Prius.

The components of Ni-MH are recyclable, but a recycling structure is not yet in place. Ni-MH batteries have a much longer life cycle than lead-acid batteries and are safe and abuse tolerant. The disadvantages of Ni-MH batteries are the relatively high cost, higher self-discharge rate compared to Ni-Cd, poor charge acceptance capability at elevated temperatures, and low cell efficiency. Ni-MH is likely to survive as the leading rechargeable battery in the future for traction applications, with the strong challenge coming only from lithium-ion batteries.

###  3.3.3 Lithium-Based Batteries

**Text**（课文）

Lithium is the lightest of all metals and presents very interesting characteristics from an electrochemical point of view. Indeed, it allows a very high thermodynamic voltage, which results in a very high specific energy and specific power.

1. Li-I Battery

Since the first announcement of the Li-I battery in 1991, the Li-I battery technology has seen an unprecedented rise to what is now considered to be the most promising rechargeable battery of the future. Although still in the stage of development, the Li-I battery has already gained acceptance for EV and HEV applications.

The Li-I battery uses a lithiated carbon intercalation material (LixC) for the negative electrode instead of metallic lithium, a lithiated transition metal intercalation oxide (Li1-xMyOz) for the positive electrode, and a liquid organic solution or a solid polymer for the electrolyte. Li-I battery has a nominal voltage of 4 V, a specific energy of 120 (W·h)/kg, an energy density of 200 (W·h)/L, and a specific power of 260 W/kg. It is anticipated that the development of the Li-I battery will ultimately move to the manganese-based type because of the low cost, abundance, and environmental friendliness of the manganese-based materials.

**New words and expressions**（单词和短语）

**1. New words**（单词）

| | |
|---|---|
| announcement [əˈnaʊnsmənt] | n. 公告；宣告；发表；通告 |
| unprecedented [ʌnˈpresɪdentɪd] | adj. 空前的；无前例的 |
| promising [ˈprɒmɪsɪŋ] | v. 许诺，答应（promise 的现在分词形式）<br>adj. 有希望的，有前途的 |
| acceptance [əkˈseptəns] | n. 接纳；赞同；容忍 |
| manganese [ˈmæŋɡəniːz] | n. [化学] 锰 |
| carbon [ˈkɑːbən] | n. [化学] 碳；碳棒；复写纸<br>adj. 碳的；碳处理的 |
| anticipate [ænˈtɪsɪpeɪt] | v. 预料，预期；预见；预计（并做准备）；期盼，期望；先于……做，早于……行动；在期限内履行（义务），偿还（债务） |
| ultimately [ˈʌltɪmətli] | adv. 最后；根本；基本上 |

## 2. Expressions（短语）

| | |
|---|---|
| unprecedented rise | 空前的提高 |
| be considered to be | 被认为是 |
| the most promising | 最有希望的 |
| liquid organic solution | 有机溶液 |

### Notes to the text（难点解析）

★1. Although still in the stage of development, the Li-I battery has already gained acceptance for EV and HEV applications. 虽然依然处于发展阶段，Li-I 蓄电池已经在电动汽车和混合动力电动汽车的应用中获得了认可。

★2. It is anticipated that the development of the Li-I battery will ultimately move to the manganese-based type because of the low cost, abundance, and environmental friendliness of the manganese-based materials. 可以预期，Li-I 蓄电池的发展将最终归结于锰基型 Li-I 电池，因为其成本低、原材料储量充裕，且锰基型材料对环境友好。

### Exercises（练习）

◆1. Translate the following passages (expressions) into Chinese（英译汉）
（1） unprecedented rise
（2） liquid organic solution

◆2. Translate the following passages (expressions) into English（汉译英）
（1） 最有希望的
（2） 被认为是
（3） 制造技术已有了空前的提高。

### Reading material（阅读材料）

The interest in secondary lithium cells soared soon after the advent of lithium primary cells in the 1970s. The nominal cell voltage for a Li-I battery is 3.6 V, which is equivalent to three Ni-MH or Ni-Cd battery cells.

Li-I batteries have high specific energy, high specific power, high energy efficiency, good high-temperature performance, and low self-discharge. The components of Li-I batteries are also recyclable. These characteristics make Li-I batteries highly suitable for EV and HEV and other applications of rechargeable batteries.

## 3.4 Supercapacitors and Ultracapacitors

### Text（课文）

Capacitors are devices that store energy by the separation of equal positive and negative electrostatic charges. The basic structure of a capacitor consists of two conductors, known as plates, separated by a dielectric, which is an insulator. The power densities of conventional capacitors are extremely high ($1,012$ W/m$^3$), but the energy density is very low [$50(W \cdot h)/m^3$].

These conventional capacitors are commonly known as "electrolytic capacitors." They are widely used in electrical circuits as intermediate energy storage elements for time constants that are of a completely different domain and are of much smaller order compared to the energy storage devices that are to serve as the primary energy sources for EVs.

Supercapacitors contain an electrolyte that enables the storage of electrostatic charge in the form of ions, in addition to conventional energy storage in electrostatic charges, like in an electrolytic capacitor. The internal functions in a supercapacitor do not involve electrochemical reaction. The electrodes in supercapacitors are made of porous carbon with high internal surface area to help absorb the ions and provide a much higher charge density than is possible in a conventional capacitor. The ions move much more slowly than electrons, enabling a much longer time constant for charging and discharging compared to electrolytic capacitors.

Power density and energy density of supercapacitors and ultracapacitors are of the order of $10^6$ W/m$^3$ and $10^4$ (W $\cdot$ h)/m$^3$, respectively. Energy density is much lower compared to those of batteries [5 to $25 \times 10^4$ (W $\cdot$ h)/m$^3$], but the discharge times are much faster (1 to 10 s compared to $5 \times 10^3$ s of batteries), and the cycle life is much more ($10^5$ compared to 100 to 1,000 of batteries).

Current research and development aim to create ultracapacitors with capabilities in the vicinity of 4,000 W/kg and 15 (W $\cdot$ h)/kg. The possibility of using supercapacitors and ultracapacitors as primary energy sources is quite far reaching, although it is likely that these can be improved to provide sufficient energy storage in HEVs. On the other hand, supercapacitors and ultracapacitors with high specific power are suitable as an intermediate energy transfer device in conjunction with batteries or fuel cells in EVs and HEVs to provide sudden transient power demand, such as during acceleration and hill climbing. The devices can also be used efficiently to capture recovered energy during regenerative braking.

### New words and expressions（单词和短语）

#### 1. New words（单词）

| | |
|---|---|
| device [dɪˈvaɪs] | n. 装置；策略；图案；设备；终端 |
| capacitor [kəˈpæsɪtə(r)] | n. [电] 电容器 |
| separation [ˌsepəˈreɪʃn] | n. 分离，分开；间隔，距离；[法] 分居；缺口 |
| electrostatic [ɪˌlektrəʊˈstætɪk] | adj. 静电的；静电学的 |
| conductor [kənˈdʌktə(r)] | n. 导体；售票员；领导者；管理人 |

| plate [pleɪt] | n. 碟；金属板；金属牌；感光底片<br>vt. 电镀；给……装甲 |
|---|---|
| dielectric [ˌdaɪɪˈlektrɪk] | n. 电介质；绝缘体<br>adj. 非传导性的；诱电性的 |
| insulator [ˈɪnsjuleɪtə(r)] | n. [物] 绝缘体；从事绝缘工作的工人 |
| conventional [kənˈvenʃənl] | adj. 符合习俗的，传统的；常见的；惯例的 |
| intermediate [ˌɪntəˈmiːdiət] | v. 充当调解人，起媒介作用<br>n. 中级生；（化合物）中间体，中间物；中介，媒介<br>adj. 中间的，过渡的；中级的，中等的 |
| domain [dəˈmeɪn] | n. 领域；域名；产业；地产 |
| porous [ˈpɔːrəs] | adj. 多孔渗水的；能渗透的；有气孔的 |
| electrons [ɪˈlektrɑn] | n. [物] 电子（electron 的复数形式） |
| vicinity [vəˈsɪnəti] | n. 邻近，附近；近处 |
| transfer [trænsˈfɜː(r)] | v. 转让；转接；移交；转移（地方）；（使）换乘；转存，转录；调动（工作）；传染，传播；使（运动员）转队；<br>n. （地点的）转移；（工作的）调动；已调动的人或东西；权力的移交；运动员转会；（公共汽车、飞机等的）转移； |
| conjunction [kənˈdʒʌŋkʃn] | n. 结合；[语] 连接词；同时发生 |
| transient [ˈtrænziənt] | n. 瞬变现象；过往旅客；候鸟<br>adj. 短暂的；路过的 |
| capture [ˈkæptʃə(r)] | vt. 俘获；夺得；捕捉，拍摄，录制<br>n. 捕获；战利品，俘虏 |
| recover [rɪˈkʌvə(r)] | n. 还原至预备姿势<br>vt. 恢复；弥补；重新获得 |

## 2. Expressions（短语）

| time constant | 时间常数 |
|---|---|
| primary energy sources | 主要能源 |
| in conjunction with | 结合使用 |

### Notes to the text（难点解析）

★1. The possibility of using supercapacitors and ultracapacitors as primary energy sources is quite far reaching, although it is likely that these can be improved to provide sufficient energy storage in HEVs. 尽管超级电容器能够为混合动力汽车提供充足的能源存储，但超级电容器成为汽车主能源的可能性还很小。

## Exercises(练习)

◆1. Translate the following passages (expressions) into Chinese(英译汉)

(1) Capacitors are devices that store energy by the separation of equal positive and negative electrostatic charges.

(2) energy density

(3) electrical circuits

◆2. Translate the following passages (expressions) into English(汉译英)

(1) 时间常数

(2) 主要能源

(3) 在电动汽车或者混合动力汽车上,将超级电容器同蓄电池或者燃料电池结合使用,可满足提供瞬时功率需求。

## Reading material(阅读材料)

Because of the frequent stop-and-go operation of EVs and HEVs, the discharging and charging profile of the energy storage is highly varied. The average power required from the energy storage is much lower than the peak power for acceleration and hill climbing in a relatively short duration. The ratio of peak power to average power can reach over 10∶1. In HEV design, the peak power capacity of the energy storage is more important than its energy capacity, and usually constrains its size reduction. Based on present battery technology, battery design has to carry out the trade-off among specific energy, specific power, and cycle life. The difficulty in simultaneously obtaining high values of specific energy, specific power, and cycle life has led to some suggestions that the energy storage system of EV and HEV should be a hybridization of an energy source and a power source. The energy source, mainly batteries and fuel cells, has high specific energy, whereas the power source has high specific power. Power sources can be recharged from the energy source during less demanding driving or regenerative braking. The power source that has received wide attention is the ultracapacitor.

## 3.5 Flywheels

### Text(课文)

The flywheel is the kind of energy supply unit that stores energy in mechanical form. Flywheels store kinetic energy within a rotating wheel-like rotor or disk made of composite materials. Flywheels have a long history of usage in automobiles, being routinely used in all of today's IC engines to store energy and smooth the power delivered by abrupt pulses of the engine. However, the amount of energy storage required in flywheels of IC engines is small and is limited by the need of the vehicle to accelerate rapidly. The flywheel is currently being looked into for use in a number of different capacities. Flywheels can be used in HEVs with a standard IC engine as a power assist device.

Alternatively, flywheels can be used to replace chemical batteries in EVs to serve as the primary energy source or could be used in conjunction with batteries. However, technological breakthroughs in increasing the specific energy of flywheels are necessary before they can be considered as the energy source for EVs and HEVs. The flywheels of today are quite complex, large and heavy. Safety is also a concern with flywheels.

The flywheel design objective is to maximize energy density. The material to be used in a flywheel must be lightweight with high tensile strength conditions that are satisfied by composite materials.

Flywheels have several advantages as an energy source, the most important of which is the high specific power. Theoretically, specific power of flywheels has been shown to be of the order of 5 to 10 kW/kg, with a specific power of 2 kW/kg being easily achievable without exceeding safe working stresses. Other performance features that make flywheels attractive can be attributed to their mechanical nature. Flywheels are not affected by temperature extremes. There are no concerns with toxic chemical processing and disposal of waste materials, making flywheels environmentally friendlier than chemical batteries. Flywheel energy storage is reliable in that it possesses excellent controllability and repeatability characteristics. The state of charge in flywheels is precisely known at all times through measurement of the rotational speed. The energy conversion process to and from a flywheel approaches 98%, compared to 75% to 80% of batteries. The service life of a flywheel is many times that of a battery, with little maintenance required. The charging of flywheels is a fraction of that required by batteries and can be less than 10 min for full recharge in a flywheel charging station. The ability to absorb or release a high amount of power in a short period of time also aids the regenerative braking process.

Despite several advantages, there are still a number of significant drawbacks with flywheels. The major difficulty in implementing a flywheel energy storage system is in the extra equipment needed to operate and contain the device. The extras are particularly difficult in EV and HEV applications, where the extra weight and expense make a big difference.

### New words and expressions（单词和短语）

#### 1. New words（单词）

| | |
|---|---|
| flywheel [ˈflaɪwiːl] | n. [机]飞轮，惯性轮；调速轮 |
| mechanical [məˈkænɪkl] | adj. 机械的；力学的；呆板的；无意识的；手工操作的 |
| form [fɔːm] | n. 形式，形状；形态，外形；方式；表格<br>vt. 构成，组成；排列，组织；产生，塑造 |
| kinetic [kɪˈnetɪk；kaɪˈnetɪk] | adj. [力]运动的；活跃的 |
| rotating [rəʊˈteɪtɪŋ] | adj. 旋转的<br>v. 旋转，转动；轮流，轮值；轮作 |

| | | |
|---|---|---|
| rotor [ˈrəʊtə(r)] | n. 转子；水平旋翼；旋转体 | |
| composite [ˈkɒmpəzɪt] | adj. 复合的，合成的；（火车车厢）综合的；（柱式）混合；菊科的<br>n. 复合材料，合成物；综合提案；菊科植物；混合柱式 | |
| routinely [ruːˈtiːnli] | adv. 例行公事地；老一套地 | |
| abrupt [əˈbrʌpt] | adj. 生硬的；突然的；唐突的；陡峭的 | |
| pulse [pʌls] | n. [电子]脉冲；脉搏<br>vi. 跳动，脉跳 | |
| assist [əˈsɪst] | v. 参加，出席；协助（做一部分工作）；（通过提供金钱或信息）帮助；在场（当助手）；使便利<br>n. 帮助；（体育比赛中的）助攻；辅助机械专置 | |
| replace [rɪˈpleɪs] | vt. 取代，代替；替换，更换；归还，偿还 | |
| breakthrough [ˈbreɪkθruː] | n. 突破；突破性进展 | |
| objective [əbˈdʒektɪv] | adj. 客观的；客观存在的<br>n. 目的；目标；（军事行动的）攻击目标；物镜；宾格 | |
| stress [stres] | n. 压力；强调；紧张；重要性；重读<br>vt. 强调；使紧张；加压力于；用重音读 | |
| achievable [əˈtʃiːvəbl] | adj. 可完成的；可有成就的；做得成的 | |
| feature [ˈfiːtʃə(r)] | n. 特色，特征；容貌；特写或专题节目<br>vt. 特写；以……为特色；由……主演 | |
| controllability [kənˌtrəʊləˈbɪlɪti] | n. [自]可控性；可控制性 | |
| repeatability [rɪˌpiːtəˈbɪlɪti] | n. 重复性；[计]可重复性；再现性 | |
| rotational [rəʊˈteɪʃənl] | adj. 转动的；回转的；轮流的 | |
| fraction [ˈfrækʃn] | n. 分数；部分；小部分；稍微 | |
| drawback [ˈdrɔːbæk] | n. 缺点，不利条件；退税 | |
| implementing [ˈɪmplɪmentɪŋ] | v. 贯彻，实行（implement 的现在分词） | |

## 2. Expressions（短语）

| | |
|---|---|
| energy supply unit | 能量供给单元 |
| power assist device | 动力辅助装置 |
| waste material | 废物 |

Chapter 3 Energy Storages

| | |
|---|---|
| safe working stress | 安全应力 |
| composite materials | 复合材料 |
| controllability and repeatability characteristic | 可控性和可重复性的特点 |
| rotational speed | 转速 |
| charging station | 充电站 |

### Notes to the text（难点解析）

★1. However, technological breakthroughs in increasing the specific energy of flywheels are necessary before they can be considered as the energy source for EVs and HEVs. 然而，在飞轮成为电动汽车或者混合动力汽车的能量源之前，需要突破的技术方面的问题是增加飞轮的比能量。

★2. The material to be used in a flywheel must be lightweight with high tensile strength conditions that are satisfied by composite materials. 在飞轮中使用的材料必须具有重量轻、拉伸强度高的特点，而复合材料能很好地满足这样的条件。

### Exercises（练习）

◆1. Translate the following passages (expressions) into Chinese（英译汉）
（1）Safety is also a concern with flywheels.
（2）The flywheels of today are quite complex, large and heavy.
（3）power assist device （4）charging station

◆2. Translate the following passages (expressions) into English（汉译英）
（1）能量供给单元
（2）复合材料
（3）飞轮可在很短的时间内吸收或释放很多的能量，这将有助于再生制动。

◆3. Directions：Answer the following questions briefly according to the text
What is the principle of the flywheel?

### Reading material（阅读材料）

The use of flywheels for storing energy in mechanical form is not a new concept. More than 25 years ago, the Oerlikon Engineering Company in Switzerland made the first passenger bus solely powered by a massive flywheel. This flywheel, weighing 1,500 kg and operating at 3,000 r/min, was recharged by electricity at each bus stop. The traditional flywheel is a massive steel rotor with hundreds of kilograms that spins on the order of ten hundred of r/min. On the contrary, the advanced flywheel is a lightweight composite rotor with tens of kilograms and rotates on the order of ten thousand of r/min; it is the so-called ultra-high-speed flywheel.

The concept of ultra-high-speed flywheels appears to be a feasible means for fulfilling the stringent energy storage requirements for EV and HEV applications, namely high specific energy, high specific power, long cycle life, high energy efficiency, quick recharge, maintenance-free characteristics, cost effectiveness, and environmental friendliness.

## 3.6　Fuel Cells

### Text（课文）

In recent decades, the application of fuel cells in vehicles has been the focus of increased attention. In contrast to a chemical battery, a fuel cell generates electric energy rather than storing it and continues to do so as long as a fuel supply is maintained. Compared with the battery-powered EVs, the fuel-cell-powered vehicles have the advantages of a longer driving range without a long battery charging time. Compared with the ICE vehicles, they have the advantages of high energy efficiency and much lower emissions due to the direct conversion of free energy in the fuel into electric energy, without undergoing combustion.

#### 3.6.1　Operating Principles of Fuel Cells

A fuel cell is a galvanic cell in which the chemical energy of fuel is converted directly into electrical energy by means of electrochemical processes. The fuel and oxidizing agent are continuously and separately supplied to the two electrodes of the cell, where they undergo a reaction. Electrolyte is necessary to conduct the ions from one electrode to the other as shown in Figure 3.5. Fuel is supplied to the anode or positive electrode, where electrons are released from the fuel under catalyst. The electrons, under the potential difference between these two electrodes, flow through the external circuit to the cathode electrode or negative electrode, where combining positive ions and oxygen, reaction products, or exhaust are produced. The chemical reaction in a fuel cell is similar to that in a chemical battery.

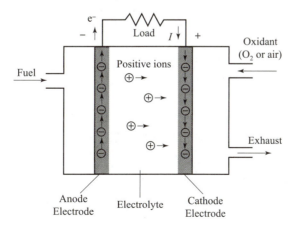

Figure 3.5　Basic operation of a fuel cell

## New words and expressions（单词和短语）

### 1. New words（单词）

| | |
|---|---|
| decade [dɪˈkeɪd] | n. 十年 |
| focus [ˈfəʊkəs] | n. 焦点；中心；清晰；焦距<br>vt. 使集中；使聚焦 |
| contrast [ˈkɒntrɑːst] | n. 明显的差异，对比，对照；明显不同的人（或事物）；（摄影或绘画中的）颜色反差；图像明暗对比度，反差<br>v. 对比，对照；显出明显的差异，与……形成对比 |
| generate [ˈdʒenəreɪt] | vt. 使形成；发生；生殖；产生物理反应 |
| conversion [kənˈvɜːʃn] | n. 转换；变换；[金融] 兑换；改变信仰 |
| undergo [ˌʌndəˈgəʊ] | vt. 经历，经受；忍受 |
| galvanic [gælˈvænɪk] | adj. 电流的；使人震惊的；触电似的 |
| process [prəˈses] | n. （为达到某一目标的）过程；（自然变化的）过程；工艺流程；诉讼程序；传票；突起；进展；（发型）直发式<br>v. 加工；审核；处理（数据）；列队行进；冲印（照片） |
| anode [ˈænəʊd] | n. 阳极（电解池）<br>n. 负极（原电池） |
| electron [ɪˈlektrɒn] | n. 电子 |
| release [rɪˈliːs] | n. 释放；发布；新发行的东西；排放；解脱；新闻稿；让予；宣泄；释放装置<br>v. 释放；放开；发泄；免除；松开；使不紧张；公开；解禁 |
| catalyst [ˈkætəlɪst] | n. [物化] 催化剂；刺激因素 |
| potential [pəˈtenʃl] | adj. 潜在的，可能的<br>n. 潜能，可能性；电势 |
| external [ɪkˈstɜːnl] | n. 外部；外观；外面<br>adj. 外部的；表面的；[药] 外用的；外国的；外面的 |
| cathode [ˈkæθəʊd] | n. 阴极（在电解池中，发生还原反应的电极） |
| exhaust [ɪgˈzɔːst] | v. 使筋疲力尽；耗尽；彻底探讨；排出（气体）<br>n. 废气；排气管 |

## 2. Expressions（短语）

| | |
|---|---|
| fuel cell | 燃料电池 |
| in contrast to | 与……相比 |
| chemical battery | 化学蓄电池 |
| rather than | 不是，而不是 |
| as long as | 只要 |
| be compared with… | 与……相比较 |
| battery-powered | 配置蓄电池 |
| driving range | 行程 |
| charging time | 充电时间 |
| galvanic cell | 原电池 |
| oxidizing agent | 氧化剂 |
| positive electrode | 正极 |
| external circuit | 外电路 |
| cathode electrode | 阴极 |
| is similar to… | 与……相似 |
| chemical reaction | 化学反应 |

### Notes to the text（难点解析）

★1. In contrast to a chemical battery, a fuel cell generates electric energy rather than storing it and continues to do so as long as a fuel supply is maintained. 与化学蓄电池形成对比，燃料电池产生电能而不储存电能，并且只要维持燃料供给，它就将继续运行。

★2. A fuel cell is a galvanic cell in which the chemical energy of fuel is converted directly into electrical energy by means of electrochemical processes. 燃料电池是一种原电池，借助于电化学过程，其内部燃料的化学能直接转换为电能。

### Exercises（练习）

◆1. Translate the following passages (expressions) into Chinese（英译汉）

(1) In recent decades, the application of fuel cells in vehicles has been the focus of increased attention.

(2) cathode electrode

(3) oxidizing agent

◆2. Translate the following passages (expressions) into English（汉译英）

(1) 正极

(2) 化学反应

### Reading material（阅读材料）

A fuel cell is an electrochemical device that produces electricity by means of a chemical reaction, much like a battery. The major difference between batteries and fuel cells is that the latter can produce electricity as long as fuel is supplied, while batteries produce electricity from stored chemical energy and, hence, require frequent recharging.

The basic structure of a fuel cell (Figure 3.5) consists of an anode and a cathode, similar to a battery. The fuel supplied to the cell is hydrogen and oxygen. The concept of fuel cell is the opposite of electrolysis of water, where hydrogen and oxygen are combined to form electricity and water. The hydrogen fuel supplied to the fuel cell consists of two hydrogen atoms per molecule chemically bonded together in the form $H_2$. This molecule includes two separate nuclei, each containing one proton, while sharing two electrons. The fuel cell breaks apart these hydrogen molecules to produce electricity.

 ### 3.6.2 Fuel Cell Technologies

### Text（课文）

It is possible to distinguish six major types of fuel cells, depending on the type of their electrolyte. They are proton exchange membrane (PEM) or polymer exchange membrane fuel cells (PEMFCs), alkaline fuel cells (AFCs), phosphoric acid fuel cells (PAFCs), molten carbonate fuel cells (MCFCs), solid oxide fuel cells (SOFCs), and direct methanol fuel cells (DMFCs). Table 3.2 lists their normal operation temperature and the state of electrolyte.

**Table 3.2  Operating Data of Various Fuel Cell Systems**

| Cell System | Operating Temperature/℃ | Electrolyte |
| --- | --- | --- |
| PEMFCs | 60–100 | Solid |
| AFCs | 100 | Liquid |
| PAFCs | 60–200 | Liquid |
| MCFCs | 500–800 | Liquid |
| SOFCs | 1,000–1,200 | Solid |
| DMFCs | 100 | Solid |

Polymer Exchange Membrane Fuel Cells

PEMFCs use solid polymer membranes as the electrolyte. The polymer membrane is perfluorosulfonic acid, which is also referred to as Nafion (Dupont). This polymer membrane is acidic; therefore the ions transported are hydrogen ions ($H^+$) or protons. The PEMFC is fueled with pure hydrogen and oxygen or air as oxidant.

The catalyst is a critical issue in PEMFCs. In early realizations, very high loadings of platinum were required for the fuel cell to operate properly. Tremendous improvements in catalyst technology have made it possible to reduce the loading from 28 mg/cm$^2$ to 0.2 mg/cm$^2$. Because of the low operating temperature of the fuel cell and the acidic nature of the electrolyte, noble metals are required for the catalyst layer. The cathode is the most critical electrode because the catalytic reduction of oxygen is more difficult than the catalytic oxidation of hydrogen.

Another critical issue in PEMFCs is water management. In order to operate properly, the polymer membrane needs to be kept humid. Indeed, the conduction of ions in polymer membranes requires humidity. If the membrane is too dry, there will not be enough acid ions to carry the protons. If it is too wet (flooded), the pores of the diffusion layer will be blocked and reactant gases will not be able to reach the catalyst.

The last major critical issue in PEMFCs is poisoning. The platinum catalyst is extremely active and thus provides great performance. The trade-off of this great activity is a greater affinity for carbon monoxide (CO) and sulfur products than oxygen. The poisons bind strongly to the catalyst and prevent hydrogen or oxygen from reaching it. The poisoning by carbon monoxide is reversible, but comes at a cost and requires the individual treatment of each cell.

## New words and expressions（单词和短语）

### 1. New words（单词）

| | |
|---|---|
| distinguish [dɪˈstɪŋgwɪʃ] | vi. 区别，区分；辨别<br>vt. 区分；辨别；使杰出，使表现突出 |
| proton [ˈprəʊtɒn] | n. [物]质子 |
| exchange [ɪksˈtʃeɪndʒ] | n. 交换；交流；交易所；兑换<br>vt. 交换；交易；兑换<br>vi. 交换；交易；兑换 |
| alkaline [ˈælkəlaɪn] | adj. 碱性的；含碱的 |
| membrane [ˈmembreɪn] | n. 膜；薄膜；羊皮纸 |
| acidic [əˈsɪdɪk] | adj. 酸的，酸性的；产生酸的 |
| issue [ˈɪʃuː; ˈɪsjuː] | n. 问题；流出；期号；发行物<br>vt. 发行，发布；发给；放出，排出<br>vi. 发行；流出；造成……结果；传下 |
| platinum [ˈplætɪnəm] | n. [化学]铂；白金；唱片集达100万张的销售量；银灰色<br>adj. 唱片集已售出100万张的 |
| catalytic [ˌkætəˈlɪtɪk] | n. 催化剂；刺激因素<br>adj. 接触反应的；起催化作用的 |

| | |
|---|---|
| reduction [rɪˈdʌkʃn] | n. 减少；下降；缩小；还原反应 |
| oxidation [ˌɒksɪˈdeɪʃn] | n. [化学] 氧化 |
| humid [ˈhjuːmɪd] | adj. 潮湿的；湿润的；多湿气的 |
| conduction [kənˈdʌkʃn] | n. [生理] 传导 |
| pore [pɔː(r)] | n. （皮肤上的）毛孔；（植物的）气孔，孔隙<br>v. 仔细打量，审视；凝视；认真研读，审阅；深思熟虑 |
| diffusion [dɪˈfjuːʒn] | n. 扩散，传播；[光] 漫射 |
| block [blɒk] | n. 块；街区；大厦；障碍物<br>vt. 阻止；阻塞；限制；封盖<br>adj. 成批的，大块的；交通堵塞的 |
| reactant [rɪˈæktənt] | n. [化学] 反应物；反应剂 |
| affinity [əˈfɪnəti] | n. 密切关系；吸引力；姻亲关系；类同 |
| reversible [rɪˈvɜːsəbl] | adj. 可逆的；可撤销的；可反转的<br>n. 双面布料 |
| sulfur [ˈsʌlfə] | v. 用硫黄处理；用硫消毒（或熏制）<br>n. 硫，硫黄；硫黄色；美洲粉蝶 |
| bind [baɪnd] | n. 捆绑；困境；讨厌的事情；植物的藤蔓<br>vt. 绑；约束；装订；包扎；凝固<br>vi. 结合；装订；有约束力；过紧 |
| poison [ˈpɔɪzn] | n. 毒药；极有害的思想；抑制剂；中子吸收剂<br>vt. 毒害；下毒；败坏；污染（地区、空气等）；抑制……的活性<br>adj. 有毒的 |

## 2. Expressions（短语）

| | |
|---|---|
| proton exchange | 质子交换 |
| phosphoric acid | 磷酸 |
| molten carbonate | 熔融碳酸盐 |
| solid oxide | 固态氧化物 |
| direct methanol | 直接甲醇 |
| perfluorosulfonic | 全氟磺酸膜 |
| issue in | 导致，关键是 |
| catalytic reduction | 还原作用 |

| catalytic oxidation | 氧化作用 |
| carbon monoxide | 一氧化碳 |

## Notes to the text（难点解析）

★1. The cathode is the most critical electrode because the catalytic reduction of oxygen is more difficult than the catalytic oxidation of hydrogen. 因氧的催化还原作用比氢的催化氧化作用更为困难，所以阴极是最关键的电极。

★2. The last major critical issue in PEMFCs is poisoning. 质子交换膜燃料电池中最后的关键是其毒化问题。

## Exercises（练习）

◆1. Translate the following passages (expressions) into Chinese（英译汉）
（1） The catalyst is a critical issue in PEMFCs.
（2） Another critical issue in PEMFCs is water management.
（3） solid oxide
（4） proton exchange

◆2. Translate the following passages (expressions) into English（汉译英）
（1） 固态聚合物
（2） 氧化作用

## Reading material（阅读材料）

The first PEMFCs were developed in the 1960s for the needs of the U.S.-manned space program. It is nowadays the most investigated fuel cell technology for automotive applications by manufacturers such as Ballard. It is operated at $60℃-100℃$ and can offer a power density of $0.35-0.6 \text{ W/cm}^2$. The PEMFC has some definite advantages in its favor for EV and HEV applications. Firstly, its low-temperature operation and hence its fast start-up are desirable for an EV and HEV. Secondly, the power density is the highest among all the available types of fuel cells. The higher the power density, the smaller the size of the fuel cell that needs to be installed for the desired power demand. Thirdly, its solid electrolyte does not change, move, or vaporize from the cell. Finally, since the only liquid in the cell is water, the possibility of any corrosion is essentially delimited. However, it also has some disadvantages, such as the expensive noble metal needed, expensive membrane, and easily poisoned catalyst and membrane.

# Chapter 4
## Management of Energy Storage Systems

## 4.1　Introduction

### Text（课文）

Energy storage systems（ESS）play an important role in EV, HEV and PHEV. The performance of these vehicles is highly dependent on the ESS. There are a few types of energy storage options available for different vehicle applications. Nickel Metal Hydride batteries have been widely used in HEVs in the past ten years. Lithium ion batteries are considered as the only viable solution for EV and PHEV at the present time. Ultracapacitors also have been investigated for use in PHEV due to their very high power density and long cycle life. Flywheel-based HEVs also have been investigated. Integrated hybrid energy storage systems that contain high energy lithium ion batteries and high power ultracapacitors could potentially provide the best solutions for EV and PHEV. Proper management of the ESS in EV, HEV, and PHEV can not only extend the life of the battery ESS, but also help improve overall fuel efficiency of the vehicle.

### New words and expressions（单词和短语）

#### 1. New words（单词）

| | |
|---|---|
| options ['ɒpʃnz] | n. 选择；期权；[计] 选择项（option 的复数）<br>v. 给予……的销售权 |
| investigate [ɪn'vestɪɡeɪt] | v. 调查；研究 |
| integrate ['ɪntɪɡreɪt] | n. 一体化；集成体<br>adj. 整合的；完全的<br>vi. 求积分；取消隔离；成为一体 |
| management ['mænɪdʒm(ə)nt] | n. 管理；管理人员；管理部门；操纵；经营手段 |
| efficiency [ɪ'fɪʃ(ə)nsɪ] | n. 效率；效能；功效 |

| | |
|---|---|
| extend [ɪkˈstend] | vt. 延伸；扩大；推广；伸出；给予；使竭尽全力；对……估价 |
| | vi. 延伸；扩大；伸展；使疏开 |

**2. Expressions（短语）**

| | |
|---|---|
| play an important role | 发挥着重要的作用 |
| dependent on | 取决，依靠 |
| long cycle life | 周期寿命长 |

## Notes to the text（难点解析）

★1. There are a few types of energy storage options available for different vehicle applications. 有几种不同类型的储能选择，可以用于不同的车辆应用。

★2. Proper management of the ESS in EV, HEV, and PHEV can not only extend the life of the battery ESS, but also help improve overall fuel efficiency of the vehicle. 对电动汽车、混合动力汽车和插电式混合动力汽车储能系统的适当管理不仅能延长电池储能系统的寿命，还可以提高汽车整体的燃料效率。

## Exercises（练习）

◆1. Translate the following passages (expressions) into Chinese（英译汉）

（1） Ultracapacitors also have been investigated for use in PHEV due to their very high power density and long cycle life.

（2） play an important role

（3） energy storage systems

★2. Translate the following passages (expressions) into English（汉译英）

（1） 锂离子电池

（2） 镍金属氢化物电池

（3） 储能系统（ESS）在电动汽车、混合动力汽车和插电式混合动力汽车中发挥着重要的作用。

## Reading material（阅读材料）

According to DOE PHEV Meeting Summary Report (2006), the battery warranty cost is believed to be one of the show-stoppers for the mass market penetration of PHEV. Tesla Motors provides only 3 years of warranty on their EV battery. Others charge \$300/year for battery warranty beyond 3 years. It is estimated that the replacement cost of the Chevy Volt battery pack is more than \$10,000, The EV and PHEV battery will have a warranty of 10/150 (10 years or 150 k miles, whichever happens earlier) in the "green states" in the United States, which is due to CARB regulations allowing a \$3,000 incentive if a PHEV battery has the 10/150 warranty. Equally, if not more important than warranty cost is the customer perception of battery life and the impact on resale value (and residual value) of the car.

## 4.2 Battery Management

### Text (课文)

Battery management systems (BMS) are widely used in systems where a group of battery cells are connected in series and/or parallel to deliver large power. In an EV, HEV, or PHEV, there are hundreds or even thousands of battery cells in a pack depending on the type of battery cells used. It is critical to monitor and control the batteries so that optimum performance of the system can be achieved and at the same time, the vehicle safety is maintained and the ESS life is extended.

A BMS can have a few levels of functionality. At the simplest level, a BMS should be able to monitor the battery parameters, such as voltage, current, temperature, state of charge (SOC), and state of health (SOH). At the next level, the BMS needs to control the charge and discharge, balance the cells, and maintain health of the battery. The other functions of the BMS include thermal management and safety protections, i.e., capability of isolation faulty battery cells in a fault condition.

### New words and expressions (单词和短语)

**1. New words (单词)**

| | |
|---|---|
| critical [ˈkrɪtɪk(ə)l] | adj. 鉴定的；[核]临界的；批评的，爱挑剔的；危险的；决定性的 |
| monitor [ˈmɒnɪtə] | n. 监视器；监听器；监控器；显示屏；班长<br>vt. 监控 |
| optimum [ˈɒptɪməm] | n. 最佳效果；最适宜条件<br>adj. 最适宜的 |
| functionality [fʌŋkʃəˈnæləti] | n. 功能；[数]泛函性，函数性 |
| parameter [pəˈræmɪtə] | n. 参数；系数；参量 |
| voltage [ˈvəʊltɪdʒ] | n. 电压 |
| current [ˈkʌr(ə)nt] | adj. 现在的；流通的，通用的；最近的；草写的<br>n. (水、气、电) 流；趋势；涌流 |
| temperature [ˈtemprətʃə(r)] | n. 温度；体温；气温；发烧 |

**2. Expressions (短语)**

| | |
|---|---|
| battery management system | 电池管理系统 |
| at the simplest level | 最简单的层次 |

| state of charge | 充电状态 |
| state of health | 健康状态 |
| thermal management | 热管理 |
| safety protection | 安全保护措施 |
| in a fault condition | 在故障情况下 |

## Notes to the text（难点解析）

★1. The other functions of the BMS include thermal management and safety protections, i. e., capability of isolation faulty battery cells in a fault condition. BMS 的其他功能还有热管理和安全保护措施，即在故障情况下能够隔离故障单体电池。

## Exercises（练习）

◆1. Translate the following passages (expressions) into Chinese（英译汉）

(1) At the simplest level, a BMS should be able to monitor the battery parameters, such as voltage, current, temperature, state of charge (SOC), and state of health (SOH).

(2) It is critical to monitor and control the batteries.

(3) battery management systems

(4) in a fault condition

◆2. Translate the following passages (expressions) into English（汉译英）

(1) 热管理

(2) 安全保护措施

(3) BMS 能够监测电池参数。

◆3. Directions：Answer the following questions briefly according to the text

What functionality can a BMS have？

## Reading material（阅读材料）

Energy management has multiple goals. It of course involves the distribution of energy (implying instantaneous power as well) depending on load demand. It also implies protection of the system in case some threshold is exceeded, for example, voltage, current, SOC, and so on. Further, since the resource is not unlimited, it involves the best allocation of resources with the objective of minimizing fuel consumption while observing various constraints. Thus good energy management leads to better fuel economy and/or lower emissions, and it also leads to enhanced life of devices. For example, by controlling the SOC properly, it may be possible to better maintain the battery's health, thus requiring less replacement. To be more precise, power management has the goal to take a holistic view of the system, not just from the point of view of fuel economy; or rather, it is to achieve a minimum life cycle cost of the system, from the point of view of operation, maintenance, and longevity, all taken together.

### 4.2.1 Parameter Monitoring

**Text** (课文)

The parameters to be monitored include battery voltage, current and temperature. We will first explore voltage monitoring.

There are two types of battery voltage measurements in a battery pack: cell voltage measurement and pack voltage measurement. For pack voltage measurement, due to the high voltage associated with the pack, it is not possible to directly use voltage division. An isolated voltage transducer is appropriate in this case. Figure 4.1 shows an isolated high voltage sensor for pack voltage measurement purposes, made by LEM.

It is important to monitor cell voltages as well. When cells are put in parallel, it is only necessary to measure one voltage for all cells that are in parallel. However, since there are hundreds of cells in series, it would not be practical to measure all cell voltages using a single microcontroller. There are two approaches in practice. One is to divide batteries into groups (modules). Then voltages of cells inside a module are measured locally using a module monitoring circuit and then sent to the central BMS. Another approach is to use "banking technology".

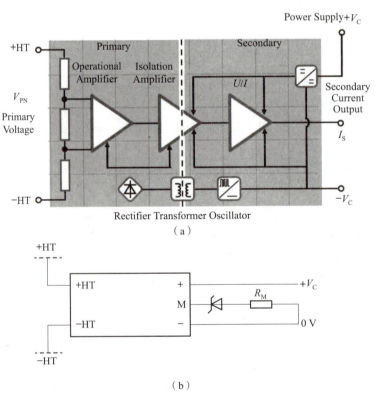

Figure 4.1　Isolated voltage sensor courtesy, LEM USA Inc.

(a) Principle of the isolated voltage sensor; (b) Configuration of the voltage sensor with a single power supply

Next, let's look at temperature monitoring. There are three temperature monitoring devices available: resistance temperature detector (RTD), thermistors, and thermocouples.

An RTD consists of a thin film of platinum on a plastic film. Its resistance varies with temperature and it can typically measure temperatures up to 850℃. It offers the very high linearity between resistance and temperature. The typical resistance is 100Ω at 0℃. RTDs are expensive so they are used mostly on precision temperature measurements. They are rarely used for temperature monitoring in battery packs.

Thermistors are made of semiconductor material or metal oxides. The resistance of thermistors decreases with increasing temperature. Therefore they are referred to as negative temperature coefficient (NTC) sensors. Thermistors are popular in battery temperature measurement. Figure 4.2 shows the thermistor resistance as a function of temperature, in logarithmic plot.

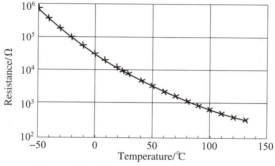

Figure 4.2  Thermistor resistance value

Thermistors can be directly connected to the A/D channels of a microcontroller (MCU), but a buffer circuit is preferred between the thermistor and the MCU as shown in Figure 4.3. A numerical table or liberalized equation is needed inside the MCU to look up the temperature for a given measurement (Table 4.1).

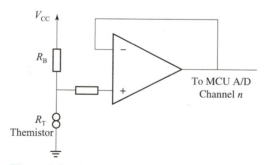

Figure 4.3  Temperature measurement circuits

Table 4.1  The battery temperature for the given measurement

| Voltage/V | 4.963 | 4.927 | 4.863 | 4.755 | 4.586 | 4.336 | 3.996 | 3.571 | 3.333 | 3.085 |
|---|---|---|---|---|---|---|---|---|---|---|
| Temperature/℃ | -50 | -40 | -30 | -20 | -10 | 0 | 10 | 20 | 25 | 30 |
| Voltage/V | 2.579 | 2.094 | 1.662 | 1.298 | 1.005 | 0.775 | 0.598 | 0.464 | 0.361 | 0.284 |
| Temperature/℃ | 40 | 50 | 60 | 70 | 80 | 90 | 100 | 110 | 120 | 130 |

Thermocouples are based on the effect that the junction between two different metals produces a voltage which increases with temperature. Since they are made of metals, they can measure temperatures up to several thousand degrees celsius. But their stability and measurement accuracy are not as good as resistor based temperature sensors.

Lastly, we will look at current monitoring. Current measurement is realized through the use of current sensors, or current transducers. There are many types of current sensors available for use in battery pack current measurement. LEM DHAB S/25 dual channel current sensor and its circuit configuration are shown in Figure 4.4.

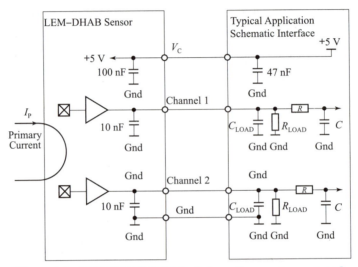

Figure 4.4  LEM DHAB S/25 dual channel current sensor and its circuit configuration, LEM USA Inc.

This current sensor has two channels of amplifier: one rated at 200 A, and the other at 25 A. The current sensor output for channel 1 is scaled at 10 mV/A, and for channel 2 is scaled at 80 mV/A. With a single 5 V power supply, the output is 2.5 V at zero current. For channel 1, 0.5 V corresponds to $-200$ A, and 4.5 V corresponds to 200 A. For channel 2, 0.5 V corresponds to $-25$ A, and 4.5 V corresponds to 25 A. The amplifier circuit for the current sensor is shown in Figure 4.5.

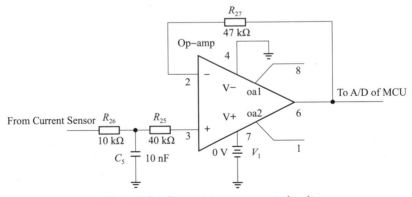

Figure 4.5  Current measurement circuit

## New words and expressions（单词和短语）

### 1. New words（单词）

| | |
|---|---|
| parameter [pəˈræmɪtə(r)] | n. 参数；系数；参量 |
| monitor [ˈmɒnɪtə(r)] | n. 监视器；监听器；监控器；显示屏；班长<br>vt. 监控 |
| explore [ɪkˈsplɔː(r)] | vi. 探索；探测；探险<br>vt. 探索；探测；探险 |
| measurement [ˈmeʒəmənt] | n. 测量；[计量] 度量；尺寸；量度制 |
| isolate [ˈaɪsəleɪt] | vt.（使）隔离，孤立；将……剔出；（某物质、细胞等）分离；区别看待（观点、问题等）<br>n. 被隔离的人（或物）；[生]（用于研究的）分离菌<br>adj. 孤独的，孤立的 |
| approach [əˈprəʊtʃ] | v. 走进；与……接洽；处理；临近，逐渐接近（某时间或事件）；几乎达到（某水平或状态）<br>n. 方法，方式；接近；接洽；（某事的）临近；路径；进场（着陆）；相似的事物 |
| module [ˈmɒdjuːl] | n. [计] 模块；组件；模数 |
| precision [prɪˈsɪʒn] | n. 精度，[数] 精密度；精确<br>adj. 精密的，精确的 |
| junction [ˈdʒʌŋkʃn] | n. 连接，接合；交叉点；接合点 |
| channel [ˈtʃæn(ə)l] | vt. 引导，开导；形成河道<br>n. 通道；频道；海峡 |
| amplifier [ˈæmplɪfaɪə] | n. [电子] 放大器，扩大器；扩音器 |

### 2. Expressions（短语）

| | |
|---|---|
| voltage monitoring | 电压监测 |
| due to | 由于 |
| isolated voltage transducer | 隔离电压传感器 |
| voltage sensor | 电压传感器 |
| microcontroller | 微控制器 |
| resistance temperature detector | 电阻温度检测器 |
| thermistor | 热敏电阻 |

| | |
|---|---|
| thermocouple | 热电偶 |
| thin film | 薄膜 |
| consist of | 组成 |
| as a function of | 根据 |
| liberalized equation | 自由方程 |
| semiconductor material | 半导体材料 |
| metal oxide | 金属氧化物 |
| negative temperature coefficient (NTC) sensors | 负温度系数（NTC）传感器 |
| degrees celsius | 摄氏度 |
| numerical table | 数值表 |
| look up | 查找 |
| current transducer | 电流传感器 |
| correspond to | 对应 |

### Notes to the text（难点解析）

★1. An isolated voltage transducer is appropriate in this case. 在这种情况下适合使用隔离电压传感器。

★2. There are two approaches in practice. One is to divide batteries into groups (modules). Then voltages of cells inside a module are measured locally using a module monitoring circuit and then sent to the central BMS. Another approach is to use "banking technology." 在实际中有两种方法：一种方法是把电池分成组（模块），然后一个模块内的电压用一个模块监控电路测量出来，送到中心的 BMS；另一种方法是利用"库技术"。

★3. RTDs are expensive so they are used mostly on precision temperature measurements. They are rarely used for temperature monitoring in battery packs. 电阻温度检测器价格昂贵，因此多用在精确温度测量中，在电池组的温度监测中很少用。

### Exercises（练习）

◆1. Translate the following passages (expressions) into Chinese（英译汉）

（1）The parameters to be monitored include battery voltage, current and temperature.

（2）Current measurement is realized through the use of current sensors, or current transducers.

（3）resistance temperature detector

（4）semiconductor material

◆2. Translate the following passages (expressions) into English（汉译英）

（1）电流传感器

（2）温度传感器

（3）用一个微控制器测量所有单体的电压是不实际的。

◆3. Fill in the blanks with the suitable words according to the text

There are _____ types of battery voltage measurements in a battery pack: cell voltage measurement and _____ voltage measurement. For pack voltage measurement, due _____ the high voltage associated with the pack, it is not _____ to directly use voltage division. An isolated voltage _____ is appropriate in this case.

◆4. Directions: Answer the following questions briefly according to the text

How many temperature monitoring devices are available? What are they?

### Reading material（阅读材料）

Almost all batteries have internal leakage (self discharge) in the idle condition. Typically the leakage current increases with temperature. For this battery pack, if the leakage current is 20 mA (which includes battery leak as well as consumption of peripheral circuits associated with the battery, such as BMS cell monitoring circuits, and cell balancing circuits), we can find out how many days for the battery to self-discharge from 100% SOC to 30% SOC.

$$40/0.02 = 2,000 = 83 \text{ (d)}$$

It means the battery will last 83 days when stored in an idle condition. It is worth to note that battery leakage tends to increase when stored at a higher temperature or extremely low temperatures.

## 4.2.2 Calculation of SOC

### Text（课文）

State of charge (SOC) calculation is one of the most important functions of a BMS. Traditionally, SOC is calculated by counting how much current (or electrons) has moved in or out of the battery:

$$\text{SOC(new)} = \text{SOC(old)} - I \times T_S / (A \cdot h)_{\text{nominal}} \tag{4.1}$$

However, this calculation is subject to many uncertainties:

◆Measurement accuracy: Current sensors have measurement accuracy and resolution. Over time, the error could be cumulated in SOC.

◆The amplifier circuit also has accuracy associated with the precision of resistors and power supplies.

◆MCU calculation rounding errors

◆MCU A/D resolution

◆Battery initial SOC which may not be known to the MCU

◆Battery loss that cannot be counted for the calculation of SOC using the above equation

◆Self-discharge cannot be counted for by the SOC algorithm.

◆Current has harmonics which could cause measurement error due to discrete sampling by the MCU.

◆Noises in the measurement loop and in the amplification circuits

◆Battery aging could impact how much energy can be charged to the battery. Hence a percentage of SOC may not truly represent how much energy is available.

Therefore, other approaches must be developed to supplement the traditional SOC calculations. One of the most popular approaches is to use battery terminal voltage to calibrate the battery SOC. In this method, the battery is tested to develop a relationship between terminal voltage and SOC for different charge/discharge current and temperature. A lookup table is then built to find SOC based on measurement of battery voltage, current, and temperature. This SOC is then compared with the calculated SOC from the Coulomb counting method. If the discrepancy exceeds a certain threshold, then attention needs to be given and some further diagnostics needs to happen. A typical SOC and voltage relationship is shown in Figure 4.6. This method can not take into account the influence of battery aging.

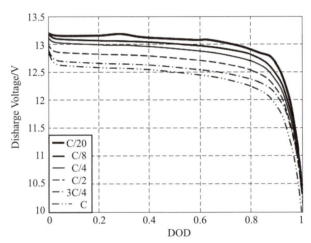

Figure 4.6 Battery SOC versus terminal voltage

The second approach is to reset SOC when the battery is fully charged. Some batteries are not allowed to be fully charged but modern lithium ion batteries can be charged full every time without affecting the battery life.

## New words and expressions（单词和短语）

### 1. New words（单词）

| | |
|---|---|
| calculation [ˌkælkjuˈleɪʃn] | n. 计算；估计；计算的结果；深思熟虑 |
| function [ˈfʌŋkʃn] | n. 功能；[数] 函数；职责；盛大的集会<br>vi. 运行；活动；行使职责 |
| accuracy [ˈækjərəsi] | n. [数] 精确度，准确性 |

| | | |
|---|---|---|
| resolution [ˌrezəˈluːʃn] | n. [物] 分辨率；决议；解决；决心 | |
| cumulate [ˈkjuːmjʊleɪt] | adj. 累积的；堆积的<br>vt. 累积；堆积<br>vi. 累积 | |
| supplement [ˈsʌplɪmənt] | n. 增补（物）；补品；增刊；（书籍的）附录；额外服务费用；补角<br>v. 增补，补充 | |
| calibrate [ˈkælɪbreɪt] | v. 校正；标定；调整；测定口径 | |
| algorithm [ˈælgərɪðəm] | n. [计][数] 算法，运算法则 | |
| equation [ɪˈkweɪʒn] | n. 方程式，等式；相等；[化学] 反应式 | |
| initial [ɪˈnɪʃl] | adj. 最初的；字首的<br>vt. 用姓名的首字母签名<br>n. 词首大写字母；原始细胞 | |
| loss [lɔːs] | n. 减少；亏损；失败；遗失 | |
| harmonics [hɑːˈmɒnɪks] | n. 和声学；泛音；数律分析法 | |
| discrete [dɪˈskriːt] | n. 分立元件；独立部件<br>adj. 离散的，不连续的 | |
| supplement [ˈsʌplɪmənt] | n. 增补（物）；补品；增刊；（书籍的）附录；额外服务费用<br>v. 增补，补充 | |
| terminal [ˈtɜːmɪnl] | n. 航空站；终点站；终端机；线接头；末端；晚期病人<br>adj. 晚期的；无可挽回的；末端的；终点的；期末的 | |
| discrepancy [dɪˈskrepənsi] | n. 不符；矛盾；相差 | |
| threshold [ˈθreʃhəʊld] | n. 入口；门槛；开始；极限；临界值 | |
| diagnostics [ˌdaɪɡˈnɒstɪks] | n. 诊断学（用作单数） | |
| reset [ˌriːˈset] | vi. 重置；清零<br>vt. 重置；重新设定；重新组合<br>n. 重新设定；重新组合；重排版 | |

## 2. Expressions（短语）

| | |
|---|---|
| state of charge | 荷电状态 |
| is subject to | 受支配 |
| rounding error | 舍入误差 |
| take into account | 考虑 |

| | |
|---|---|
| measurement error | 测量误差 |
| discrete sampling | 离散采样 |
| be associated with… | 与……有关 |
| measurement loop | 测量回路 |
| battery aging | 电池老化 |

### Notes to the text（难点解析）

★1. However, this calculation is subject to many uncertainties. 然而，这个计算受很多不确定因素的影响。

★2. Battery loss that cannot be counted for the calculation of SOC using the above. 使用上述方程不能把电池损耗算进SOC的计算中。

### Exercises（练习）

◆1. Translate the following passages (expressions) into Chinese（英译汉）

（1）Therefore, other approaches must be developed to supplement the traditional SOC calculations.

（2）Battery aging could impact how much energy can be charged to the battery.

（3）take into account

（4）rounding errors

◆2. Translate the following passages (expressions) into English（汉译英）

（1）受支配

（2）测量误差

（3）一种流行的方法是用电池端电压来校准电池SOC。

◆3. Directions：Answer the following questions briefly according to the text

Can you tell us several uncertainties in SOC calculation?

### Reading material（阅读材料）

Lastly, advanced mathematical models can be used to predict battery SOC, such as Kalman Filtering, etc. The Kalman filter makes an optimum trade-off between believing the sensor reading and believing the model to achieve the best possible state estimate. The key is to filter the noise and combine with a good mathematical model. Kalman Filtering treats the measurement noise as a random variable and removes measurement noise from the system. In Kalman Filtering, we estimate signal $X$ for each $K$ (state) using

$$X_K = K_K Z_K + (1 - K_K) Z_{K-1} \tag{4.2}$$

where $Z_K$ is the measurement value that has error, and $K_K$ is the Kalman Gain which needs to be determined for different systems. A good mathematical model is a critical part of the Kalman Filter based SOC estimation.

### 4.2.3　Fault and Safety Protection

**Text（课文）**

The proposed circuit in Figure 4.7 (a) can be used to balance the battery cells during charging and to isolate faulty cells during charging or discharging. There are two transistors associated with each battery cell. These transistors are typical low on-state resistance MOSFETs, with typical resistance at the milliohms range.

During normal operation, the parallel-connected transistors are turned off and the series-connected resistors are turned on, as shown in Figure 4.7 (b). During fault conditions, assume $B_1$ has a fault, transistor $T_{1P}$ which is parallel-connected to the faulty cell ($B_1$ as shown in Figure 4.7 (c)) is turned on while the series connected transistor $T_{1S}$ for the same cell is turned off.

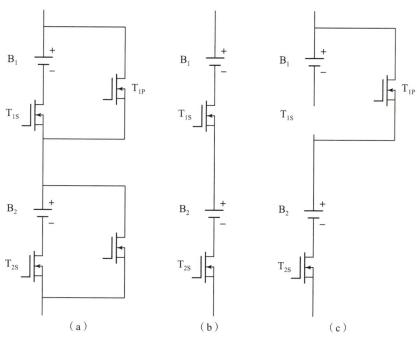

Figure 4.7　A balance and isolation circuit to manage battery pack in a PHEV
(a) Configuration; (b) Normal operation; (c) $B_1$ fault or bypass

During charging, the balancing can be performed using the same circuit. When $B_1$ is full, $T_{1P}$ is turned on and $T_{1S}$ is turned off, so all charging current goes through the bypass transistor $T_{1P}$. This is more suitable for constant current charging because when one cell is discounted from the battery string, the whole pack voltage is reduced by one cell. Therefore, the charger voltage has to be adjusted accordingly.

The advantage of this circuit is that it does not consume any power (other than the transistor loss) during balancing, and it can isolate any faulty cell during the usage of the battery pack. The disadvantage is that the loss on the series connected transistors can be very large during high current operations. Hence, this design is not suitable for large power applications. For example, if the MOSFET voltage at 200 A is 0.2 V; ($R_{DS\_ON} = 0.001\ \Omega$ which costs \$2), the loss on the single MOSFET will be $200^2 \times 0.001 = 40$ (W). For a pack that is composed of 100 cells in series, the loss will be 4 kW at peak. However, when the current is reduced to 60 A, the pack loss due to the transistors will be only 360 W. However, the pack will only be able to supply 24 kW assuming each cell is rated at 4 V.

### New words and expressions（单词和短语）

#### 1. New words（单词）

| | |
|---|---|
| transistor [trænˈzɪstə(r)] | n. 晶体管（收音机） |
| balance [ˈbæləns] | n. 平衡；余额；匀称<br>vt. 使平衡；结算；使相称<br>vi. 保持平衡；相称；抵销 |
| bypass [ˈbaɪpɑːs] | v. 绕过，避开；忽视，不顾（规章制度）；设旁路，迂回<br>n. 旁路，支路；旁通管，分流术 |
| perform [pəˈfɔːm] | vt. 执行；完成；演奏<br>vi. 执行，机器运转；表演 |
| discount [ˈdɪskaʊnt] | n. 折扣；贴现率<br>vt. 打折扣；将……贴现；贬损；低估；忽视<br>vi. 贴现；打折扣出售商品 |
| adjust [əˈdʒʌst] | vt. 调整，使……适合；校准<br>vi. 调整，校准；适应 |
| accordingly [əˈkɔːdɪŋli] | adv. 因此，于是；相应地；照着 |
| consume [kənˈsjuːm] | vt. 消耗，消费；使……着迷；挥霍<br>vi. 耗尽，毁灭；耗尽生命 |
| assume [əˈsjuːm] | vi. 设想；承担；采取<br>vt. 假定；僭取；篡夺；夺取；擅用；侵占 |

#### 2. Expressions（短语）

| | |
|---|---|
| be associated with… | 与……有关联 |
| turn off | 关断 |
| turn on | 打开 |
| parallel-connected | 并联的 |

| | |
|---|---|
| series-connected | 串联的 |
| fault condition | 故障情况 |
| constant current | 电流恒定 |
| charger voltage | 充电电压 |
| be suitable for | 适合 |

### Notes to the text（难点解析）

★1. The proposed circuit in Figure 4.7（a） can be used to balance the battery cells during charging and to isolate faulty cells during charging or discharging. 图 4.7（a）中的电路可以在充电期间用来均衡电池组单位，并且在充电或放电期间隔离故障单体。

★2. During normal operation, the parallel-connected transistors are turned off and the series-connected resistors are turned on. 在正常运行时，并联的晶体管关断，串联的电阻导通。

### Exercises（练习）

◆1. Translate the following passages（expressions）into Chinese（英译汉）

（1）This is more suitable for constant current charging because when one cell is discounted from the battery string, the whole pack voltage is reduced by one cell.

（2）It can isolate any faulty cell during usage of the battery pack.

（3）turn on

（4）faulty cell

◆2. Translate the following passages（expressions）into English（汉译英）

（1）关断

（2）并联的晶体管

（3）缺点是在电流很大时，串联的晶体管损耗会很大。

3. Directions：Answer the following questions briefly according to the text.

Can you analyze circuit shown in Figure 4.7？

### Reading material（阅读材料）

The fundamental problem is this: different cells in the string all get the same chaining current for the same length of time (they are in series so it cannot be otherwise), but individual cells have different capacities and start with different residual charge, so they will almost certainly need slightly more or less current/charge duration. The problem gets worse as the string gets longer.

 **4.2.4　Charge Management**

### Text（课文）

Proper charge and discharge of batteries can maintain healthy condition of the battery system.

Consequently, improper charge and discharge can impact the battery life and capacity.

Batteries in the EV, HEV, and PHEV are charged in three scenarios: during plugin charge, during regenerative braking, and opportunity charge using engine power. The plugin charge is usually over an extended period of time at a lower charge rate. But the regenerative braking can happen at a much higher current level over very short time duration.

Plugin charge usually goes through five phases:

➢ Diagnosis phase. When the car is plugged in, the BMS and charger will perform a series of testing to make sure the battery is capable of receiving charge. A small current, typically $C/20$ is injected to the battery. This phase can last a few minutes with the charging current gradually ramped up to the second phase.

➢ Constant current charging phase. Once the battery passes the diagnosis, the battery is charged with constant current, usually at $C/5$ for regular charging, and $C/2 \sim 2C$ for fast charging.

➢ Constant voltage or reduced current charging phase. During the constant current charging phase, once one of the cells reaches the maximum voltage, the charging current is reduced. At this point, the battery can either be charged at a reduced current, or enter the constant voltage charging phase.

➢ Balancing phase. However, depending on the imbalance of the battery cells, the constant voltage phase can take a long time. During this phase, the balancing circuit is activated for the cells that have reached the threshold. Once all battery cells reach the preset voltage threshold, the charge is stopped and the charger can be turned off.

➢ Maintenance phase. Some batteries need a maintenance phase in which a very small amount of current is being injected to the battery to make up the leakage loss. Some battery packs have been designed to use this small current to keep the battery warm in cold weather (Figure 4.8).

While the management of plugin charge is relatively straight forward, management of the charging of battery during regenerative braking can be very difficult. This is due to the fact that a large current is being injected to the battery to generate the desired braking torque, as well as the heat generated inside the battery due to battery internal resistance.

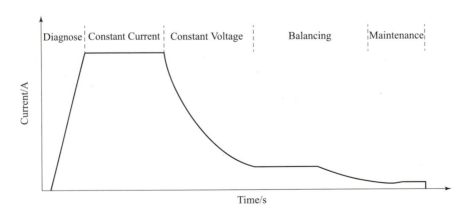

Figure 4.8 Plugin charge management

## New words and expressions（单词和短语）

### 1. New words（单词）

| | |
|---|---|
| proper [ˈprɒpə(r)] | adj. 适当的；本身的；特有的；正派的<br>adv. 完全地<br>n. (Proper) 人名；(英、德) 普罗珀 |
| maintain [meɪnˈteɪn] | vt. 维持；继续；维修；主张；供养 |
| impact [ˈɪmpækt] | n. 影响；效果；碰撞；冲击力<br>vt. 挤入，压紧；撞击；对……产生影响<br>vi. 影响；撞击；冲突；压紧 (on, upon, with) |
| scenario [səˈnɑːrɪəʊ] | n. 方案；情节；剧本；设想 |
| phase [feɪz] | n. 月相；时期，阶段<br>vt. 分阶段进行；使定相 |
| diagnosis [ˌdaɪəɡˈnəʊsɪs] | n. 诊断 |
| maintenance [ˈmeɪntənəns] | n. 维护，维修；保持；生活费用 |

### 2. Expressions（短语）

| | |
|---|---|
| healthy condition | 健康状态 |
| plugin charge | 插电式充电期间 |
| regenerative braking | 可再生制动期间 |
| engine power | 发动机功率 |
| goes through | 经过 |
| is capable of | 能力 |
| is injected to | 流入 |
| constant voltage | 恒电压 |
| make up | 弥补 |
| braking torque | 制动转矩 |
| battery internal resistance | 电池内部电阻 |

## Notes to the text（难点解析）

★1. The plugin charge is usually over an extended period of time at a lower charge rate. But the regenerative braking can happen at a much higher current level over very short time duration. 插电式充电通常是在较长的时间内以较低的充电速率进行的。但可再生制动会在很短的时间内

以很高的电流进行。

★2. At this point, the battery can either be charged at a reduced current, or enter the constant voltage charging phase. 在这个点，电池组或者以减小的电流充电，或者进入恒电压充电阶段。

### Exercises（练习）

◆1. Translate the following passages (expressions) into Chinese（英译汉）

（1）This is due to the fact that a large current is being injected to the battery to generate the desired braking torque, as well as the heat generated inside the battery due to battery internal resistance.

（2）constant current

（3）regenerative braking

◆2. Translate the following passages (expressions) into English（汉译英）

（1）恒电压

（2）制动转矩

（3）由于单体组中单体之间的不平衡，恒电压阶段将持续很长时间。

◆3. Directions：Answer the following questions briefly according to the text

Can you analyze five phases about plugin charge?

## 4.3 Battery Cell Balancing

### Text（课文）

Battery cells are connected in parallel or series to form the battery pack in an HEV, EV, or PHEV. When battery cells are connected in series to form a string, the available energy of the string is determined by the cell that has the least energy. Similarly, when charging the battery, the amount of energy which can be transferred to the string is determined by the cell that has the most energy.

There will be small differences in capacity and internal impedance for hundreds or thousands of cells that are used to form the string. Over time, these differences can be enlarged due to the usage patterns, especially due to the different operating temperatures.

Hence it is important to balance the cells during operation of the battery pack. There are two categories of balancing methods available: passive balancing and active balancing.

For passive balancing, the energy of the high energy cells are discharged to a resistor or transistor and dissipated as heat. For active balancing, the energy from the high energy cells are discharged to charge the lower energy cells.

For passive balancing, there are typically resistor based and transistor or IC based balancing circuits. Both methods can be used during charge or in idle condition.

Figure 4.9 shows resistor based passive balancing of a three-cell string. The resistors/transistors are in parallel with each battery cell. When the voltage across any cell is less than the designed voltage (in this case, 3.65 V), the transistor is off hence no current goes through the bypass circuit. All charging current goes through the battery to charge the battery. Once the cell voltage reaches 3.65 V, the transistor is turned on and current flowing through the resistor/transistor starts to increase. In this case, the cells that are below 3.65 V are still charged but the cell that reaches 3.65 V or above is bypassed and stopped charging. Once all cells in the string reach 3.65 V, the charge process will stop.

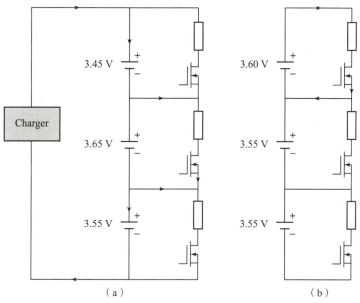

**Figure 4.9  Resistive charge balancing method**
(a) Balancing during charge; (b) Balancing during idle

The advantage of this balancing method is that the circuit can be simple and small hence the packaging can be easy. The voltage can be very accurate, up to a few millivolts. The disadvantages are: (1) The balancing is essentially a voltage based balancing method and the energy contents in each cell may still be different even if the cells have the same open circuit voltage; and (2) The energy that flows through the resistor/transistor is wasted as heat. Not only does this decrease the charge efficiency, but also creates difficulties for the thermal management of the battery pack. The typical bypass current is designed to be no more than a few amperes.

Active balancing, on the other hand, can be very efficient. There are two types of active balancing circuits. One is the traditional capacitor or inductor based cell balancing, and the other is DC/DC converter based cell balancing. Active balancing provides high efficiency but increases the complexity for the wiring and control algorithm development, and can be expensive if it is built into a battery pack.

A DC/DC converter based cell balancing combines the advantages of a DC/DC converter and the inductive balancing scheme as shown in Figure 4.10. In this circuit, the input of DC/DC converter can be switched to any cell and the output can be switched to any other cell through the selective switches. During charge, discharge, or idle time, when the DC/DC converter is activated, the control algorithm will search for the lowest voltage and the highest voltage among all cells. Once the highest and lowest voltage cells are found, the DC/DC converter is controlled to charge the lowest cell using the energy from the highest cell, until the cell reaches the average voltage. This process will continue until all cells have the same voltage.

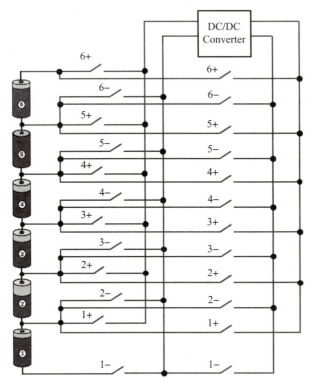

Figure 4.10　DC/DC converter based balancing method

## New words and expressions（单词和短语）

### 1. New words（单词）

| | |
|---|---|
| string [strɪŋ] | n. 线，弦，细绳；一串，一行<br>vt. 悬挂；系；扎；用线（或细绳等）串，把……连在一起 |
| impedance [ɪmˈpiːdns] | n. [电]阻抗 |
| passive [ˈpæsɪv] | n. 被动语态<br>adj. 被动的，消极的；被动语态的 |
| active [ˈæktɪv] | n. 主动语态；积极分子<br>adj. 积极的；活跃的；主动的；有效的；现役的 |
| wiring [ˈwaɪərɪŋ] | n. [电]接线，架线；线路；金属线缝术<br>v. 装电线（wire 的现在分词） |
| dissipate [ˈdɪsɪpeɪt] | vi. 驱散；放荡<br>vt. 浪费；使……消散 |

| | | |
|---|---|---|
| algorithm [ˈælgərɪðəm] | n. | [计][数]算法，运算法则 |
| switch [swɪtʃ] | n. | 开关；转变；（铁道的）转辙器，道岔；（树上砍下的）细软枝条 |
| | v. | 改变（立场、方向等）；替换；转换；调换；调（班） |
| complexity [kəmˈpleksəti] | n. | 复杂，复杂性；复杂错综的事物 |

### 2. Expressions（短语）

| | |
|---|---|
| the least energy | 最小能量 |
| the most energy | 最多能量 |
| be transferred to | 传输 |
| internal impedance | 内阻 |
| operating temperature | 运行温度 |
| passive balancing | 被动式均衡 |
| active balancing | 主动式均衡 |
| in idle condition | 闲置状态 |
| be switched to | 切换到 |
| control algorithm | 控制算法 |
| same voltage | 相同的电压 |

### Notes to the text（难点解析）

★1. When battery cells are connected in series to form a string, the available energy of the string is determined by the cell that has the least energy. Similarly, when charging the battery, the amount of energy which can be transferred to the string is determined by the cell that has the most energy. 当电池被串联形成一个串时，这个串的可用能量取决于含有最小能量的电池。同样，当为电池组充电时，能够传输到电池组的能量取决于剩余能量最多的那个电池。

★2. For passive balancing, the energy of the high energy cells are discharged to a resistor or transistor and dissipated as heat. 对于被动式平衡，能量高的电池单体通过电阻或晶体管放电，能量以热量形式耗散。

### Exercises（练习）

◆1. Translate the following passages (expressions) into Chinese（英译汉）

（1）Once all cells in the string reach 3.65 V, the charge process will stop.

（2）Not only does this decrease the charge efficiency, but also creates difficulties for the thermal management of the battery pack.

（3）internal impedance

（4）in idle condition

◆2. Translate the following passages (expressions) into English (汉译英)

(1) 相同的电压

(2) 被动式均衡

(3) DC/DC 变换器就被控制利用最高电压单体的能量向电压最低的电池单体充电，直到单体到达平均电压。

### Reading material（阅读材料）

In order to limit the heat generated in the process of balancing, the charge current needs to be reduced at the time the cell balancing circuit is activated. Therefore the process of balancing control can he illustrated in Figure 4.11 and Figure 4.12 for the charge controller and balancer controller, respectively. In this example, the battery is charged full at 3.65 V (open circuit voltage) and 100% at 4.0 V (floating voltage). The balancing starts at cell voltage 3.65 V. The charge current during the balancing phase is reduced by a percentage when $V_{max}$ = 3.65 V, and reduced to 1.65 A at $V_{max}$ = 4.2 V.

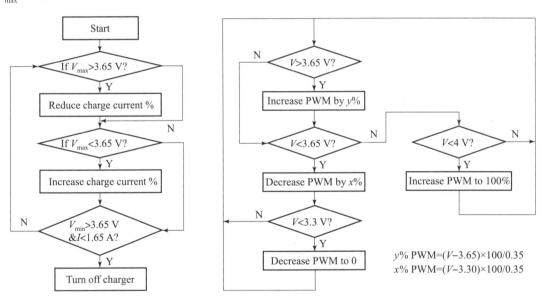

Figure 4.11  Charger control algorithm designed for cell balancing

Figure 4.12  Balancer control algorithm designed for cell balancing

The charger algorithm will activate the balancing circuit when a cell voltage reaches 3.65 V, and at the same time, it reduces the charging current to 1.65 A. However, if the maximum cell voltage drops below 3.65 V, the balancing circuit is deactivated and the charging current restored. The hysteresis of 3.3 V to 3.65 V, and 3.65 V and 4.0 V, is to prevent the circuit from being in an unstable condition. The balancing control algorithm will increase the turn-on time for the transistor so more current will go through the bypass circuit.

# Chapter 5
## Electric Propulsion Systems

**Text** (课文)

Electric propulsion systems are at the heart of EVs and HEVs. They consist of electric motors, power converters and electronic controllers. The electric motor converts the electric energy into mechanical energy to propel the vehicle or vice versa, to enable regenerative braking and/or to generate electricity for the purpose of charging the on-board energy storage. The power converter is used to supply the electric motor with proper voltage and current. The electronic controller commands the power converter by providing control signals to it, and then controls the operation of the electric motor to produce proper torque and speed, according to the command from the driver. The functional block diagram of an electric propulsion system is illustrated in Figure 5.1.

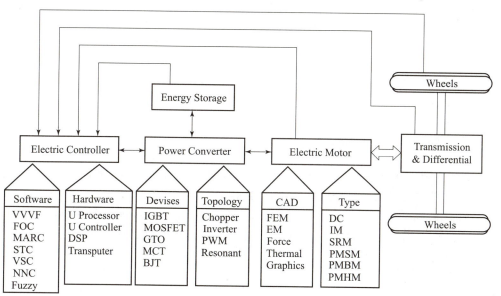

Figure 5.1 Functional block diagram of a typical electric propulsion system

The choice of electric propulsion systems for EVs and HEVs mainly depends on a number of factors, including the driver's expectation, vehicle constraints, and energy source. The driver's expectation is defined by a driving profile, which includes the acceleration, maximum speed, climbing capability, braking, and range. The vehicle constraints, including volume and weight, depend on the vehicle type, vehicle weight, and payload. The energy source relates to batteries, fuel cells, ultracapacitors, flywheels, and various hybrid sources. Thus, the process of identifying the preferred feature and package options for electric propulsion has to be carried out at the system level. The interaction of subsystems and the likely impacts of system trade-offs must be examined.

### New words and expressions（单词和短语）

#### 1. New words（单词）

| | |
|---|---|
| constraint [kən'streɪnt] | n. [数] 约束；局促，态度不自然；强制 |
| profile ['prəʊfaɪl] | n. 侧面；轮廓；外形；剖面；简况<br>vt. 描……的轮廓；扼要描述<br>vi. 给出轮廓 |
| payload ['peɪləʊd] | n. （导弹、火箭等的）有效载荷，有效负荷；收费载重，酬载；（工厂、企业等）工资负担 |

#### 2. Expressions（短语）

| | |
|---|---|
| power converter | 功率变换器 |
| electronic controller | 电子控制器 |
| mechanical energy | 机械能 |
| vice versa | 反之亦然 |
| electric propulsion system | 电驱动系统 |
| functional block diagram | 功能模块框图 |

### Notes to the text（难点解析）

★1. The power converter is used to supply the electric motor with proper voltage and current. 功率变换器用来对电动机提供特定的电压和电流。

★2. The driver's expectation is defined by a driving profile, which includes the acceleration, maximum speed, climbing capability, braking, and range. 驾驶员的期望值由包括加速性能、最高车速、爬坡能力、制动性能和行驶里程在内的行驶循环予以定义。

### Exercises（练习）

◆1. Translate the following passages (expressions) into Chinese（英译汉）

(1) Electric propulsion systems are at the heart of EVs and HEVs.

(2) The electric motor converts the electric energy into mechanical energy to propel the vehicle.

(3) functional block diagram

(4) mechanical energy

◆2. Translate the following passages (expressions) into English (汉译英)

(1) 再生制动

(2) 电能

(3) 这些系统由电动机、功率变换器和电子控制器构成。

### Reading material (阅读材料)

The electronic controller can be further divided into three functional units—sensor, interface circuitry and processor. The sensor is used to translate the measurable quantities, such as current, voltage, temperature, speed, torque, and flux, into electric signals through the interface circuitry. These signals are conditioned to the appropriate level before being fed into the processor. The processor output signals are usually amplified via the interface circuitry to drive power semiconductor devices of the power converter.

## 5.1 Electric Motors

###  5.1.1 Advantage of Electric Motors

#### Text (课文)

Let us note first of all that the mechanical torque of the electric motor results from the action of a magnetic induction flux on an electric current. In an electric motor, the flux imposes the dimensions of the magnetic material (iron); the current imposes the diameter of the wire (generally made of copper) which constitute the coil-windings.

Thus, electric-motor dimensions depend largely on the torque characteristics which we want to obtain. The motor power is equal to the product of the torque by the rotation speed, such that at a given power, the size of the motor is small as its rotation speed is high.

Whatever its nature is—DC motor or AC motor—the electric motor presents a certain number of advantages:

It can provide a torque to all speeds and in particular when stationary. This property permits the elimination of the clutch in the torque transmission chain with the help of a suitable supply control voltage for a DC motor, or with help of the inverter in the case of an AC motor.

It can support short loads, and provide significant overtorques, about 2 to 4 times' the nominal torque, during the acceleration or starting period.

It presents a high thermal inertia; the maximum power is higher than the nominal continuous output. The continuous power/maximum power depends on the size of the motor and its cooling mode. In general, for motors used in electric traction, this ratio is about 1.3.

## New words and expressions（单词和短语）

### 1. New words（单词）

| | |
|---|---|
| dimension [daɪˈmenʃn] | n. 方面；[数] 维；尺寸；次元；容积<br>adj. 规格的<br>vt. 标出尺寸 |
| flux [flʌks] | n. [流] [机] 流量；变迁；不稳定；流出<br>vt. 使熔融；用焊剂处理<br>vi. 熔化；流出 |
| impose [ɪmˈpəʊz] | vt. 强加；征税；以……欺骗<br>vi. 利用；欺骗；施加影响 |
| diameter [daɪˈæmɪtə(r)] | n. 直径 |
| wire [ˈwaɪə(r)] | n. 电线；金属丝；电报<br>vt. 拍电报；给……装电线<br>vi. 打电报 |
| stationary [ˈsteɪʃənri] | n. 不动的人；驻军<br>adj. 固定的；静止的；定居的；常备军的 |
| elimination [ɪˌlɪmɪˈneɪʃn] | n. 消除；淘汰；除去 |

### 2. Expressions（短语）

| | |
|---|---|
| mechanical torque | 机械转矩 |
| magnetic induction | 磁感应 |
| nominal torque | 额定转矩 |
| thermal inertia | 热惯性 |
| cooling mode | 冷却方式 |

## Notes to the text（难点解析）

★1. Thus, electric motor dimensions depend largely on the torque characteristics which we want to obtain. 因此，电动机的尺寸很大程度上取决于我们所需的转矩特性。

★2. It can provide a torque to all speeds and in particular when stationary. 它都可以在任意转速下输出转矩，特别是在静止状态起动时能够提供较大转矩。

## Exercises（练习）

◆1. Translate the following passages (expressions) into Chinese（英译汉）

（1）Such that at a given power, the size of the motor is small as its rotation speed is high.

(2) The continuous power/maximum power depends on the size of the motor and its cooling mode.

(3) DC motor

(4) AC motor

★2. Translate the following passages (expressions) into English (汉译英)

(1) 机械转矩

(2) 额定转矩

★3. Directions: Answer the following questions briefly according to the text

What are the advantages of the electric motor ?

### Reading material (阅读材料)

In a DC motor the rotational speed is limited:

➢ mechanically by removing risks on binder windings and commutated segments;

➢ electrically by the commutation of the current between the commutator segments.

In practice the electric motors used in road-vehicle drive train systems have unit powers lower than 50-60 kW and their supply voltage most of the time remains lower than 200 VDC.

Under these conditions it is possible to manufacture engines with a DC motor, which turn at 5,000 r/min. Motors with AC current, because of the absence of a collector, can reach rotation speeds higher than those of the DC motor: 10,000 r/min and a perfectly feasible speed for the powers concerned in conventional road vehicles. As such, the specific power of an AC motor is higher than that of a DC motor.

 ### 5.1.2 Classification of Electric Motors

### Text (课文)

Differing from the industrial applications of motors, the motors used in EVs and HEVs usually require frequent starts and stops; high rates of acceleration/deceleration; high torque and low-speed hill climbing; low torque and high-speed cruising, and a very wide speed range of operation. The motor drives for EVs and HEVs can be classified into two main groups, namely the commutator motors and commutatorless motors, as illustrated in Figure 5.2.

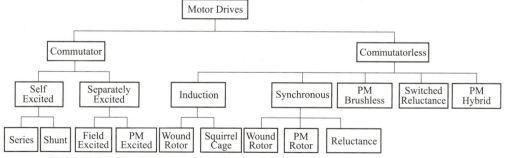

Figure 5.2  Classification of electric motor drives for EV and HEV applications

## 1. DC Motors

### Text（课文）

Commutator motors mainly are the traditional DC motors, which include series excited, shunt excited, compound excited, separately excited, and permanent magnets (PMs) excited motors. DC motors need commutators and brushes to feed current into the armature, thus making them less reliable and unsuitable for maintenance-free operation and high speed. In addition, winding-excited DC motors have low specific power density. Nevertheless, because of their mature technology and simple control, DC motor drives have been prominent in electric propulsion systems.

### New words and expressions（单词和短语）

#### 1. New words（单词）

| | |
|---|---|
| commutator [ˈkɒmjuteɪtə(r)] | n. [电]换向器；整流器 |
| armature [ˈɑːmətʃə(r)] | n. 电枢（电机的部件）；盔甲，甲胄；防卫器官 |
| prominent [ˈprɒmɪnənt] | adj. 突出的，显著的；杰出的；卓越的 |

#### 2. Expressions（短语）

| | |
|---|---|
| commutator motor | 有换向器电动机 |
| series excited | 串励 |
| shunt excited | 并励 |
| compound excited | 复励 |
| separately excited | 他励 |
| permanent magnets (PMs) excited | 永磁（PM）励磁 |

### Notes to the text（难点解析）

★1. Nevertheless, because of their mature technology and simple control, DC motor drives have been prominent in electric propulsion systems. 然而，由于技术成熟和控制简单，直流电动机驱动一直在电驱动系统中有着突出的地位。

### Exercises（练习）

◆1. Translate the following passages (expressions) into Chinese（英译汉）

（1）commutator motors

（2）series excited

◆2. Translate the following passages (expressions) into English（汉译英）

（1）并励

（2）永磁（PM）励磁

(3) 复励

(4) 他励

◆3. Directions: Answer the following questions briefly according to the text

What can DC motor be classified?

## 2. Induction Motors

### Text（课文）

Technological developments have recently pushed commutatorless electric motors into a new era. Advantages include higher efficiency, higher power density, and lower operating cost. They are also more reliable and maintenance-free compared to commutator DC motors; thus, commutatorless electric motors have now become more attractive.

Induction motors are widely accepted as a commutatorless motor type for EV and HEV propulsion. This is because of their low cost, high reliability and maintenance-free operation. However, conventional control of induction motors such as variable-voltage variable-frequency cannot provide the desired performance. With the advent of the power electronics and microcomputer era, the principle of field-oriented control (FOC) or vector control of induction motors has been accepted to overcome their control complexity due to their nonlinearity. However, these EV and HEV motors using FOC still suffer from low efficiency at light loads and limited constant-power operating range.

### New words and expressions（单词和短语）

#### 1. New words（单词）

| | |
|---|---|
| vector [ˈvektə(r)] | n. 矢量；带菌者；航线 |
| | vt. 用无线电导航 |
| nonlinearity [ˌnɒnlɪnɪˈærəti] | n. [数] 非线性；非线性特征 |

#### 2. Expressions（短语）

| | |
|---|---|
| new era | 新时代 |
| induction motor | 异步电动机 |
| with the advent of | 随着……的到来 |
| power electronic | 电力电子 |
| vector control | 矢量控制 |
| field-oriented control (FOC) | 磁场定向控制 |
| variable-voltage variable-frequency | 变压变频 |
| constant-power | 恒功率 |

## Notes to the text（难点解析）

★1. Vector control of induction motors has been accepted to overcome their control complexity due to their nonlinearity. 矢量控制原理已被用来克服由于异步电动机非线性带来的控制难度。

## Exercises（练习）

◆1. Translate the following passages (expressions) into Chinese（英译汉）

(1) Induction motors are widely accepted as a commutatorless motor type for EV and HEV propulsion.

(2) They have been accepted as having great potential to compete with induction motors for EV and HEV applications.

(3) maintenance-free

◆2. Translate the following passages (expressions) into English（汉译英）

(1) 异步电动机

(2) 变压变频

### 3. PM Synchronous Motors

## Text（课文）

By replacing the field winding of conventional synchronous motors with PMs, PM synchronous motors can eliminate conventional brushes, slip rings, and field copper losses. Actually, these PM synchronous motors are also called PM brushless AC motors, or sinusoidal-fed PM brushless motors, because of their sinusoidal AC current and brushless configuration. Since these motors are essentially synchronous motors, they can run from a sinusoidal or pulsed waveform modulation supply (PWM supply) without electronic commutation. These motors are generally simple and inexpensive, but with relatively low output power. Similar to induction motors, these PM synchronous motors usually use FOC for high-performance applications. Because of their inherently high power density and high efficiency, they have been accepted as having great potential to compete with induction motors for EV and HEV applications. Figure 5.3 shows the Leroy-Somer Synchronous Motor.

Figure 5.3　Leroy-Somer Synchronous Motor

## New words and expressions（单词和短语）

### 1. New words（单词）

| | |
|---|---|
| synchronous [ˈsɪŋkrənəs] | adj. 同步的；同时的 |
| eliminate [ɪˈlɪmɪneɪt] | vt. 消除；排除 |
| sinusoidal [ˌsaɪnəˈsɔɪdəl] | adj. 正弦曲线的 |
| modulation [ˌmɒdjəˈleɪʃn] | n. [电子] 调制；调整 |
| commutation [ˌkɒmjuˈteɪʃn] | n. 减刑；交换；经常来往；代偿 |
| inherently [ɪnˈherəntli] | adv. 内在地；固有地；天性地 |

### 2. Expressions（短语）

| | |
|---|---|
| field winding | 励磁绕组 |
| copper losses | 铜耗 |
| synchronous motor | 同步电动机 |

## Notes to the text（难点解析）

★1. PM synchronous motors can eliminate conventional brushes, slip rings, and field copper losses. 永磁同步电动机可排除传统的电刷、集电环以及励磁绕组的铜耗。

## Exercises（练习）

◆1. Translate the following passages (expressions) into Chinese（英译汉）
(1) field winding
(2) synchronous motors
★2. Translate the following passages (expressions) into English（汉译英）
(1) 铜耗
(2) 正弦交变电流

## Reading material（阅读材料）

When PMs are mounted on the rotor surface, they behave as nonsalient synchronous motors because the permeability of PMs is similar to that of air. By burying those PMs inside the magnetic circuit of the rotor, the saliency causes an additional reluctance torque, which leads to facilitating a wider speed range at constant power operation. On the other hand, by abandoning the field winding or PMs while purposely making use of the rotor saliency, synchronous reluctance motors are generated.

## 4. PM Brushless DC (BLDC) Motors

### Text (课文)

By virtually inverting the stator and rotor of PM DC motors (commutator), PM brushless DC (BLDC) motors are generated. It should be noted that the term "DC" may be misleading, since it does not refer to a DC current motor. Actually, these motors are fed by rectangular AC current and hence are also rectangular-fed PM brushless motors. The most obvious advantage of these motors is the removal of brushes. Another advantage is the ability to produce a large torque because of the rectangular interaction between current and flux. Moreover, the brushless configuration allows more cross-sectional area for the armature windings. Since the conduction of heat through the frame is improved, an increase in electric loading causes higher power density. Different from PM synchronous motors, these PM BLDC motors generally operate with shaft position sensors.

### New words and expressions (单词和短语)

#### 1. New words (单词)

| | |
|---|---|
| stator [ˈsteɪtə] | n. 固定片，定子 |
| rotor [ˈrəʊtə(r)] | n. 转子；水平旋翼；旋转体 |
| misleading [ˌmɪsˈliːdɪŋ] | v. 使产生错误想法（或印象）；欺骗；给……带错路；把……引入歧途（mislead 的现在分词）<br>adj. 误导的；引入歧途的；让人产生错误观念的 |
| rectangular [rekˈtæŋɡjələ(r)] | adj. 矩形的；成直角的 |
| removal [rɪˈmuːvl] | n. 免职；移动；排除；搬迁 |
| brush [brʌʃ] | n. 刷子；画笔；毛笔；争吵；冲突；灌木丛地带；矮树丛；狐狸尾巴<br>vt. 刷；画 |
| conduction [kənˈdʌkʃn] | n. [生理] 传导 |
| sensor [ˈsensə(r)] | n. 传感器 |

#### 2. Expressions (短语)

| | |
|---|---|
| armature winding | 电枢绕组 |
| electric loading | 电负荷 |
| shaft position sensor | 转轴位置检测器 |

### Notes to the text (难点解析)

★1. By virtually inverting the stator and rotor of PM DC motors (commutator), PM brushless DC (BLDC) motors are generated. 实际上，通过转换永磁直流电动机（有刷电动机）定子和

转子的位置，就可得到永磁无刷直流电动机（BLDC）。

## Exercises（练习）

◆1. Translate the following passages (expressions) into Chinese（英译汉）

（1）These PM BLDC motors generally operate with shaft position sensors.

（2）PM brushless motors

（3）armature windings

◆2. Translate the following passages (expressions) into English（汉译英）

（1）转轴位置检测器

（2）定子和转子

### 5. Switched Reluctance Motors（SRMs）

## Text（课文）

Switched reluctance motors (SRMs) have been recognized to have considerable potential for EV and HEV applications. Basically, they are direct derivatives of single-stack variable-reluctance stepping motors. SRMs have the definite advantages of simple construction, low manufacturing cost and outstanding torque-speed characteristics for EV and HEV applications. Although they possess simplicity in construction, this does not imply any simplicity of their design and control. Because of the heavy saturation of pole tips and the fringe effect of pole and slots, their design and control are difficult and subtle. Traditionally, SRMs operate with shaft sensors to detect the relative position of the rotor to the stator. These sensors are usually vulnerable to mechanical shock and sensitive to temperature and dust. Therefore, the presence of the position sensor reduces the reliability of SRMs and constrains some applications. Recently, sensorless technologies have been developed in the Power Electronics and Motor Drive Laboratory—again, at Texas A&M University. These technologies can ensure smooth operation from zero speed to maximum speed.

## New words and expressions（单词和短语）

### 1. New words（单词）

| | |
|---|---|
| derivatives [dɪˈrɪvətɪvz] | n. 派生物；衍生物；派生词；衍生字（derivative 的复数） |
| reluctance [rɪˈlʌktəns] | n. ［电磁］磁阻；勉强；不情愿 |
| saturation [ˌsætʃəˈreɪʃn] | n. 饱和；色饱和度；浸透；磁化饱和 |
| fringe [frɪndʒ] | n. 边缘；穗；刘海 <br> adj. 边缘的；附加的 <br> vt. 加穗于 |
| slot [slɒt] | n. 位置；狭槽；水沟；硬币投币口 <br> vt. 跟踪；开槽于 |

| | | |
|---|---|---|
| subtle [ˈsʌtl] | | adj. 微妙的；精细的；敏感的；狡猾的；稀薄的 |
| vulnerable [ˈvʌlnərəbl] | | adj. 易受攻击的，易受……的攻击；易受伤害的；有弱点的 |
| dust [dʌst] | | n. 灰尘；尘埃；尘土<br>vt. 撒；拂去灰尘 |

### 2. Expressions（短语）

| | |
|---|---|
| switched reluctance motor | 开关磁阻电动机（SRM） |
| PM brushless DC (BLDC) motor | 永磁无刷直流电动机（BLDC） |
| mechanical shock | 机械振动 |

### Notes to the text（难点解析）

★1. These sensors are usually vulnerable to mechanical shock and sensitive to temperature and dust. 这些检测器通常容易因机械振动而受损，并对温度和尘埃敏感。

### Exercises（练习）

◆1. Translate the following passages (expressions) into Chinese（英译汉）

(1) Therefore, the presence of the position sensor reduces the reliability of SRMs and constrains some applications.

(2) outstanding torque-speed characteristics

◆2. Translate the following passages (expressions) into English（汉译英）

(1) 无位置检测器技术

(2) 开关磁阻电动机

### Reading material（阅读材料）

For a purely electric vehicle application, the permanent magnets solution is preferred for many reasons: output in the electric vehicle use area, compactness, mass and noise level.

On the other hand, for a general-purpose use (alternator starter, pure hybrid and electric) and since the cost criterion becomes the determining parameter, the choice of the switch reluctance motor seems relevant compared to the synchronous and asynchronous solutions because of the lower manufacturing cost of the motor and the lowest cost of power electronics, taking into account the weaker control currents for this type of motor.

However, the use of this very promising technology requires two main challenges：

➢ control of noises and vibrations；

➢ reduction of the torque ripple.

Table 5.1 is the comparison of electric motor technologies.

Table 5.1 Comparison of electric motor technologies

(Power 30 kW, Voltage DC200 V, Battery Torque 150 N·m)

| Item | DC Motor | AS Motor | Motor Syn. Bob | Motor Ayn. Magnet | Switched Reluctance |
|---|---|---|---|---|---|
| Max Efficiency | Good | Fairly Average | Good | Fairly Average | Medium |
| Average Efficiency | Average | Good | Good | Fairly Average | Good |
| Max Speed | Fairly Average | Good | Good | Good | Good |
| PE Cost | Fairly Average | Fairly Average | Average | Average | Good |
| Motor Cost | Fairly Average |  | Average | Average | Fairly Average |
| Torque/Speed | Average | Average | Fairly Average | Fairly Average | Good |

## 5.2 Electronic Structure

**Text**（课文）

The most common architecture corresponds to a direct connection with the battery as presented by the diagram in Figure 5.4. Architectures as voltages of converter and motor are defined by battery voltage, all the criteria (like performances and costs) can not always reach.

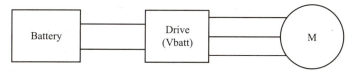

Figure 5.4 Direct electric drive system

Another solution consists in adding a buffer DC/DC converter (Figure 5.5) whose main functions are voltage adaptation of the inverter + motor (choice of the optimized work voltage of the semiconductors, passive electronic parts and engine), and battery decoupling (active filtering, minimization of the requirement in capacitive elements).

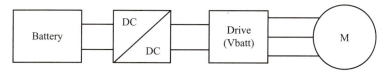

Figure 5.5 Electric drive with DC/DC converter

**New words and expressions**（单词和短语）

**1. New words**（单词）

architecture [ˈɑːkɪtektʃə(r)]　　　　　　n. 建筑学；建筑风格；建筑式样；架构

| | |
|---|---|
| criteria [kraɪˈtɪərɪə] | n. 标准，条件（criterion 的复数） |
| buffer [ˈbʌfə(r)] | n. [计] 缓冲区；缓冲器，[车辆] 减震器<br>vt. 缓冲 |
| semiconductor [ˌsemɪkənˈdʌktə(r)] | n. [电子] [物] 半导体 |
| decoupling [diːˈkʌplɪŋ] | n. 去耦<br>v. 去耦（decouple 的现在分词） |
| capacitive [kəˈpæsɪtɪv] | adj. 电容性的 |
| filtering [ˈfɪltərɪŋ] | v. [化工] 过滤，滤除（filter 的 ing 形式） |

**2. Expressions（短语）**

| | |
|---|---|
| passive electronic part | 无源电子部件 |
| active filtering | 有源滤波 |

### Reading material（阅读材料）

The use of an electric traction motor in autonomous road vehicles implies the presence on board of an electric energy source, which can be:

➤ a battery with an appropriate capacity for the desired range of the vehicle in the case of an all-electric vehicle;

➤ battery of lower capacity, associated with a range extender (association of a thermal engine and an alternator) or with a fuel cell in the case of a hybrid electric vehicle.

This very brief presentation enables us to notice that in the majority of electric vehicles we will be confronted with the compatibility of DC-current energy sources and alternative-current sources and inside the same category with compatibilities between the voltages of the sources and receivers. This compatibility issue thus implies the presence of on board electric road vehicles with electronic converters whose role will make it possible to remove the operating incompatibilities.

## 5.3 Electronic Converters

### 5.3.1 Components of Electronic Converters

### Text（课文）

The electronic static inverters which equip electric or hybrid vehicles to modify the electrical energy presentation mode, use associations of electronic power semiconductors, diodes, thyristors, IGBT, which work in commutation i. e. they operate in on or off mode to limit the losses.

If we take a closer look at the operation of power semiconductors, we observe that it is the role they play during commutations which constitutes the main feature of these components. We can distinguish as follows:

➢ non-controllable components: the diodes;

➢ components controllable only with the setting in a thyristor conducting state. These semiconductors can be put in a state of conduction by a control impulse sent onto their "trigger" during an arbitrary moment but they cannot return to the blocked state following a blocking sent onto the trigger. To return to the blocked state, the current crossing them must be cancelled under the very effect of the source or the load, thus causing a "natural" current commutation;

➢ components controllable when placed in conducting state and in blocked state.

For this type of current the change from blocked to conducting state and vice versa is caused by a current impulse sent onto their control electrode:

① trigger for the GTD and other IGCT;

② gate for IGBT, and field-effect transistors of the MOS type;

③ base for the bipolar transistors.

In electric vehicles, the most used semiconductors are diodes, IGBT and MOS. Thyristors are used only in rectifying assemblies.

## New words and expressions（单词和短语）

### 1. New words（单词）

| | |
|---|---|
| static [ˈstætɪk] | n. 静电；静电干扰<br>adj. 静态的；静电的；静力的 |
| constitute [ˈkɒnstɪtjuːt] | vt. 组成，构成；建立；任命 |
| diode [ˈdaɪəʊd] | n. [电子] 二极管 |
| thyristor [θaɪˈrɪstə] | n. 半导体闸流管 |
| trigger [ˈtrɪɡə(r)] | n. 扳机；起因，引起反应的事；触发器，引爆装置<br>v. 触发，引起；开动（装置） |
| arbitrary [ˈɑːbɪtrəri] | adj. [数] 任意的；武断的；专制的 |
| commutation [ˌkɒmjuˈteɪʃn] | n. 减刑；交换；经常来往；代偿 |
| bipolar [ˌbaɪˈpəʊlə(r)] | adj. 有两极的，双极的 |

### 2. Expressions（短语）

| | |
|---|---|
| on or off mode | 开或关的组合模式 |
| power semiconductor | 功率半导体 |
| non-controllable components | 不可控部件 |

| conducting state | 导通状态 |
|---|---|
| blocked state | 截止状态 |
| field-effect transistor | 场效应晶体管 |

### Notes to the text（难点解析）

★1. These semiconductors can be put in a state of conduction by a control impulse sent onto their "trigger" during an arbitrary moment but they cannot return to the blocked state following a blocking sent onto the trigger. 在任意时刻发送一个控制脉冲到触发器，这些半导体可以切换为导通状态，然而发截止指令到触发器时这些半导体并不能回到截止状态。

### Exercises（练习）

◆1. Translate the following passages（expressions）into Chinese（英译汉）

（1）For this type of current the change from blocked to conducting state and vice versa is caused by a current impulse sent onto their control electrode.

（2）non-controllable components

◆2. Translate the following passages（expressions）into English（汉译英）

（1）截止状态

（2）场效应晶体管

◆3. Directions：Answer the following questions briefly according to the text

How can we distinguish the semiconductor from commutations which constitutes the main feature of these components?

### Reading material（阅读材料）

In this operating mode, the semiconductor can：

➢ sometimes be "conducting" i. e. equivalent to a closed mechanical switch which lets the current pass with a direct voltage drop between weak terminals；

➢ sometimes be "blocked" i. e. equivalent to an open mechanical switch supporting a voltage between terminals, raised with a virtually-zero leakage current；

➢ pass very quickly from the "conducting" state to "blocked" state；these are in fact the different changes of state seen at the component or on the circuit, which includes the component that we call "commutation."

 5.3.2 Rectifiers

### Text（课文）

**1. Definition**

Rectifiers are energy converters which transform an alternative-current electric source into a

DC-current electric source.

## 2. Introduction

We can distinguish:

➢ diode rectifiers: These converters establish a rigid relation between the output DC voltage and the input alternative voltage;

➢ thyristor rectifiers which make it possible to vary continuously the relationship between the DC voltage recovered on their output terminals and the alternating voltage applied on their input terminals—while acting on the starting angle of the thyristors;

➢ rectifiers associated with diodes and thyristors;

➢ groupings of thyristor rectifiers intended to improve performance and decrease disturbances;

➢ PWM (pulse with modulation) rectifiers which associate IGBT and diodes and which have the advantage of slightly disturbing their alternative input sources.

## 3. Use of rectifiers in electric vehicles

In an electric vehicle, rectifiers are used to convert alternative-current electric energy provided either by the public network, or by an on board alternator coupled with a thermal engine; in DC-current electric energy storable in an electric chemical battery and/or super caps.

If energy is provided by the public network, the rectifier system is called a "charger" with a single-phase structure. If energy is provided by an alternator, the rectifier is in general a three-phase type.

### New words and expressions（单词和短语）

#### 1. New words（单词）

| | |
|---|---|
| rectifier [ˈrektɪˌfaɪə] | n. [电] 整流器；改正者，矫正者 |
| transform [trænsˈfɔːm] | vt. 改变，使……变形；转换<br>vi. 变换，改变；转化 |
| alternative [ɔːlˈtɜːnətɪv] | n. 二中择一；供替代的选择<br>adj. 供选择的；选择性的；交替的 |
| distinguish [dɪˈstɪŋgwɪʃ] | vi. 区别，区分；辨别<br>vt. 区分；辨别；使杰出，使表现突出 |
| rigid [ˈrɪdʒɪd] | adj. 严格的；僵硬的，死板的；坚硬的；精确的 |
| vary [ˈveəri] | vi. 变化；变异；违反<br>vt. 改变；使多样化；变奏 |

| | |
|---|---|
| terminal [ˈtɜːmɪnl] | n. 航空站；终点站；终端机；线接头；末端；晚期病人<br>adj. 晚期的；无可挽回的；末端的；终点的；期末的 |
| disturbance [dɪˈstɜːbəns] | n. 干扰；骚乱；忧虑 |

### 2. Expressions（短语）

| | |
|---|---|
| alternative-current | 交流 |
| DC voltage | 直流电压 |
| alternative voltage | 交流电压 |
| vary continuously | 连续改变 |
| starting angle | 起始角 |
| pulse with modulation | PWM 脉冲调制电路 |
| public network | 公共电网 |
| on board alternator | 车载交流发电机 |
| single-phase | 单相 |
| three-phase | 三相 |

### Notes to the text（难点解析）

★1. Rectifiers are energy converters which transform an alternative-current electric source into a DC-current electric source. 整流器是把交流电转化成直流电的能量装置。

★2. PWM (pulse with modulation) rectifiers which associate IGBT and diodes and which have the advantage of slightly disturbing their alternative input sources. 由 IGBT 和二极管组合而成的 PWM 整流器，具有对输入控制源干扰较小的优点。

### Exercises（练习）

◆1. Translate the following passages (expressions) into Chinese（英译汉）

（1）alternative-current electric source

（2）diode rectifiers

（3）PWM (pulse with modulation) rectifiers

（4）DC voltage

◆2. Translate the following passages (expressions) into English（汉译英）

（1）连续改变

（2）车载发电机

（3）公共电网

（4）晶闸管整流器

###  5.3.3 Choppers

**Text** (课文)

**1. Definition**

A chopper is a current converter which makes it possible from a DC voltage source (at constant voltage value) to adjust and control voltages and currents, different from the input values and adapted to the necessary needs to supply various receivers (motors, batteries, etc).

**2. Description**

In its basic version, an electronic chopper is composed:

➢ of a controllable switch (IGBT, MOSFET, GTO, etc.);

➢ of a freewheel diode;

➢ of passive components, coils and capacitors, which provide the functions of filtering input and output chopper currents. The mass and volume of these components depend for a large part on the operating frequency of the power switch;

➢ of the controlled device.

**3. Usage of choppers in electric vehicles**

In an electric vehicle choppers have two essential applications:

➢ firstly, they are essential in the supply of propulsion motors when these are DC motors;

➢ secondly, they are necessary to adapt the main battery voltage to that of the electronic auxiliaries and 12V network used (sensors, regulators, etc.).

The use of a chopper indeed makes it possible to maintain the motor current with the desired value while ensuring the progressive adjustment of the motor voltage without notable loss. The chopper allows us to regulate the torque and the speed of the motor and thus of the vehicle in traction but also during electric braking. This braking can be energy recovery, rheostatic or combined—i. e. associated with electric braking and a part of mechanical braking. Of course, specific provisions must be taken to carry out the necessary controls and protections, for example the use of a filter situated between the battery and the chopper itself to ensure the decoupling of the voltage source consisting of the battery and the traction motor.

**New words and expressions** (单词和短语)

**1. New words** (单词)

chopper ['tʃɒpə(r)]　　　n. [电子]斩波器；斧头；切碎机
　　　　　　　　　　　　vt. 用直升机运送
　　　　　　　　　　　　vi. 乘直升机飞行

| adjust [əˈdʒʌst] | vt. 调整，使……适合；校准 |
| --- | --- |
| | vi. 调整，校准；适应 |

| receiver [rɪˈsiːvə(r)] | n. （电话）听筒；无线电接收机；（破产公司的）官方接管人；接受者，收受者；购买（或接受）赃物的人；接球手；接受罐，聚集器；机匣 |
| --- | --- |

| switch [swɪtʃ] | n. 开关；转变；交换机；（铁道的）转辙器，道岔 |
| --- | --- |
| | v. 改变（立场、方向等）；替换；转换；调换；调（班）；（用枝条）击打；摆动 |

| coil [kɔɪl] | n. 线圈；一圈（绳索）；卷；（自动售货机中的）成卷邮票；蚊香；宫内节育环；（汽车发动机的）盘管；混乱 |
| --- | --- |
| | v. 盘绕，把……卷成圈，成圈状 |

| capacitor [kəˈpæsɪtə(r)] | n. [电] 电容器 |
| --- | --- |
| frequency [ˈfriːkwənsi] | n. 频率；频繁 |
| adjustment [əˈdʒʌstmənt] | n. 调整，调节；调节器 |
| rheostat [ˈriːəstæt] | n. [电] 变阻器 |
| provision [prəˈvɪʒn] | n. 规定；条款；准备；[经] 供应品 |
| | vt. 供给……食物及必需品 |
| situate [ˈsɪtʃueɪt] | vt. 使位于；使处于；把……放在（特殊的环境中），把……跟（具体情境）联系 |
| | adj. 位于……的 |
| protection [prəˈtekʃn] | n. 保护；防卫；护照 |

### 2. Expressions（短语）

| constant voltage value | 固定的电压值 |
| --- | --- |
| freewheel diode | 续流二极管 |
| power switch | 功率开关 |
| operating frequency | 操作频率 |
| essential application | 必不可少的应用 |
| electric braking | 电制动 |
| energy recovery | 能量回收 |
| mechanical braking | 机械制动 |

## Notes to the text（难点解析）

★1. A chopper is a current converter which makes it possible from a DC voltage source (at constant voltage value) to adjust and control voltages and currents, different from the input values and adapted to the necessary needs to supply various receivers (motors, batteries, etc). 斩波器是将电压值固定的直流电，转换为电压值可变可调的直流电源的装置，输出的电压不同于输入电压并且可以适应各接收器的所需电压（电动机、电池等）。

## Exercises（练习）

◆1. Translate the following passages (expressions) into Chinese（英译汉）

（1）They are essential in the supply of propulsion motors when these are DC motors.

（2）The chopper allows us to regulate the torque and the speed of the motor and thus of the vehicle in traction but also during electric braking.

（3）energy recovery

（4）power switch

◆2. Translate the following passages (expressions) into English（汉译英）

（1）斩波器

（2）续流二极管

◆3. Directions: Answer the following questions briefly according to the text

What is the chopper?

## Reading material（阅读材料）

Indeed, we cannot consider the brutal connection of a DC motor on fixed-voltage energy source batteries for example—for two reasons:

➢ no adjustment of the motor torque or speed would be possible;

➢ the direct electric motor supply would be destructive from both an electric (overcurrent) and a mechanics (overtorque), point of view.

The use of a current chopper located between the energy source and the DC motor makes it possible to solve these two constraints and it brings significant progress with respect to the starting-up processes: insertion of a variable resistor in series between the source and the motor.

### 5.3.4　Inverters

## Text（课文）

**1. Definition**

An inverter is a converter of DC current to alternative current.

**2. Usage of inverters in electric-powered vehicles**

In electric vehicles driven by an AC motor, it is not possible to directly connect this type of motor to the continuous voltage source that the battery constitutes. It is necessary to interpose between the energy source and the traction motor (s) a conversion (called an inverter) which transforms electrical DC current into electrical AC current and which makes it possible to carry out the control of the motor torque and the speed regulation of the vehicle both in the traction mode and in the braking mode.

Continuous-to-alternate conversion can be produced in multiple ways but the characteristics of road vehicles and the rationalization of industrial solutions have resulted in favoring an inverter structure with six bidirectional switches constituted by the association of an IGBT and a diode assembled in anti-parallel and controlled according to a standard PWM function. This type of assembly makes it possible to associate a voltage source (like a battery) and a receiver of the power controlled in current (asynchronous motor, synchronous motor wound or with permanent magnet). It should be noted that in a PWM inverter, the output voltage is a succession of voltage pulses (square pulses of voltage) of variable width so that the average value of the fundamental of this wave is sinusoidal over the period of stamping. The moments of switches' shutdown and opening are generally given in real-time by means of appropriate control electronics.

This control method has two important advantages:

—it pushes the output voltage harmonics back towards the high frequencies, which facilitates voltage filtering;

—it makes it possible to vary the value of the fundamental output voltage.

### New words and expressions（单词和短语）

#### 1. New words（单词）

| | |
|---|---|
| interpose [ˌɪntəˈpəʊz] | v. 提出（异议等）；使插入；使干涉；干预；调停 |
| rationalization [ˌræʃnəlaɪˈzeɪʃn] | n. 合理化 |
| assembly [əˈsembli] | n. 装配；集会，集合<br>n. 汇编，编译 |
| succession [səkˈseʃn] | n. 连续；继位；继承权；[生态] 演替 |
| sinusoidal [ˌsaɪnəˈsɔɪdəl] | adj. 正弦曲线的 |
| stamping [ˈstæmpɪŋ] | n. 冲击制品<br>v. 冲压 |
| shutdown [ˈʃʌtdaʊn] | n. 关机；停工；关门；停播 |
| harmonics [hɑːˈmɒnɪks] | n. 和声学；泛音；数律分析法 |

#### 2. Expressions（短语）

| | |
|---|---|
| traction motor | 牵引电动机 |

| | |
|---|---|
| carry out | 实施 |
| in traction mode | 驱动工况 |
| in braking mode | 制动工况 |
| anti-parallel | 逆平行 |
| asynchronous motor | 异步电动机 |
| synchronous motor wound | 同步绕线转子电动机 |
| voltage filtering | 电压滤波 |

## Notes to the text（难点解析）

★1. It should be noted that in a PWM inverter, the output voltage is a succession of voltage pulses (square pulses of voltage) of variable width so that the average value of the fundamental of this wave is sinusoidal over the period of stamping. 需要明确的是，在 PWM 逆变器中，输出电压是一系列不等宽的脉冲电压（矩形脉冲电压），但在一个周期内该波形的均值变化与正弦波等效。

## Exercises（练习）

◆1. Translate the following passages (expressions) into Chinese（英译汉）

（1）An inverter is a converter of DC current to alternative current.

（2）asynchronous motor

（3）voltage filtering

◆2. Translate the following passages (expressions) into English（汉译英）

（1）驱动工况

（2）制动工况

（3）在交流电动机驱动的电动汽车上，电动机是不能与电池组成的电源直接相连的。

◆3. Directions：Answer the following questions briefly according to the text

What is the inverter?

# Chapter 6
## Recharging Systems for Electric Vehicles

### Text（课文）

The type of charger and the nature of the recharging infrastructure strongly depend on the kind of vehicle and its use. Charging technology plays a key role in maximizing battery performance. A proper battery charging technique ensures battery safety and increases system reliability. The primary requirement of the charging process is to provide a fast and efficient way of charging without degrading the battery. Some of the factors to be taken into account while charging the battery are：

1）Avoiding overcharging and undercharging.
2）Fast charging without affecting the battery life.
3）Maintaining a good quality of charging current.

### New words and expressions（单词和短语）

#### 1. New words（单词）

| | |
|---|---|
| charger ['tʃɑːdʒə(r)] | n. 充电器；军马；袭击者；委托者；控诉者 |
| infrastructure ['ɪnfrəstrʌktʃə(r)] | n. 基础设施；公共建设；下部构造 |
| degrade [dɪ'greɪd] | vt. 贬低；使……丢脸；使……降级；使……降解<br>vi. 降级，降低；退化 |

#### 2. Expressions（短语）

| | |
|---|---|
| battery life | 电池寿命 |
| charging current | 充电电流 |
| battery performance | 电池性能 |
| fast charging | 快速充电 |

### Notes to the text（难点解析）

★1. Charging technology plays a key role in maximizing battery performance. 充电技术在提高电池性能方面起着关键作用。

★2. A proper battery charging technique ensures battery safety and increases system reliability. 适当的电池充电技术能确保电池安全，增加系统可靠性。

### Exercises（练习）

◆1. Translate the following passages（expressions）into Chinese（英译汉）

（1） Avoiding overcharging and undercharging

（2） fast charging

（3） charging current

## 6.1　What Is Battery Charging

### Text（课文）

During vehicle use the battery transforms chemical energy stored in its electrodes by an oxidation/reduction reaction into electric energy. At the time of the recharge the process is reversed. The charger imposes a higher voltage than the battery voltage and an opposite current. The current provided by the charger will be controlled with precision in order to impose charging conditions required by the battery.

This requires a certain number of measurements（voltage, current, temperature）which are interpreted by the electronics of the charger. The simplest systems are only controlled by the battery voltage：the current is kept constant as long as the battery voltage does not exceed an initial threshold.

Beyond this first threshold, the battery voltage is kept constant. After this phase, we start the balancing charge where a lower current is applied. All battery manufacturers recommend a specific charge algorithm according to the battery service operation, which should be respected to optimize the operating life of their product.

The selected charge algorithm will take account of the batteries' service requirements. Indeed, optimum management of the batteries requires a close link between the manufacturer of the battery and the integrator of the vehicle that defines the charger specifications.

### New words and expressions（单词和短语）

**1. New words（单词）**

| | |
|---|---|
| oxidation [ˌɒksɪˈdeɪʃn] | n. ［化学］氧化 |
| opposite [ˈɒpəzɪt] | n. 对立面；反义词<br>prep. 在……的对面<br>adj. 相反的；对面的；对立的<br>adv. 在对面 |
| measurement [ˈmeʒəmənt] | n. 测量；［计量］度量；尺寸；量度制 |

interpret [ɪnˈtɜːprət]　　　　　　　　　vi. 解释；翻译
　　　　　　　　　　　　　　　　　　vt. 说明；口译

## 2. Expressions（短语）

| | |
|---|---|
| oxidation/reduction reaction | 氧化/还原反应 |
| chemical energy | 化学能 |
| balancing charge | 均衡充电 |
| charge algorithm | 充电策略 |
| optimum management | 优化管理 |

### Notes to the text（难点解析）

★1. The current provided by the charger will be controlled with precision in order to impose charging conditions required by the battery. 由充电器提供的电流能够被进行精确控制，以保证满足电池所要求的充电条件。

★2. Indeed, optimum management of the batteries requires a close link between the manufacturer of the battery and the integrator of the vehicle that defines the charger specifications. 在实践中，电池的优化管理就要求电池的制造商和车辆制造者紧密沟通以决定最佳的充电规范。

### Exercises（练习）

◆1. Translate the following passages（expressions）into Chinese（英译汉）

（1）The charger imposes a higher voltage than the battery voltage and an opposite current.

（2）oxidation/reduction reaction

（3）electric energy

◆2. Translate the following passages（expressions）into English（汉译英）

（1）化学能

（2）充电策略

（3）电压超出上述的预设阈值时，电池端电压将保持恒定。

◆3. Directions：Answer the following questions briefly according to the text

What is battery charging?

### Reading material（阅读材料）

Charging algorithm can be defined as the combination of what was mentioned up to here and controlling all or part of the parameters affecting battery performance and life cycle in such a way to achieve battery pack charging safely, efficiently, and terminated on time. Managing the charging procedure of a high power battery pack with hundreds of cells involves many issues. To control all of these parameters, efficient and accurate algorithms with reliable safety and backup circuits are required. The trend toward fast charging with huge amounts of current flowing to the battery pack producing lots of heat requires accurate and reliable supervisory control algorithms to ensure safe charge. Managing such complex task can be handled with advanced control techniques like fuzzy logic, supervisory control, decentralized control and so on.

## 6.2 The Various Types of Chargers

### Text (课文)

**1. The external charger supplying the battery directly**

This is the traditional charge method used for all industrial traction battery applications. Each pack of industrial vehicle batteries is connected to this type of charge.

The traditional recharging of traction batteries is done by an external charger connected directly to the battery by cables using grips or low-voltage connectors. It is this method which was adopted for the first electric vehicles at the beginning of the 20th century, and remains today the method preferred for industrial trucks and other industrial vehicles.

**2. The on-board charger**

For urban electric cars we prefer on-board chargers (Figure 6.1), which allow recharging on all electrical outlets having a gauge and adequate protection.

The convenience of this solution for the customer largely compensates for the disadvantages related to the on-board additional weight and the increase in cost of each vehicle.

Moreover, the charger is perfectly suited to the battery. The use of external chargers for electric cars will be reserved for fast charging requiring heavy, voluminous equipments.

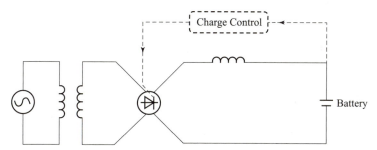

Figure 6.1  Diagram of an on-board charger using a 50 Hz transformer

The main constraints of this type of charger:
➢ volume;
➢ insulation between the network and the battery;
➢ the shape of the absorbed current;
➢ the use of a domestic plug (also dealt with in standardization);
➢ the maximization of the power available on a domestic wall-plug.

Today, chargers are of the switching-system type (PWM, Figure 6.2).

Make-up of a current electronic charger:

1) conditioning of the network current (rectifier);

2) power oscillator;

3) high-frequency transformer and rectification.

The evolution of chargers in the future will see an increase in power, and/or a reduction in volume and a reduction in costs.

If we accept a non-insulated charger, we can consider the use of the motor inverter and motor coil to carry out the charge function.

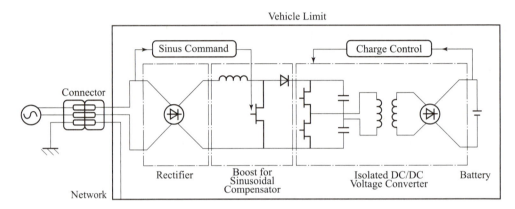

Figure 6.2　PWM charger

### 3. Fast charging

Fast charging allows 80% of a battery to be recharged in 20 minutes, which requires an external system and high power (20 kV·A and 400 A).

### 4. On-board fast charging

Physical limits to fast charging:

➤ maximum current permitted by the battery;

➤ limits to the charging (between 50% and 80%);

➤ limits according to the type of battery;

➤ maximum current permitted by connectors.

Type of circuit used for the charger:

50 Hz and high-frequency transformer, three-phase current, compensation of the power-factor. The need for a particular dialog protocol between the vehicle and the charging station.

### New words and expressions（单词和短语）

#### 1. New words（单词）

external [ɪkˈstɜːnl]　　　　　　　　n. 外部；外观；外面

　　　　　　　　　　　　　　　　adj. 外部的；表面的；[药] 外用的；外国的；外面的

| grip [ɡrɪp] | n. 紧握；柄；支配；握拍方式；拍柄绷带 |
| | vt. 紧握；夹紧 |
| | vi. 抓住 |
| connector [kəˈnektə(r)] | n. 连接器，连接头 |
| gauge [ɡeɪdʒ] | n. 计量器；标准尺寸；容量规格；针织物的细度 |
| | vt. 测量；估计；给……定规格 |
| adequate [ˈædɪkwət] | adj. 充足的；适当的；胜任的 |
| compensate [ˈkɒmpenseɪt] | vt. 补偿，赔偿；付报酬 |
| | vi. 补偿，赔偿；抵消 |
| constraint [kənˈstreɪnt] | n. [数] 约束；局促，态度不自然；强制 |
| domestic [dəˈmestɪk] | n. 国货；用人 |
| | adj. 国内的；家庭的；驯养的；一心只管家务的 |
| standardization [ˌstændədaɪˈzeɪʃn] | n. 标准化；[数] 规格化；校准 |
| rectification [ˌrektɪfɪˈkeɪʃn] | n. 改正，矫正；[化工] 精馏；[电] 整流；[数] 求长 |
| dialog [ˈdaɪəlɒɡ] | n. 对话；会话 |
| protocol [ˈprəʊtəkɒl] | n. 协议；草案；礼仪 |
| | vt. 拟定 |
| | vi. 拟定 |

## 2. Expressions（短语）

| industrial truck | 工业货车 |
| on-board charger | 车载充电器 |
| electrical outlet | 电插座 |
| deal with | 处理 |
| switching-system | 开关元件控制 |
| high-frequency transformer | 高频变压器 |
| power-factor | 功率因数 |
| charging station | 充电站 |

## Notes to the text（难点解析）

★1. The convenience of this solution for the customer largely compensates for the disadvantages related to the on-board additional weight and the increase in cost of each vehicle. 对于顾客来说，

这种解决方案的便利性在很大程度上弥补了该方案增加了车辆重量和提高了购车成本的缺点。

★2. The need for a particular dialog protocol between the vehicle and the charging station. 车辆和充电站之间需要特定的连接协议。

### Exercises（练习）

◆1. Translate the following passages（expressions）into Chinese（英译汉）

（1）It is this method which was adopted for the first electric vehicles at the beginning of the 20th century.

（2）insulation between the network and the battery

（3）three-phase current

（4）power-factor

◆2. Translate the following passages（expressions）into English（汉译英）

（1）高频变压器

（2）快速充电

（3）民用插座

◆3. Directions：Answer the following questions briefly according to the text.

What is the on-board charger?

### Reading material（阅读材料）

When the number of electric vehicles exceeded the number of thermal cars, recharging was done directly via external chargers installed in garages.

The recharging of traction batteries for the majority of industrial applications is performed by an external charger connected to the electric network. The connection between the charge equipment and batteries is carried out by two flexible wires with a two-pin specific connector. In addition to the two high-power contacts, the connector can comprise a link for protection wires ground link and for the realization of additional controls with auxiliary contacts.

It is the method which is most generally adopted for the recharging of utility vehicle fleets and small golf cars. This system shown in Figure 6.3, rustic but robust, was useful for the first experiments on electric vehicles whose technology was directly based on industrial vehicles.

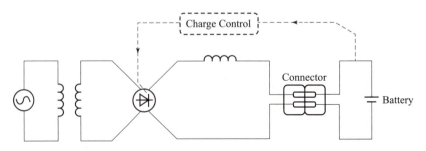

Figure 6.3　Diagram of a traditional charger using a 50 Hz transformer

## 5. Induction charger

### Text（课文）

Recharging by induction makes it possible to transfer energy to the vehicle without requiring physical contact between the vehicle and the charger. Energy is transmitted by a magnetic field through a transformer with separable primary coil and secondary coil. Although it is possible to carry out an energy exchange with transformers operating at the frequency of the electric network (50 Hz or 60 Hz) it is more common to use a high-frequency oscillating circuit to provide this function in order to reduce the volume of the transformer coils. Indeed, the power that can be transmitted through a transformer air gap is proportional to the induction (field intensity), the transfer and the frequencies. It is thus useful to increase the operating frequencies of the systems and to maximize the power of the field in order to reduce the volume of the coils.

The operating principle of chargers with high-frequency induction is similar to that already indicated for on-board electronic chargers and the electric diagram can appear more or less identical.

The diagram is divided into two as shown in Figure 6.4:

the network rectifier, the power-factor corrector and the high-frequency oscillator are housed in the equipment on the ground;

the connection between the vehicles and the charger is carried out by the transformer without Ohmic contact;

the high-frequency rectifier and the charge detection system are housed in the vehicle.

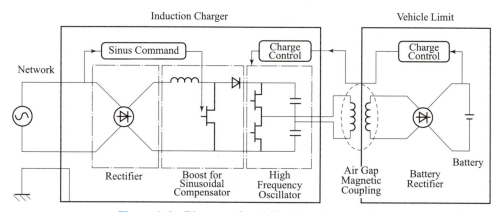

Figure 6.4　Diagram of an induction charge system

It is noted that this diagram requires an information exchange protocol, as is the case for the fast charger.

Note: the diagram of 50 Hz supply with the rectifier is given as an example. This functionality can be carried out in various ways (three-phase current supply, passive filtering, etc.). We can use other types of high-frequency oscillators.

Application of inductive recharging for automated connection as shown in Figure 6.5.

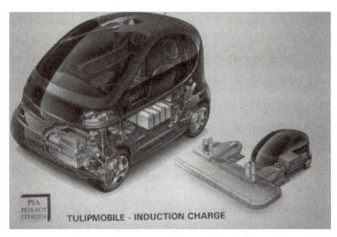

Figure 6.5　Induction charge system: Tulip prototypes from PSA Peugeot Citroen

## New words and expressions（单词和短语）

### 1. New words（单词）

| | |
|---|---|
| proportional [prəˈpɔːʃnl] | n. [数] 比例项<br>adj. 比例的，成比例的；相称的，均衡的 |
| detection [dɪˈtekʃn] | n. 侦查，探测；发觉，发现；察觉 |
| automate [ˈɔːtəmeɪt] | vt. 使自动化，使自动操作<br>vi. 自动化，自动操作 |

### 2. Expressions（短语）

| | |
|---|---|
| induction charger | 感应充电器 |
| primary coil | 一次线圈 |
| secondary coil | 二次线圈 |
| oscillating circuit | 振荡电路 |
| high-frequency | 高频 |
| air gap | 气隙 |
| field intensity | 场强度 |
| more or less identical | 几乎相同 |
| ohmic contact | 接触电阻 |

## Notes to the text（难点解析）

★1. Energy is transmitted by a magnetic field through a transformer with separable primary coil and secondary coil. 能量是由可分离的一次线圈和二次线圈组成的变压器形成的磁场传输的。

★2. It is more common to use a high-frequency oscillating circuit to provide this function in order to reduce the volume of the transformer coils. 但是使用的更普遍的是高频振荡电路，以便能够减小变压器线圈的体积。

### Exercises（练习）

◆1. Translate the following passages（expressions）into Chinese（英译汉）

（1）Recharging by induction makes it possible to transfer energy to the vehicle without requiring physical contact between the vehicle and the charger.

（2）on-board electronic chargers

（3）high-frequency induction

◆2. Translate the following passages（expressions）into English（汉译英）

（1）接触电阻

（2）高频整流器

（3）感应充电器

◆3. Directions：Answer the following questions briefly according to the text.

What is induction charger?

### 6. Wireless charging

### Text（课文）

Wireless charging involves the use of power and energy transfer at a much longer distance. It is different from inductive charging which involves a transformer with closely placed primary and secondary windings. Although inductive charging can eliminate the direct electric contact, it still needs a plug, cable, and physical connection of the inductive coupler. Wear and tear of the plug and cable could cause danger as well.

Wireless charging could eliminate the cable and plug altogether. In this scenario, a driver can pull the car over to a specially designed parking lot and the car battery is automatically charged without the pulling of any cable or plug as shown in Figure 6.6. It provides the safest approach for EV battery charging.

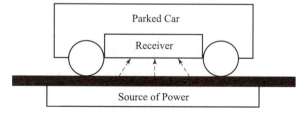

Figure 6.6　Wireless charging of a PHEV/EV on a parking floor

There have been a few different experiments carried out for wireless energy transfer. The most promising technology is using electromagnetic resonance as shown in Figure 6.7. In this setup, there is a pair of antennas with one inside the parking structure as the transmitter and one inside the car as the receiver. The two antennas are designed to resonate at the controlled frequency. The limitations are the level of power transfer, and efficiency due to the large air gap between the two antennas.

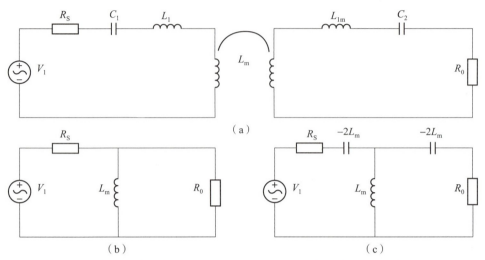

Figure 6.7 Circuits for electromagnetic resonance-based wireless charging:
(a) circuit; (b) equivalent circuit at resonance frequency condition1;
(c) equivalent circuit at resonance frequency at condition 2

## New words and expressions（单词和短语）

### 1. New words（单词）

| scenario [səˈnɑːrɪəʊ] | n. 方案；情节；剧本；设想 |
| resonance [ˈrezənəns] | n. [力]共振；共鸣；反响 |
| antennas [ænˈtenəz] | n. [电讯]天线，[动]触角（antenna 的复数形式） |
| transmitter [trænzˈmɪtə(r)] | n. [电讯]发射机，[通信]发报机；传达人；递质 |
| receiver [rɪˈsiːvə(r)] | n. (电话)听筒；无线电接收机；(破产公司的)官方接管人；接受者；收受者；购买（或接受）赃物的人；接球手；接受罐，聚集器；机匣 |

### 2. Expressions（短语）

| wireless charging | 无线充电 |
| physical connection | 物理连接 |
| inductive coupler | 感应耦合器 |
| parking lot | 停车场 |
| wireless energy transfer | 无线能量传递 |
| electromagnetic resonance | 电磁谐振 |

### Notes to the text(难点解析)

★1. The car battery is automatically charged without the pulling of any cable or plug. 汽车的电池自动充电,无须任何插头和电线。

★2. In this setup, there is a pair of antennas with one inside the parking structure as the transmitter and one inside the car as the receiver. 在这种设置中,有一对天线,其中一个天线放在停车场作为发射装置,另一个天线放在车内作为接收装置。

### Exercises(练习)

◆1. Translate the following passages (expressions) into Chinese(英译汉)

(1) Wireless charging could eliminate the cable and plug altogether.

(2) physical connection

(3) secondary winding

◆2. Translate the following passages (expressions) into English(汉译英)

(1) 无线充电

(2) 停车场

(3) 两个天线被设计成在可控频率内谐振。

◆3. Directions:Answer the following questions briefly according to the text

What is the wireless charging?

## 6.3　Recharging Efficiency

### Text(课文)

Like all physical transformations, charge and discharge do not have an efficiency of 100% because the chemical processes are not perfectly reversible and the battery has certain internal impedance which dissipates part of the energy in heat. We retain two efficiency coefficients:

The electric efficiency of the battery

The electric efficiency of the battery, which is given by the relationship between the energy actually provided by the battery during the discharge and the electric energy provided by the charger to reach the initial state of the battery. This energy, measured in Watt is given by the integral of the "voltage by current" multiplication at the battery terminals at the time of the charge and the discharge. This value is lower than the faradic battery efficiency, and can pass from 70% for certain lead-acid batteries to 95% for new-technology batteries used under optimal conditions.

The efficiency of the battery-plus-charger system

It is obtained by measuring the relationship between the total energy provided by the battery at the time of the recharging and the electric network energy provided to the charger to reach the initial charge state of the battery. This coefficient thus takes account of all off the losses of the "battery +

charger" system. The efficiency of the charger is very dependent on the employed technology and their charge operating process. It is thus a culmination of all the efficiencies.

### New words and expressions（单词和短语）

#### 1. New words（单词）

| | |
|---|---|
| coefficient [ˌkəʊɪˈfɪʃənt] | n. [数] 系数 |
| integral [ˈɪntɪɡrəl] | adj. 积分的；完整的，整体的；构成整体所必需的<br>n. 积分；部分；完整 |
| culmination [ˌkʌlmɪˈneɪʃn] | n. 顶点；高潮 |

#### 2. Expressions（短语）

| | |
|---|---|
| initial state | 初始状态 |
| perfectly reversible | 完全可逆 |

### Notes to the text（难点解析）

★1. Like all physical transformations, charge and discharge do not have an efficiency of 100% because the chemical processes are not perfectly reversible and the battery has certain internal impedance which dissipates part of the energy in heat. 与所有的自然现象一样，充放电过程不能达到100%的效率。因为该化学过程不是完全可逆的，并且电池具有内部阻抗会耗散损失一部分的能量。

### Exercises（练习）

◆1. Translate the following passages (expressions) into Chinese（英译汉）

（1）The efficiency of the charger is very dependent on the employed technology and their charge operating process.

（2）electric network energy

（3）initial state

### Reading material（阅读材料）

The faradic efficiency, which is equal to the relationship between the number of coulombs (the integral of the current) provided by the battery during the discharge and the number of coulombs necessary at the time of the recharge to reach the initial charge state of the battery before the beginning of the discharge. It is the coefficient generally indicated by manufacturers. This is close to 1 for new batteries (nickel-metal hydrive, lithium ion). It is a little lower for lead-acid batteries and open nickel-cadmium batteries, which require a longer overload phase.

## 6.4 Recharging in Complete Safety

### Text (课文)

#### Standardization

The electric car is at the crossroads of two worlds. When it moves, it is a car which must be conceived to respect all the regulations of the automotive world. When it is being recharged, it is also comparable to electric equipment and must respect the corresponding regulations and standards. But it is not equipment like domestic devices because it is subjected to a harsh environment and must resist stronger constraints than those met in domestic usage. The questions relating to electric safety during recharging were largely discussed during the 1990s and gave rise to a series of standards describing charge equipment specifically. These standards are the result of an international dialog which succeeded in establishing a common text which covers the various types of networks throughout the world and which adapts to the various practices of each country. Indeed, not all electrical communications resemble each other and the methods of protection available are not identical.

#### Hydrogen emissions

The regulation asks for an absence of hydrogen release under conditions of normal charge.

#### Various plugs used for recharging

The standardized 16-and 32-amp home plugs.

#### The standard power-plug

The plug on the vehicle must allow normal charge on a 16 A plug and fast charge on specific terminals. Integration on the vehicle is an essential aspect. Specific plugs have been developed and standardized.

Charge stations in public spaces

For example, many chargers are available in France such as: underground chargers, recharging at the place of residence, and calibration of the plugs (Figure 6.8 and Figure 6.9).

Figure 6.8　Maréchal socket on electric vehicles

Difficulties relating to the installation of chargers in public spaces:

1) analysis of the recharging cost;

2) the cost of installation;

3) the cost of invoicing;

4) difficulties caused by the invoicing.

Figure 6.9　Charge stations

## New words and expressions（单词和短语）

### 1. New words（单词）

| crossroad [ˈkrɒsrəʊdz] | n. 十字路口；交叉路口；聚会的中心地点 |
|---|---|
| conceive [kənˈsiːv] | vi. 怀孕；设想；考虑<br>vt. 怀孕；构思；以为；持有 |
| harsh [hɑːʃ] | adj. 严厉的；严酷的；刺耳的；粗糙的；刺目的；丑陋的 |
| resist [rɪˈzɪst] | n. [助剂] 抗蚀剂；防染剂<br>vt. 抵抗，忍耐，忍住<br>vi. 抵抗，抗拒；忍耐 |
| establish [ɪˈstæblɪʃ] | v. 建立，创立；确立；获得接受；查实，证实 |
| calibration [ˌkælɪˈbreɪʃn] | n. 校准；刻度；标度 |
| residence [ˈrezɪdəns] | n. 住宅，住处；居住 |
| invoicing [ˈɪnvɔɪsɪŋ] | n. 发票；[物价] 货品计价<br>v. 开发票（invoice 的 ing 形式） |

### 2. Expressions（短语）

| charge equipment | 充电设备 |
|---|---|
| power-plug | 电源插头 |

| | |
|---|---|
| public spaces | 公共场所 |
| place of residence | 居民区 |

### Notes to the text（难点解析）

★1. When it moves, it is a car which must be conceived to respect all the regulations of the automotive world. When it is being recharged, it is also comparable to electric equipment and must respect the corresponding regulations and standards. 在行驶的时候它是汽车，必须遵守汽车行业的所有规范；当充电时，它也作为电气设备，必须遵守相应的法规和标准。

★2. The regulation asks for an absence of hydrogen release under conditions of normal charge. 法规要求，在正常充电的情况下电池不得排出氢气。

### Exercises（练习）

◆1. Translate the following passages (expressions) into Chinese（英译汉）

（1）The plug on the vehicle must allow normal charge on a 16 A plug.

（2）public spaces

（3）place of residence

◆2. Translate the following passages (expressions) into English（汉译英）

（1）充电成本

（2）充电站

◆3. Directions: Answer the following questions briefly according to the text

What are the difficulties relating to the installation of chargers in public spaces?

### Reading material（阅读材料）

The standards distinguish various recharging modes.

Four modes of direct recharging (using connectors) are defined. The recharging must be done at home, in the workshops of companies and in the street. As an example, in the USA the domestic voltage is only 110 V but electric vehicles have higher performance and require a higher on-board energy (the electric ranger has 30 kW・h of on-board battery) than small French sedans which comprise a battery of only 11 kW・h and are supplied from a network having a voltage of 230 V.

## 6.5　Charging Methods

### Text（课文）

Charging in general is the action of putting energy back to the battery, i. e., restoring energy. It is important to know that different chemistries may require completely different charging methods. Other factors affecting choosing the charging method are capacity, required time, or other factors. The most common techniques are mentioned here:

### 6.5.1 Constant Voltage Charge

As it is clear from the name "Constant Voltage" or CV is when a constant voltage is applied to the battery pack. This voltage is a preset value given by the manufacturer. This method is accompanied with a current limiting circuit most of the time, especially for the beginning periods of charging where the battery easily takes high rates of current comparing to its capacity. The current limitation value mainly depends on the capacity of the battery. This method is usually used for lead-acid batteries, also for Li-ion batteries while using current limiter to avoid overheating the battery especially in the first stages of the charging process.

### 6.5.2 Constant Current Charge

Constant current charging method is applying a constant current to the battery with low percentage of current ripples independent of the battery state of charge or temperature. The abbreviation for this method is CC in the literature. This is achieved by varying the voltage applied to the battery using control techniques such as current mode control to keep the current constant. In the split rate CC different rates of current are applied based on SOC, time of charge, voltage, or combination of them in different stages of charging. This gives more accurate and balanced charging and circuits should be used to avoid over-voltage of the cells.

### 6.5.3 Taper Current Charge

This method can be used when the source is non-regulated. It is usually implemented with a transformer with a high output voltage comparing to the battery voltage. A resistance should be used to limit the current flowing to the battery. A diode can also be used to ensure unidirectional power flow to the battery. In this method the current starts at full rating and gradually decreases as the cell gets charged. This technique is only applicable to Sealed Lead-Acid (SLA) batteries.

### 6.5.4 Pulse Charge

This technique involves using short time current or voltage pulses for charging. By changing the width of pulses the average of the current or voltage can be controlled. Pulse charging provides two significant advantages: (Ⅰ) it reduces charging time, (Ⅱ) the conditioning effect of this technique highly improves the life cycle. The intervals between pulses are called rest times, which play an important role, and they provide some time for chemical reactions inside the battery to take place and stabilize. Since in this method high rates of current or voltage can be used, it reduces undesirable chemical reactions that happen at the electrodes, such as gas formation and crystal growth, which are the most important reasons of life cycle reduction in batteries.

### 6.5.5 Reflex Charge

During charging procedure some gas bubbles appear on the electrodes, especially amplified during fast charging. This phenomenon is called "burping." Applying very short discharge pulses or negative pulses which can be achieved for example by short circuiting the battery for very small time intervals compared to charging time intervals in a current limited fashion, typically 2–3 times bigger than the charging pulses during the charging rest period resulting in depolarizing the cell will speed up the stabilization process and hence the overall charging process. This technique is called with other names such as "Burp Charging" or "Negative Pulse Charging."

### 6.5.6 Float Charge

For some applications when the charging process is complete and the battery is fully charged, the batteries should be maintained at 100% SOC for a long time to be ready for time of use. Uninterruptable Power Supplies (UPS) are one of such applications where the batteries should always remain fully charged. However, because of self-discharge of batteries, they get discharged over time; for example, they may lose 20% or 30% of their charge per month. To compensate for self-discharge, a constant voltage which is determined based on the battery chemistry and ambient temperature is applied permanently. This voltage is called "Float Voltage." This technique is not recommended for Li-ion and Li-Po batteries and it is not necessary for EVs/PHEVs which are frequently used every day.

### New words and expressions（单词和短语）

#### 1. New words（单词）

| | |
|---|---|
| limiter ['lɪmɪtə] | n. [机] [电] 限制器，[电子] 限幅器；限制者 |
| ripple ['rɪpl] | n. 波纹；涟漪；[物] 涟波<br>vt. 在……上形成波痕 |
| abbreviation [əˌbriːvɪ'eɪʃn] | n. 缩写；缩写词 |
| taper ['teɪpə(r)] | v. （使）逐渐变窄；（使）成锥形；逐渐变弱（或减轻）；（中央银行）缩减资产购买<br>n. （点火用的）木条，纸媒；细长蜡烛；逐渐缩小（或变细）；弱光；锥形物；（比赛前）练习的减少<br>adj. 逐渐变窄的；划分等级的 |
| implement ['ɪmplɪm(ə)nt] | n. 工具，器具；手段<br>vt. 实施，执行；实现，使生效 |

| | | |
|---|---|---|
| applicable [əˈplɪkəbl] | adj. 可适用的；可应用的；合适的 | |
| intervals [ˈɪntevls] | n. 间隔；[声] 音程（interval 的复数） | |
| stabilize [ˈsteɪbəlaɪz] | vt. 使稳固，使安定<br>vi. 稳定，安定 | |
| reflex [ˈriːfleks] | n.（对刺激的）本能反应；反射（作用）；反映物；反映形式；反射光<br>adj. 本能反应的；（角）大于 180 度的；（光）被反射的；反折的；反省的 | |
| bubble [ˈbʌbl] | n. 气泡，泡沫，泡状物；透明圆形罩，圆形顶<br>vt. 使冒泡；滔滔不绝地说<br>vi. 沸腾，冒泡；发出气泡声 | |
| phenomenon [fəˈnɒmɪnən] | n. 现象；奇迹；杰出的人才 | |
| burp [bɜːp] | n. 打嗝；饱嗝儿<br>vi. 打嗝；打饱嗝<br>vt. 使打嗝 | |
| depolarize [diːˈpəʊləraɪz] | vt. 去偏光；去偏极 | |
| float [fləʊt] | n.（酒吧等用于给顾客找零的）备用零钱；彩车，花车；浮板；漂浮物；鱼漂；浮子<br>v. 使漂浮，浮动；漂流，飘动；飘移；安排（贷款）提出，提请考虑（想法或计划）；（货币汇率）自由浮动实行 | |
| ambient [ˈæmbɪənt] | adj. 周围的；外界的；环绕的；产生轻松氛围的<br>n. 周围环境；一种背景音乐 | |

## 2. Expressions（短语）

| | |
|---|---|
| charging method | 充电方式 |
| constant voltage | 恒压 |
| battery pack | 电池包 |
| preset value | 预置值 |
| current limiting circuit | 限流电路 |
| current limiter | 限流器 |
| constant current | 恒流 |
| balanced charging | 平衡充电 |

| | |
|---|---|
| over-voltage | 过电压 |
| taper current | 锥电流 |
| rest time | 时间间隙 |
| gas bubble | 气泡 |
| discharge pulse | 放电脉冲 |
| negative pulse | 负脉冲 |
| short circuit | 短路 |
| rest period | 休止期 |
| Uninterruptable Power Supplie (UPS) | 不间断电源 (UPS) |
| float voltage | 浮动电压 |

### Notes to the text（难点解析）

★1. In the split rate CC different rates of current are applied based on SOC, time of charge, voltage, or combination of them in different stages of charging. 分割型比率电流是利用CC充电方式来实现不同比率的电流，这项技术在不同的充电状态下是SOC、充电时间、充电电压或三者综合一起考虑的。

★2. By changing the width of pulses the average of the current or voltage can be controlled. 同时电流或电压的平均值可以通过改变脉冲宽度来进行控制。

### Exercises（练习）

◆1. Translate the following passages (expressions) into Chinese（英译汉）
（1）Charging in general is the action of putting energy back to the battery.
（2）This method can be used when the source is non-regulated.
（3）constant voltage
（4）constant current

◆2. Translate the following passages (expressions) into English（汉译英）
（1）浮压充电
（2）限流器
（3）此技术也被称为"打嗝充电"或"负脉冲充电"。

◆3. Directions：Answer the following questions briefly according to the text
How many are there charging methods? What are the charging methods?

### Reading material（阅读材料）

1. Depending on the battery type to be charged, this preset voltage value is chosen. For example, for Li-ion cells the value of 4.200 ± 50 mV is desirable, so the present value for the whole

battery pack can be obtained by multiplying this value with number of cells in series. An accurate set point is necessary, since over-voltage can damage the cells and under-voltage causes partial charge which will reduce life cycle over time. Therefore, the circuit used for charging, which can be a simple buck, boost, or buck/boost topology depending on the voltage ratio of input and output, should be accompanied with a controller to compensate for source and load changes over time. When the cell reaches the preset voltage value, this causes the battery to be in a standby mode, ready for later use. The amount of this idle time should not be very long and should be limited based on the manufacturer recommendations.

2. In some cases, for prolonging dead batteries, CC method with high rates and low duration can be utilized to extend the lifetime of the battery. But, this is a very cautious procedure and must be done carefully. Ni-Cd and Ni-MH batteries are charged using CC. Ni-MH batteries can be easily damaged due to over-charging, so, they should be accurately monitored during charging.

## 6.6　Termination Methods

### Text（课文）

When the charging is in procedure, it is very important to decide when to terminate the charging. This is because of two main reasons. One is to avoid undercharge, i.e., making sure the battery is fully charged, not partially, in order to use the full capacity of the batteries. The other one is to avoid overcharging which is very dangerous especially in the case of high energy density Lithium-based battery packs. If not terminated on time, the overcharging of batteries can lead to over gassing of the cells, especially in liquid electrolyte cells which results in increase in the volume of individual cells, a situation that cannot be tolerated in a rigidly packed battery pack. Another issue is overheating of the cells especially in Lithium-based batteries which can easily lead to the explosion and firing of the whole pack; Lithium is a very active material and easily combines with oxygen in the air. The only thing needed to begin the combination is enough heat.

Choosing different termination criteria leads to different termination methods. Selecting the type of termination of charging process depends on different factors such as the application and the environment where the battery is used. The conventional termination methods that can be used are mentioned here:

### 6.6.1　Time

Using time is one of the simplest methods which is mainly used as a backup for fast charging or normally used for regular charging for specific types of batteries. This method is very simple and inexpensive, but because of diminishing battery capacity over time due to aging, the time should be reset for a reduced capacity aged battery to avoid overcharging of old batteries.

**6.6.2　Voltage**

As mentioned before, the voltage can be used as a termination factor, i. e., terminating the charging process when the battery voltage reaches a specific value. This method has some inaccuracies, because the real open-circuit voltage is obtained when the battery is left disconnected for some time after charging. This is because chemical reactions happening inside the battery need some time to stabilize. Nevertheless, this method is widely used. In addition, this technique is usually used with constant current techniques to avoid overheating damage to the battery.

 **6.6.3　Voltage Drop ($dV/dT$)**

In some chemistries like Ni-Cd when using constant current method, the voltage increases up to the fully charged state point and then the voltage begins to decrease. This is due to oxygen build-up inside the battery. This decrease is significant, so the derivative of the voltage versus time can be measured to indicate overcharge. When this parameter becomes negative it shows that we have passed the fully charged state and the temperature begins to rise. After this point the charging method can be switched to trickle, or float charge, or be terminated completely.

 **6.6.4　Current**

In the last stages of charging, if constant voltage method is used, the current begins to decrease as the battery reaches fully charge state. A preset current value such as $C/10$ rate can be defined and when the current goes below this value the charging would be terminated.

 **6.6.5　Temperature**

In general, during charging the battery temperature increases to some extent, however, extra increase in temperature is a sign of overcharge. Using temperature sensors highly adds to the cost of the system. Nevertheless, for some chemistries such as Ni-MH, methods such as voltage drop is not recommended, since the voltage drop after full charge state is not significant to be relied on. In this case, temperature increase is a good indication of overcharge and can be used.

**New words and expressions**（单词和短语）

**1. New words**（单词）

| termination [ˌtɜːmɪˈneɪʃn] | n. 结束，终止 |
| procedure [prəˈsiːdʒə(r)] | n. 程序，手续；步骤 |

| | |
|---|---|
| undercharge [ˌʌndəˈtʃɑːdʒ] | n. 充电不足；低的索价；填不够量的火药<br>vt. 充电不足；索价低于常价；弹药装填不足 |
| partially [ˈpɑːʃəli] | adv. 部分地；偏袒地 |
| overcharging [ˈovəˈtʃɑdʒ] | v. 过度充电；收费过高（overcharge 的现在分词形式） |
| individual [ˌɪndɪˈvɪdʒuəl] | n. 个人，个体<br>adj. 个人的；个别的；独特的 |
| rigidly [ˈrɪdʒɪdli] | adv. 严格地；坚硬地；严厉地；牢牢地 |
| explosion [ɪkˈspləʊʒn] | n. 爆炸；爆发；激增 |
| criteria [kraɪˈtɪəriə] | n. 标准，条件（criterion 的复数） |
| diminish [dɪˈmɪnɪʃ] | vt. 使减少；使变小<br>vi. 减少，缩小；变小 |
| reset [ˌriːˈset] | vi. 重置；清零<br>vt. 重置；重新设定；重新组合<br>n. 重新设定；重新组合；重排版 |
| disconnect [ˌdɪskəˈnekt] | vt. 拆开，使分离<br>vi. 断开 |
| derivative [dɪˈrɪvətɪv] | n. 派生物；金融衍生产品；派生词；（化学）衍生物；导数<br>adj.（艺术家或艺术作品）模仿的；受……影响的 |
| trickle [ˈtrɪkl] | n. 滴，淌；细流<br>vt. 使……滴；使……淌；使……细细地流<br>vi. 滴；细细地流；慢慢地移动 |

### 2. Expressions（短语）

| | |
|---|---|
| be fully charged | 完全充电 |
| full capacity | 满容量 |
| high energy density | 高能量密度 |
| termination method | 充电的终止方式 |
| regular charging | 常规充电 |
| open-circuit voltage | 开路电压 |

### Notes to the text（难点解析）

★1. The other one is to avoid overcharging which is very dangerous especially in the case of high energy density Lithium-based battery packs. 二是避免过充电，特别是在高能量密度的锂基电池的情况下，这是非常危险的。

★2. In addition, this technique is usually used with constant current techniques to avoid overheating damage to the battery. 此外,该技术通常与恒流技术一起使用,这样可以避免电池过热。

### Exercises (练习)

◆1. Translate the following passages (expressions) into Chinese (英译汉)

(1) However, extra increase in temperature is a sign of overcharge.

(2) In the last stages of charging, if constant voltage method is used, the current begins to decrease as the battery reaches fully charge state.

(3) open-circuit voltage

(4) regular charging

◆2. Translate the following passages (expressions) into English (汉译英)

(1) 充电的终止方式

(2) 完全充电

(3) 设置电池的充电时间可以作为其中的一种最简单的方法。

◆3. Directions: Answer the following questions briefly according to the text.

Why do we say it is very important to decide when to terminate the charging when the charging is in procedure?

### Reading material (阅读材料)

#### Charging Algorithm

As mentioned before, lead-acid batteries have mature technology and infrastructure that already exist, but they still have poor life cycles in the order of 300-400 cycles. A lot of efforts have been put into research for increasing the life cycle of lead-acid batteries because of their advantages such as low cost and availability. This chemistry has a common charging algorithm which includes four different stages or three based on the application, as indicated in Figure 6.10.

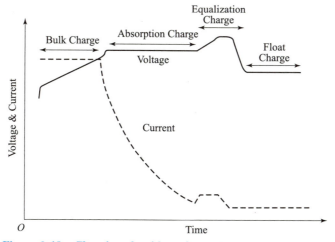

Figure 6.10　Charging algorithm of a typical Lead-acid battery

In the first stage a predefined constant current is applied to the battery pack which charges the cells rapidly. In this stage the cell voltages increase gradually because of SOC increase. This stage is called "Bulk Charge" stage. The process is continued until a predefined maximum voltage is reached. These values are all recommended by the manufacturer in the datasheet. In the next stage called "Absorption Charge" stage, a constant voltage is applied to the battery pack. At this stage the current decreases gradually until it reaches a predefined C rate value and the cells are approximately charged but not equalized because of cell imbalance. At this stage a relatively higher voltage than constant voltage in absorption charge stage can be applied to the pack for some time to balance all the cells inside the pack. This stage is called "Equalization Charge" stage. The equalization can also be achieved with other techniques as mentioned before. After some prescribed time, the charger applies a lower constant voltage in order to keep the battery in a ready-to-use state. This is called "Float Charge" stage and depending on the application it can be considered or omitted.

# 第 1 章
## 新能源汽车概述

## 1.1 环境影响

在现代社会，交通运输便捷地运送货物和人员，促进了经济和社会的发展，但它却极大地依赖化石燃料。交通运输对石油的极大依赖使汽车快速发展带来的问题日益突出。这不仅在于地球上的石油资源有限，而且在于燃油制品产生的排放导致了气候变化、城市空气质量恶化和政治冲突等诸多问题。因此全球能源体系和环境方面问题的出现，在很大程度上归咎于个人交通运输。

个人交通运输为人们选择出行的地点和时间提供了方便。然而，这种自由的选择引发了一些冲突，使得人们越来越担心环境问题和自然资源的可持续使用问题。全世界大量汽车的使用，已经产生并正在继续引发严重的环境与人类生存问题。大气污染、全球变暖以及地球石油资源的迅速递减，成为当前人们首要关注的问题。

阅读材料：

据美国交通运输部估计，世界上现有大约 8 亿辆汽车，其中约有 2.5 亿辆行驶在美国的道路上。2009 年，中国取代美国成为世界上最大的汽车制造国和汽车市场，年生产量和销售量分别达 1 379 万辆和 1 364 万辆。随着进一步的城镇化、工业化和全球化，世界范围内私人汽车数量的快速增长是必然的。

### 1.1.1 大气污染

目前，所有车辆依靠碳氢化合物类燃料的燃烧，以获得其驱动力所必需的能量。燃烧是燃料与空气之间的反应，它释放出热量和燃烧生成物。热量经发动机转换为机械功率，而燃烧生成物则排入大气。碳氢化合物是由碳和氢原子组成分子的化学化合物。理想情况下，碳氢化合物的燃烧仅生成二氧化碳和水，不会损害环境。

事实上，在热力发动机内碳氢化合物类燃料的燃烧绝非理想化的，以传统化石燃料为能量源的车辆还会产生其他的排放物，包括汽油燃烧产生的一氧化碳（CO）和氮氧化物（NO、$NO_2$ 和 $NO_x$）、来自蒸发和未完全燃烧气体中的碳氢化合物和挥发性有机化合物（VOCs）、柴油燃烧产生的硫氧化物和颗粒物（炭烟）等。这些排放物造成空气污染，最终会影响人和动物的健康。

**阅读材料：**

当然，绿色植物通过光合作用"消化"二氧化碳，二氧化碳是植物生存中必需的组成部分。动物不会因呼吸二氧化碳而受到损害，除非空气中二氧化碳的浓度增加到使氧气几乎消失的程度。

### 1.1.2 全球变暖

全球变暖是"温室效应"的结果，而"温室效应"系由二氧化碳和其他气体（如大气中的甲烷）所引发的。这些气体截获了由地面反射的日光的红外辐射，因而在大气中截留了能量，并使之升温。地球温度的升高导致对其生态系统中多数生态的破坏，并引发影响人类的许多自然界的灾害。

因全球变暖引发的生态破坏，某些受损害物种的消失关系到一些人口的自然资源供应的稳定性。同样，这也关联着某些物种从温暖的海洋迁徙到以前较冷的北部海洋，在那里这些物种会潜在地毁灭固有的物种及其赖以生存的体系。地中海可能正在发生这类情况，那里现已观察到来自红海的梭子鱼。

由于自然界灾难引起的伤害之广，使人们对自然界灾难的关注多于对生态灾害的关注。全球变暖被认为是招致如"厄尔尼诺（El Nino）"气象征兆的原因，该气象征兆干扰了南太平洋区域，并定期地引发龙卷风、洪水和干旱。极地冰盖的融化是全球变暖的另一主要的后果，它提升了海平面，而且可引发沿海区域持久的洪水，有时则是整个地区发生洪水。

二氧化碳是碳氢化合物和煤燃烧的生成物。运输工具对二氧化碳的排放占有大量的份额（1980—1999年为32%）。二氧化碳排放量的分布如图1-1所示。

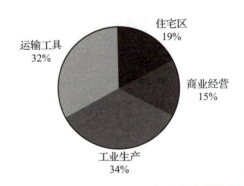

图1-1 1980—1999年二氧化碳排放量的分布

**阅读材料：**

显然，目前运输工具是二氧化碳排放的主要来源。应该注意，发展中国家正在迅速增加其运输工具的总量，而这些国家占有很大份额的世界人口。

### 1.1.3 石油资源

运输工具应用的大部分燃料为源于石油的液态燃料。石油是从地下采掘的矿物燃料,是活性物质分解的生成物,这些物质几百万年前(600万~400万年前的奥陶纪系)被埋藏在稳定的地质层中。该过程经百万年才完成,这便是以地下采掘的燃料形成的地球资源之所以有限的原因。

已经证实的储藏量是指"经地质和工程信息可靠地预示的储藏量,它们是在现阶段经济和运行条件下,今后由已知的储油层可被开采的储藏量"。因此,并不能构成地球总储藏量的指标。已经证实的储藏量如英国石油(British Petroleum)2001年的估算值(表1-1中以$10^9$t计之)所示。表1-1中关于每一地区的R/P比值是指若以当前水平连续生产,则已知储藏量可开采的年数。

表1-1 已知的石油储藏量(2000年)

| 区 域 | 已知的石油储藏量(2000年)($10^9$ t) | R/P比值 |
|---|---|---|
| 北美地区 | 8.5 | 13.8 |
| 南美和中美地区 | 13.6 | 39 |
| 欧洲 | 2.5 | 7.7 |
| 非洲 | 10 | 26.8 |
| 中东地区 | 92.5 | 83.2 |
| 苏联 | 9.0 | 22.7 |
| 亚太地区 | 6.0 | 15.9 |
| 全世界 | 142.1 | 39.9 |

在气候不成为重要问题的地区中,当今抽出的位于地表面层附近的石油是易于提取的。人们认为,像西伯利亚或美国和加拿大的极地带这样的地区,位于地壳下面的储油量要多得多。在上述地区内,气候和对生态的关注是抽油或勘探油的主要障碍。因政治和技术原因,估算地球的石油总储量是一项困难的任务。由美国地质勘探局(US Geological Survey)在2000年估计的尚未勘探的石油资源列于表1-2中。

表1-2 美国地质勘探局对尚未勘探的石油资源的估计(2000年)

| 区 域 | 尚未勘探的石油资源(2000年)($10^9$t) |
|---|---|
| 北美地区 | 19.8 |
| 南美和中美地区 | 14.9 |
| 欧洲 | 3.0 |
| 撒哈拉沙漠以南的非洲地区和南极洲 | 9.7 |
| 中东和北美地区 | 31.2 |

续表

| 区　域 | 尚未勘探的石油资源（2000年）（$10^9$ t） |
|---|---|
| 苏联 | 15.7 |
| 亚太地区 | 4.0 |
| 全世界（潜在的增长量） | 98.3（91.5） |

虽然R/P比值不包括将来的发现，但其意义深远。很明显，该值基于已知的储藏量，由此可易于为今天所理解。未来的储藏量的发现是推测的，且近期被发现的石油是不易于开采的。R/P比值也基于开采量保持为常量的前提。然而，十分明显，石油消耗量（对应的生产量）与发达国家和发展中国家的经济增长同步逐年增加。其中，石油消耗量随着某些人口大量聚居国家的迅速发展很可能呈现巨大的增长额，特别是在亚太地区。图1-2描绘了近20年来石油消耗量的发展趋势。石油消耗量以每日消耗油的千桶数给出（1桶约合8 t油）。

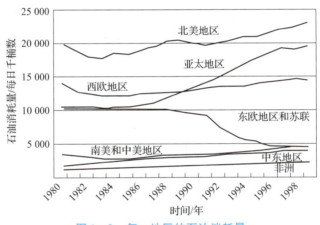

图1-2　每一地区的石油消耗量

不考虑东欧地区和苏联在石油消耗量上的下降，如图1-3所示，全球石油消耗量的发展趋势在明显增长。增长最快的地区是亚太地区，全世界大多数人口居住在该地区。期待中的石油消耗量激增，将伴随着污染物扩散和二氧化碳排放量成正比增加。

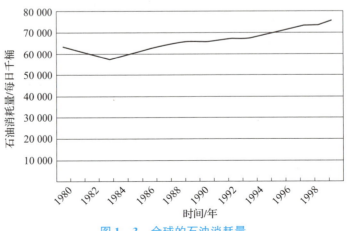

图1-3　全球的石油消耗量

**阅读材料：**

其过程大致如下：活性物质（主要是植物）死亡，并慢慢地被沉积物所覆盖。在时间进程中，这些累积的沉积物形成半固体层，且变态为岩石。活性物质就被截获在一个密闭的空间内，在该处高压和高温作用下，取决于它们的类别，被缓慢地变换为碳氢化合物或变换为煤。

## 1.2 可持续发展的交通运输

从长远的角度来看，当前的个人交通运输模式是不可持续发展的。这是因为地球上的化石燃料储藏量有限，而这些化石燃料却提供了整个交通运输所需能量的97%。为了理解如何获得交通运输的可持续发展这个问题，让我们先看一看能源的获取方式和车辆的驱动方式。

我们能够获取的能源形式可分为三类：可再生能源、基于化石燃料的不可再生能源以及核能。可再生能源包括水力、太阳能、风能、海洋能、地热能、生物能等。不可再生能源包括煤、石油和天然气。核能虽然很丰富，但也是不可再生的，这是因为地球上的铀和其他放射性元素也是有限的。另外，人们对于长远的核能安全（例如最近在日本因地震和海啸引起的重大核泄漏事故）和核污染存有忧虑。生物能是可再生能源，因为它能够从木材、农作物、植物纤维素、废弃物和垃圾堆中提取出来。电能和氢能是二次能源，它们能够利用各种一次能源如可再生能源和不可再生能源产生出来。汽油、柴油和合成气是从化石燃料中提炼出来的能量载体。

图1-4所示的是不同类型的能源形式、能量载体和汽车类型。传统汽油机/柴油机汽车依赖于从化石燃料中提炼的液体燃料。HEVs虽然比传统汽车更高效节能，但仍以化石燃料为主要能源。因此，传统汽车和HEVs均是不可持续发展的。纯电动汽车依赖电能，燃料电池汽车依赖氢能。电能和氢能均可从可再生能源中获得。因此只要有可再生能源来产生这两种能量，它们就是可持续发展的。PHEVs虽然不是完全可持续发展的，但是同时具备了传统汽车和纯电动汽车的优点。PHEVs能够通过使用电网的电能来代替化石燃料的使用。对于可持续发展来说，它不是最终的解决方案，但提供了一条通往可持续发展的道路。

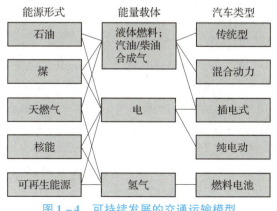

图1-4 可持续发展的交通运输模型

**阅读材料：**

电驱动车辆具有很多优点，也面临很多挑战。在汽车上，电能效率比燃烧效率更高。从油井到车轮的研究表明，在电动汽车上直接使用石油燃烧产生的电能可行驶的里程为每加仑（3.8 L）汽油行驶 108 mile（173 km），而传统的内燃机汽车仅能够行驶 33 mile（53 km）。做一个简单的比较，对一辆小型汽车来说，使用电能每英里需要花费 2 美分（在美国每千瓦时电价格为 0.12 美元），而使用汽油每英里需要花费 10 美分（每加仑汽油价格为 3.3 美元）。

一方面，电能可以从水力发电、风能、太阳能和生物能等可再生能源中产生。另一方面，当前的电网在夜晚非用电高峰时期有富余，在晚上利用这部分富余电能为电动汽车充电是非常理想的。

## 1.3　电动汽车的发展史

电动汽车有一段有趣的历史。它出现在发现电和机电能量转化的方法之后，后来被燃油汽车代替。随着对环境污染关注的日益增加以及电驱动交通的成功使用，公众对电动汽车的兴趣也与日俱增，并希望它可以具备传统内燃机汽车的行驶性能。

### 1.3.1　早期

追溯到 19 世纪 30 年代，在电磁感应定律、电动机和发电机发明之前，交通工具都是靠蒸汽驱动。早在 1820 年，法拉第使用一个通电的线圈和磁铁论证了电动机的原理，直到 1831 年，他发现了电磁感应定律，这项重大发现促进了电动机和发电机的发展，使电力交通的推广成为可能。下面为电动汽车从早期发展到 20 世纪初鼎盛时期的总结：

1830 年之前——蒸汽驱动交通

1831 年——法拉第定律，不久发明了直流电动机

1834 年——搭载不可再充电电池的电动汽车，用于短途行驶

1851 年——不可再充电的电动汽车时速达 19 mile/h（1 mile = 1 609.344 m）

1859 年——蓄电池研制成功

1874 年——蓄电池驱动车辆研制成功

19 世纪 70 年代早期——直流发电机发电

1885 年——发明燃油三轮汽车

1900 年——售出 4 200 辆汽车，其中 40% 蒸汽驱动，38% 电驱动，22% 燃油驱动

1912 年——有 34 000 辆电动汽车登记注册，是燃油汽车数量的两倍

20 世纪 20 年代——电动汽车消失，内燃机汽车成为主流交通工具

电动汽车在短期盛行之后退出市场的原因有：

1）1911 年发明了起动机，使燃油汽车起动方便。

2）亨利 T 型车（燃油汽车）在大量生产中改进，使其价格从 1909 年的 850 美元降到了 1925 年的 260 美元，而电动汽车价格较贵。

3）郊区充电设施不完善，但加油很方便。

**阅读材料：**

以下为一些早期电动汽车的参数：

1897 年：French Krieger 公司 EV，总重为 2 230 lb（1 lb = 0.453 592 37 kg），最高车速为 15 mile/h，续驶里程为 50 mile（充满电）

1900 年：French B. G. S. 公司 EV，最高车速为 40 mile/h，续驶里程为 100 mile（充满电）

1915 年：Woods EV，最高车速为 40 mile/h，续驶里程为 100 mile（充满电）

1915 年：Lansden EV，总重为 2 460 lb，续驶里程为 93 mile（充满电），额定载重量为 1 t

### 1.3.2 20 世纪 70 年代

20 世纪 70 年代初能源危机使汽油的价格显著上升，电动汽车受到越来越多的青睐。1973 年阿拉伯国家石油禁运，这更增加了对新能源的需求，也就使人们对电动汽车产生了很大的兴趣。对于国家来说，其需要减少对国外石油的依赖。1975 年，352 辆电动货车试用于美国的邮政服务业。1976 年，美国国会颁布公法 94 – 413，规定电动汽车和混合动力汽车的研究、开发和示范条例。这项条例制订了一个联邦计划，用来推进电动汽车及混合动力汽车技术的发展和阐述电动汽车商业化的可行性。美国能源部（DOE）制定了电动汽车的性能规范，见表 1 – 3。

表 1 – 3　1976 年电动汽车的性能规范

| 分　类 | 私　用 | 商　用 |
| --- | --- | --- |
| 0 ~ 50 km/h 的加速时间 | < 15 s | < 15 s |
| 25 km/h 的爬坡度 | 10% | 10% |
| 20 km/h 的爬坡度 | 20% | 20% |
| 加速 5 min 后的前进速度 | 80 km/h | 70 km/h |
| 续驶里程：纯电动汽车 | 50 km，C 循环 | 50 km，B 循环 |
| 续驶里程：混合动力汽车 | 200 km，C 循环 | 200 km，B 循环 |
| 混合动力汽车的非电能消耗量（应小于总能量消耗的75%） | < 1.3 MJ/km | < 9.8 MJ/km |
| 电量消耗 80% 时的再充电时间 | < 10 h | < 10 h |

下面是对一辆 20 世纪 70 年代通用汽车公司电动汽车的研究：

系统及其特点：

电机：他励直流电机，34 hp，2 400 r/min

电池组：Ni – Zn，120 V，735 lb

辅助蓄电池：Ni – Zn，14 V

电机驱动：使用普通晶闸管的电枢直流斩波器，使用双极结型晶体管的磁场直流斩波器

最高车速：60 mile/h

续驶里程：60~80 mile

加速性能：0~55 mile 需 27 s

汽车沿用改进后的 Chevy Chevette 的车身和底盘，它主要作为 Ni-Zn 电池的试验车辆。经过 35 500 mile 的道路试验，证明它可以上路行驶。

### 1.3.3　20 世纪 80 年代和 90 年代

20 世纪 80—90 年代，高频大功率半导体开关和微处理器技术迅速发展，提高了电力变换器的设计水平，从而可以更高效地驱动电机。同时，应用在飞轮储能系统中的磁轴承也有所发展，但它并未在主流的电动汽车开发项目中得到使用。

过去的 20 年里，法律的制定对零排放车辆（ZEV）的发展起到了很大的推动作用。1990 年，美国加州空气资源委员会推出一项法规，指出到 1998 年，凡是销量超过 35 000 辆的汽车公司，必须保证其中 2% 的汽车为零排放车辆。到 2001 年，这个比例提高到 5%，2003 年增加到 10%。这项法规的提出对大型汽车制造商开发纯电动汽车起到了很大的推动作用。不过，由于实用性的限制以及汽车制造商能力有限，其无法完成 1998 年和 2001 年的规定指标，委员会便放宽了政策，要求到 2003 年 4% 为零排放车辆，余下的 6% 为零排放车辆或部分零排放车辆，这就要求通用汽车公司在美国加州销售约 14 000 辆纯电动汽车。

随着对环境的重视和潜在的能源危机，美国政府机关、联邦实验室及大型汽车制造商提出很多倡议，用来推进零排放车辆的发展。1993 年成立的新一代汽车合作计划（PNGV）就是其中之一，它是联邦实验室和汽车工业部门联合提出的，用来支持和开发纯电动汽车和混合动力汽车。自由汽车倡议是美国能源部和汽车工业部门最新联合提出的。

近年来，电动汽车的发展趋势如下所述：

➢ 大型汽车制造商开发热情高涨。

➢ 新成立的制造商为电动汽车的发展带来活力。

➢ 新标准更适合其发展。

➢ 全球范围内开发热情高。

➢ 混合动力汽车兴起。

➢ 私营企业和小型企业也开始从生产内燃机汽车转变到生产电动汽车。

以下对一辆 20 世纪 90 年代的通用汽车公司电动汽车进行分析：

（1）Saturn EV1

➢ 1995 年，由通用汽车公司生产的商业化纯电动汽车。

➢ 售价 30 000 美元，在美国加利福尼亚州和亚利桑那州出租。

➢ 系统及其特点：

电机：三相感应电机

电池组：铅酸蓄电池

电机驱动：使用绝缘栅双极晶体管（IGBTs）的 DC/AC 逆变器

最高车速：75 mile/h

续驶里程：高速公路行驶为 90 mile，城市行驶为 70 mile

加速时间：0~60 mile 需 8.5 s

功率消耗：城市行驶为 30（kW·h）/（100 mile），高速公路行驶 25（kW·h）/（100 mile），此车用作电动汽车大批量生产的试验车。

**阅读材料：**

GM Impact 3（1993 完成）

➢ 以 1990 年美国洛杉矶车展中参展的 Impact 为平台进行开发。

➢ 容纳两人、两个车门的小轿车，可上路安全行驶。

➢ 最初生产 12 辆进行试验，到 1995 年生产了 50 辆，由 1 000 名潜在消费者进行评估。

➢ 系统及其特点：

电机：一台三相感应电机，137 hp，12 000 r/min

电池组：铅酸蓄电池（26 个），12 V，串联连接（312 V），869 lb

电机驱动：使用绝缘栅双极型晶体管（IGBTs）的 DC/AC 逆变器

最高车速：75 mile/h

续驶里程：高速公路行驶为 90 mile

加速时间：0~60 mile 需 8.5 s

整车重量：2 900 lb

此车用作电动汽车大批量生产的试验车。

### 1.3.4 电动汽车的市场前景

前面提到的电动汽车，我们只是关注它们作为乘用车时的优缺点，却未考虑它们可以有一些不用上路的特殊应用，且不受续驶里程短的影响。电动汽车使用清洁技术，且在使用中花费小，所以近几年来，它成功地进入非道路车辆市场。例如，用于载客和地面支持的机场车辆，高尔夫手推车和公园游览车，工业用车辆如铲车、起重车，残疾人专用车，用于封闭大场地的地面运输车辆等。

续驶里程短和基础设施不完善是阻碍电动汽车被公众接受的主要因素。要解决续驶里程的问题，需对蓄电池、燃料电池以及其他新能源存储装置进行大量的研究和开发。另一个方法是在公众范围内，宣传全球变暖的危害以及电动汽车的优势，且大多数人每天的出行距离少于 50 mile，而如今的技术已经足够满足这项需求。

为了满足电动汽车的需要，必须尽快建立完善的基础设施。所需的基础建设有：

➢ 充电设施——住宅区充电站和公共充电站。

➢ 电动汽车插头、软线、插座等安全问题的相关标准。

➢ 出售和分配规范。

➢ 服务和技术支持。

➢ 零部件供应。

如今，电动汽车的价格仍是其进军汽车市场的很大劣势。连混合动力汽车的电池更换费用都较高，且使用寿命短。若电动汽车的销售量增加，则它的价格将有所下降，当然政府的鼓励和津贴支持也会起到很大的作用。

电动汽车的广泛应用会改善电子工程师的就业前景。与电动汽车相关的新工作将出现在以下领域：

- 电力电子工业和电机驱动：电动汽车中电气系统的设计与开发。
- 电力工业：电动汽车使用所需的额外资源，以满足增长的功用需求。
- 电动汽车基础设施：充电站的设计与开发，氢能发电、储能和分配系统。

**阅读材料：**

不幸的是，电动汽车市场在90年代后期崩溃。是什么导致电动汽车工业失败的呢？原因很复杂，取决于你怎么看待这个问题。下面所列因素为电动汽车在20世纪90年代崩溃的主要原因：

1）电动汽车的局限性：如较短的续航里程（与汽油机汽车300 mile以上的续航里程相比，大部分电动汽车只能跑60~100 mile）；较长的充电时间（8 h以上）；昂贵的成本（比汽油机汽车贵了40%）；大部分电动汽车可提供的行李舱有限。

2）便宜的汽油：对于电动汽车车主来说，放弃使用便宜的汽油，而去投资买一款昂贵的电动汽车是没有意义的。

3）消费者：消费者认为驾驶大的运动型多功能车辆（Sports Utility Vehicle，SUV）和皮卡更安全，并且能够方便地扩展其他众多功能，如牵引功能。因此，消费者更喜欢大的SUV而不是小的高效汽车（部分原因归咎于低的汽油价格）。

4）汽车公司：虽然汽车制造商花费了数十亿美元用来研发和规划电动汽车，但市场反响并不好。他们在那段时间是赔钱卖电动汽车。同时，维修和保养对汽车经销商来说是额外的负担。责任保险是他们最担心的，虽然并没有证据显示电动汽车比汽油机汽车危险。

5）汽油公司：对汽油公司和石油工业来说，电动汽车是一个巨大的威胁。汽油公司和石油工业公司游说联邦政府和加州政府放弃电动汽车提案是导致电动汽车在20世纪90年代消失的主要原因之一。

6）政府：CARB在最后时刻否定电动汽车提案改而支持氢能汽车议案。

7）电池技术：20世纪90年代大部分电动汽车使用铅酸蓄电池。这种电池大而笨重，需要很长的充电时间。

8）基础设施：电池的充电基础设施有限。

## 1.4 混合动力电动汽车的历史

令人意想不到的是，混合动力电动汽车的概念几乎与汽车概念一样年代悠久。然而，其原始目的并非有效地降低燃油的消耗量，而是辅助内燃机汽车以保证其合格的性能水平。事实上，早期内燃机工程技术的进步不及电机工程技术。

早期混合动力电动汽车的制造是为了辅助当时功率偏小的内燃机汽车，或是为了增进电动汽车的续驶里程。混合动力电动汽车利用了基本的电动汽车应用技术，且使之实用化。尽管在其设计中体现了很多的创造性，在第一次世界大战后，早期的混合动力电动汽车还是不可能与汽油发动机已获重大改进的内燃机汽车相竞争。就功率密度而言，汽油发动机取得了惊人的进步，发动机变得更小、更有效，并且不再需要电动机予以辅助。使用电动机的附加成本以及与酸性蓄电池组相伴随的公害性，是第一次世界大战后混合动力电动汽车从市场中消失的关键因素。

然而，这些早期设计必须解决的最大问题是电动机控制的难点。而在20世纪60年代中期以前，电力电子技术尚未达到适合应用的水平，且早期的电动机是利用机械开关和电阻器控制的，它们都受制于有限的运行范围，与汽车有效的运行要求是不相容的。因此，采用混合动力电动汽车的运行方式是在很多困难情况下实现上述相容性的唯一方法。

Victor Wouk 博士被公认为推进混合动力电动汽车的近代研究者。1975 年，他与同事们一起制造了一辆 Buick Skylark 型并联式混合动力电动汽车。该车发动机是马达旋转式发动机，它与手动变速器配合，并由一台固定于传动装置前端的 15 hp 的他励直流电动机予以辅助。8 个 12 V 的汽车蓄电池组用于能量的储存，最高速度可达 80 mile/h（129 km/h），在 16 s 内可从零速度加速至 60 mile/h。

1967 年，为 Linear Alpha 公司工作的 Ernest H. Wakefield 博士更新了串联式混合动力电动汽车的设计。其中，输出功率为 3 kW 的一个小型发动机交流发电机组用于保持蓄电池组的充电状态。然而，由于技术上的原因，这一实验很快终止。在 20 世纪 70—80 年代初，采用概念上与 1899 年法国的 Vendovelli 与 Priestly 设计相类似的行程扩展器，研究了其他的方法。这些行程扩展器意图在于增进电动汽车的续驶里程，以影响市场的需求。其他的混合动力电动汽车原型分别由 Electric Auto 和 Briggs & Stratton 两公司在 1982 年和 1980 年制成，它们都是生产并联式混合动力电动汽车。

尽管存在 1973 年和 1977 年两次石油危机以及不断增加的环境忧虑，这并没有促使混合动力电动汽车成功地进入市场。研究者们的工作聚焦于电动汽车，许多电动汽车的原型在 20 世纪 80 年代制成。在该期间，对混合动力电动汽车兴趣的不足可归因于实用的电力电子技术、现代电动机和蓄电池应用技术的欠缺。事实上，20 世纪 80 年代见证了传统内燃机汽车体积减小、催化排气净化器引入以及燃料喷射普及化等技术的进展。

在 20 世纪 90 年代，当电动汽车难以达到节能目标的事实变得很明朗时，人们对混合动力电动汽车的概念产生了很大的兴趣。福特汽车公司启动了福特混合动力电动汽车挑战计划，该计划展示了源于大学的增进混合形式汽车产品的努力。

全世界汽车制造业生产的混合动力电动汽车原型取得了巨大的进步，它们在燃油经济性方面超过了对应的内燃机汽车。在混合动力电动汽车的发展和商品化中，最有影响的成果来自日本制造厂。1997 年丰田公司在日本推出了 Prius 混合动力电动汽车，本田公司也推出了 Insight 和 Civic 混合动力电动汽车。这些混合动力电动汽车目前在全世界得到了有效的应用，实现了燃油消耗量的优化。丰田公司的 Prius 和本田公司的 Insight 混合动力电动汽车具有历史性的价值，它们是回应私家车燃油消耗难题的当代首批商品化的混合动力电动汽车。

**阅读材料：**

欧洲方面的成果由法国的 Renault Next 显示，该车是一辆小型的并联式混合动力电动汽车，它采用了一个 750 cm$^3$ 的火花点火发动机和两个电动机。这一原型车的燃油经济性达到 29.4 km/L（70 mile/US gal），其最高速度和加速性能已可与传统内燃机汽车相比拟。大众汽车公司也制造了原型车 Chico，其基础是一辆装备有镍氢蓄电池组和一台三相异步电动机的小型电动汽车，由此安装了一台小型的双缸汽油发动机，用以给蓄电池组再充电，并为高速巡航提供附加的动力。

## 1.5 燃料电池电动汽车的历史

早在1839年，William Grove（常称其为燃料电池之父）已发现通过反向的水的电解即可产生电。直到1889年才有两位研究者，即Charles Langer和Ludwig Mond，创造了术语"燃料电池"，并利用空气和煤气力图设计制作第一个实用的燃料电池。当20世纪初期进一步意图发展燃料电池以使煤或碳可转换为电能时，内燃机的到来暂时压制了发展正在形成的该应用技术的任何希望。

1932年Francis Bacon成功研制了也许是第一台燃料电池装置，该装置含有用碱性电解液和镍电极构成的氢氧燃料电池，其中有Mond和Langer所采用的廉价的触媒作用的替代物。由于一些实质性的技术困难，直至1959年Bacon和公司才首次示范其实用的5kW燃料电池系统。Hairy Karl Ihrig在同一年展示了当时令人满意的装备有20hp燃料电池的牵引车。

1970年，历史上第一辆装配燃料电池的汽车是由Karl Kordesch改装的配有碱性燃料电池的Austin A40。这辆汽车在车顶安置了25（N·m³）压缩氢气的储气罐，以保证300km的续航里程。这款概念车在没有出现明显问题的情况下行驶了三年。

除这个让人激动的结果之外，后来出现的概念车都配备了20世纪80年代末的最重要研究成果，即"酸性聚合物电池"或者"PEM"电池。20世纪90年代初期的戴姆勒-奔驰公司，现在的戴姆勒-克莱斯勒公司是在此领域最具有活力和创造性的厂商。从此之后，世界上大量的制造厂商也都参与了进来。

在最近十年间，包括主要的汽车制造厂商在内的一些制造厂商，以及很多的美国公司已经支持正在进行的燃料电池应用技术的研发，以应用于燃料电池电动汽车和其他的用途，氢的生成、储存和配置是当前面临的最大挑战。事实上，燃料电池电动汽车进入市场仍然需要经历相当长的过程。

**阅读材料：**

在20世纪50年代后期，美国国家航空航天局（NASA）也开始制造应用于太空飞行任务的紧凑型发电机，并且不久即为涉及燃料电池应用技术的数百个研究合同提供资金。在成功供电给几个太空飞行任务后，目前燃料电池在空间计划中已具有确认无疑的作用。

# 第 2 章
## 新能源汽车类型

## 2.1 纯电动汽车

### 2.1.1 纯电动汽车结构

传统汽车是由内燃机驱动的,而电动汽车(EV)是通过储存在储能系统(ESS)中的电能来驱动的。电动汽车的储能系统包括电池、超级电容或者飞轮。当主要的储能系统为电池组时,电动汽车也被称为纯电动汽车或者电池电动汽车(BEV)。图 2-1 展示了纯电动汽车的结构。

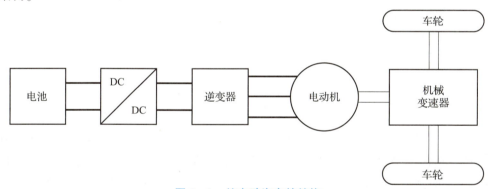

图 2-1 纯电动汽车的结构

电池供电的电动汽车由用来储存电能的电池、电动机以及逆变器构成。电池通过随车自带的或者是安装在充电地点的充电器来充电。逆变器负责控制流入或者流出电动机的功率流的方向和大小以控制汽车的速度和运动方向。值得一提的是,在汽车制动过程中,电池由再生能量进行充电。DC/DC 变换器用于匹配电池组的电压和变频器的直流母线,可以任选。这里显示的机械变速器是变速器与减速器的通称。与传统汽车相比,电动汽车和其他先进的车辆不需要传统汽车所需的自动变速器。

电动汽车续驶里程有限的限制条件,促进了燃料电池汽车(FCEV)的研发。以燃料电池供电的电动汽车与纯电动汽车除了能量来源不同外,有着几乎相同的配置,如图 2-2 所示。氢燃料是必需的,存放在车上。燃料电池汽车在很长的一段时间内代表着真正的零排放车辆。本田 FCX 是第一款在美国得到使用认证的燃料电池电动汽车。

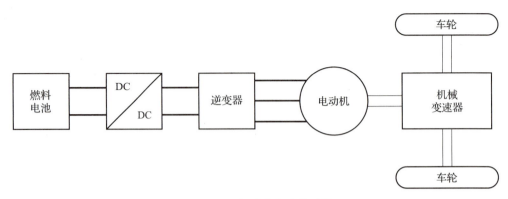

图 2-2　燃料电池汽车的结构

　　用于电动汽车的牵引电动机通常分为直流电动机、交流异步电动机或永磁电动机。然而，直流电动机自身存在的缺陷迫使电动汽车的研究人员将注意力转向交流异步电动机。免维护和低成本的交流异步电动机已吸引了众多电动汽车的开发人员，然而高速电动机的体积和重量问题同时存在。高功率密度是永磁电动机的一个主要优势，尽管电动机的成本高，但是在解决电动汽车的推进问题时还是很有吸引力的。

阅读材料：

　　电动汽车具有胜过传统内燃机车辆（ICEV）的许多优点，例如零排放、高效率、与石油无关以及安静、平稳地运行。电动汽车和内燃机车辆的运行与基本原理是类似的。然而，两者之间有一些差异，例如，汽油箱对应于蓄电池组，内燃机对应于电动机的应用以及不同的传动装置的要求。

## 2.1.2　EV 结构的概念性图示

　　现代电驱动系概念性地示于图 2-3 中。该电驱动系由三个主要的子系统组成：电动机驱动、能源和辅助子系统。电动机驱动子系统由车辆控制器、电力电子变换器、电动机、机械传动装置和驱动组成；能源子系统包含能源、能量管理单元和能量的燃料供给单元；辅助子系统由动力转向单元、车内气候控制单元和辅助电源组成。

　　基于来自加速和制动踏板的控制输入，车辆控制器向电力电子变换器给出正确的控制信号，变换器行使控制电动机与能源之间的功率流的功能。起因于 EV 再生制动所导致的反向功率流，以及该再生能量可储存于能源之中，构成了有接收能量能力的能源。大多数的 EV 蓄电池组、超级电容器组以及飞轮组都可容易地具有接收再生能量的能力。能量管理单元与车辆控制器相配合，控制再生制动及其能量的回收，它也与能量的燃料供给单元一起控制燃料供给单元，并监控能源的使用性能。辅助电源为所有的 EV 辅助设备，尤其是车内气候控制和功率控制动力转向单元，提供不同电压等级的所需功率。

　　由于在电驱动特性和能源方面的多样性，可有各种可能的 EV 结构形式，如图 2-4 所示。

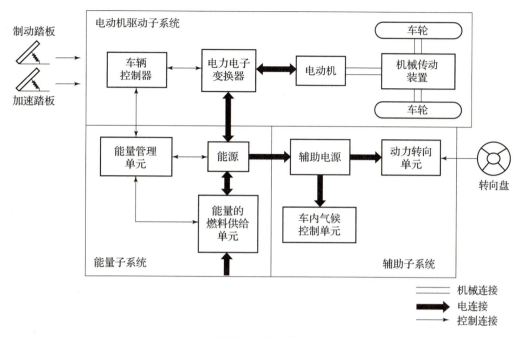

图 2-3 通用 EV 结构的概念性图示

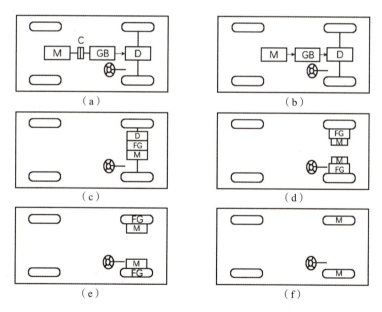

C—离合器；D—差速器；FG—固定挡的齿轮传动装置；GB—变速器；M—电动机

图 2-4 可能的 EV 结构形式

(a) 配置多挡传动装置和离合器的传统驱动系；(b) 无离合器需求的单挡传动装置；
(c) 固定挡的传动装置和差速器的集成；(d) 两个独立的电动机和带有驱动轴的固定挡传动装置；
(e) 配置两个独立电动机和固定挡传动装置的直接驱动；(f) 两个分离的轮式驱动形式

1）图 2-4（a）表明了第一种可供结构选择，其中电驱动装置替代了传统车辆驱动系的内燃机，它由电动机、离合器、变速器和差速器组成。

2）如图 2-4（b）所示，借助于电动机在大范围转速变化中所具有的恒功率特性，可用固定挡的齿轮传动装置替代多速变速器，并缩减对离合器的需要。这一结构不仅减小了机械传动装置的尺寸和重量，而且由于不需要换挡，故可简化驱动系的控制。

3）如图 2-4（c）所示，类似于图 2-4（b）中的驱动系，电动机、固定挡的齿轮传动装置和差速器可进一步集成为单个组合件，其两侧的轴连接两边的驱动轮。整个驱动系由此得以进一步的简化和小型化。

4）在图 2-4（d）中，机械差速器被两个牵引电动机所替代。该两电动机分别驱动相应侧的车轮，并当车辆沿弯曲路径行驶时，两者以不同的转速运转。

5）如图 2-4（e）所示，为进一步简化驱动系，牵引电动机可安置在车轮内。这种配置是通常所说的轮式驱动。一个薄型行星齿轮组可用以降低电动机转速，并增大电动机转矩。该薄型行星齿轮组具有高减速比以及输入和输出轴纵向配置的优点。

6）如图 2-4（f）所示，通过完全舍弃电动机和驱动轮之间任何的机械传动装置，应用于轮式驱动的低速外转子型电动机可直接连接至驱动轮。此时，电动机的转速控制等价于轮速控制，即车速控制。然而，这一配置要求电动机在车辆起动和加速运行时具有高转矩性能。

**阅读材料：**

离合器和变速器可由自动传动装置予以替代，离合器用以将电动机的动力连接到驱动轮，或从驱动轮处脱开。变速器提供一组传动比以变更转速——功率（转矩）曲线匹配载荷的需求。差速器是一种机械器件（通常是一组行星齿轮），当车辆沿着弯曲的路径行驶时，它使两侧车轮以不同的转速驱动。

### 2.1.3 EV 系统级原理图

一辆完整的纯电动汽车不仅包括驱动需要的电驱动零部件和电力电子器件，也包括其他一些使整个系统有效工作的子系统。在图 2-5 中，需要蓄电池（或者燃料电池）提供电能。图左边的模块提供动力驱动电动机。电动机是纯电动汽车的动力传动部件，在图右边用 EVPT 标识。对于每一个零部件，蓄电池或者 EVPT，均有一个控制器。蓄电池控制器能够控制充电或者放电，相似地，EVPT 控制器通过电力电子器件能够控制电动机的转速或力矩。应当注意的是，虽然图中所示的各模块布置在不同的地方，但事实上其物理布置是很紧密的。原因有二：其一出于整体包装的需要；其二将它们放在一起能够缩短高电流和高电压线的长度。同样的，虽然图中各种控制器如 FC 控制器（燃料电池控制器或蓄电池控制器）和 EVPT 控制器，分开布置以在功能上进行区分，但事实上它们能够放置在同一个物理盒子中，并且能够共用相同的微处理器来实现自己的功能。这些巧妙的设计涉及成本和包装。另外，还有一个盒子叫"接口"。这是一个接收信号和功率的控制器盒，既包括驱动需要的高压，也包括某些在低压下工作的特定设备所需要的低压。通过这个接口的功能，将这些信号传递到 EVPT 电动机或高压电池中。同样地，当在物理上集成整个系统时，这些功能模块能够进行合并。

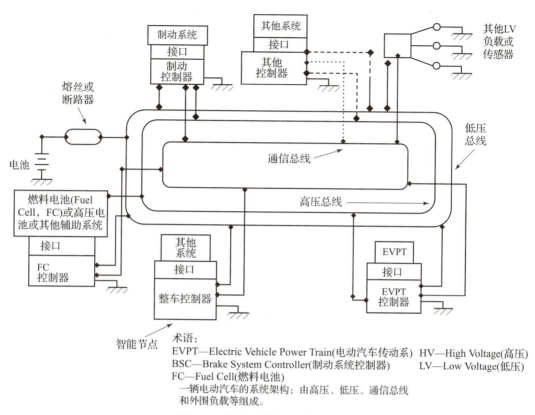

术语：
EVPT—Electric Vehicle Power Train（电动汽车传动系）　HV—High Voltage（高压）
BSC—Brake System Controller（制动系统控制器）　LV—Low Voltage（低压）
FC—Fuel Cell（燃料电池）
一辆电动汽车的系统架构：由高压、低压、通信总线和外围负载等组成。

图 2-5　纯电动汽车系统级原理图

除了上述模块，还有其他各种模块，例如整车控制器，它能接收汽车车速、驾驶员踏板位置等信号，然后确定电动机是否需要额外的力矩。基于这些信息，它将合适的力矩请求信号送给 EVPT 控制器。相似地，制动控制器也能接收相关的制动踏板位置信号、车速信号等，从而确定需要多大的制动力矩。整车控制器也能接收蓄电池荷电状态信号，判断是否能够进行再生制动。如果可能的话，它也能送信号给 EVPT 控制器，进行上述的判断。所有这些表明，各种控制器模块和进行相应动作的子系统之间的连续信息流和信号非常重要。

不同模块之间的信息传递通常通过控制器局域网（CAN）总线实现。它基于一种计算机网络，使用一根单线，包含各种信息或者多路通信信号。当多路信号共享时，需要用到某种通信协议。也就是说，当要使用物理介质时，有几种基于优先级的信号流试图共享相同的介质。对于相对较慢的信号，例如关闭车门锁的信号，它能够等待，而对于极其重要的功能信号如制动和转向信号，事关安全，需要立即被传递。有一些更先进的协议允许这样的操作。另外，对于安全攸关的功能，有必要附加基于硬件的备用通信机制，以防失效。

**阅读材料：**

从技术角度来看，纯电动汽车还有一个优点。在内燃机中，曲轴往复运转，产生脉动转矩。飞轮被用来平滑转矩的脉动特性，以免产生振动。而在纯电动汽车中，电动机产生平滑转矩，不再需要飞轮，既节约了材料和制造成本，又减轻了质量。一方面，内燃机的效率（从汽油到曲轴输出转矩）很低。其中，汽油发动机的效率为 30%~37%，柴油发动机的效率为40%左右。等到将动力传递至车轮，效率只有5%~10%。另一方面，电动机的效率很高，达到90%以上。将动力从蓄电池传递至电动机驱动轴，整个效率约为70%，仍然比内燃机的效率高得多。

## 2.2 混合动力电动汽车

混合动力电动汽车（HEV）通常有两种或两种以上的动力源。在最常见类型的混合动力电动汽车中，发动机通常与电池、电动机或者发电机连接。根据动力总成系统组件的配置情况，混合动力电动汽车可以分为四种不同的类型：并联式、串联式、混联式以及复联式混合动力电动汽车。

### 2.2.1 并联式混合

在并联式混合动力电动汽车中，电动机和发动机均通过机械耦合装置如离合器等连接到变速器。所以汽车可以由发动机来驱动，也可以由电动机或者由两者一起驱动。并联式混合动力电动汽车的电动机功率需求低于同样大小的纯电动汽车。并联式混合动力电动汽车的结构如图2-6所示。

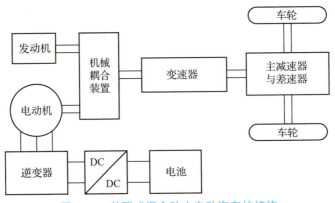

图2-6 并联式混合动力电动汽车的结构

并联式混合动力电动汽车具有以下优点。首先，并联式混合动力电动汽车只需要两个推进组件——内燃机和电动机。电动机也可以作为发电机运行。其次，对于短途行程的应用来说，发动机和电动机可以根据较低功率设计。对于长途行程，发动机可以根据最大功率设计，而电动机/发电机仍然可以根据最大功率的一半设计。然而，电动机与发动机功率耦合会导致机械结构与动力总成控制较为复杂。但同时正是这种复杂性，使动力总成控制更加灵活，以优化燃油经济性与车辆动力性能。

机械耦合是通过采用滑轮、齿轮、离合器或者发动机与电动机之间共用一根轴来实现的。电动机与发动机之间的机械耦合可以配置成共用一个变速器，或者分别使用不同的变速器甚至是使用不同的传动轴。机械传动也不再受限于传动的自动变速器。例如，行星轮系已经被引进用于并联式混合动力电动汽车，取代了传统的无级变速器（CVT）。并联式混合动力电动汽车结构的灵活性为混合动力电动汽车燃油经济性的优化提供了最大的优势。

**阅读材料：**

并联式混合动力电动汽车具有两个驱动源——内燃机和电动机，因此具备如下的工作模式：

1）电动机单独工作模式：当蓄电池电量充足，并且车辆需求功率较小时，发动机关闭，电动机和电池提供能量驱动汽车。

2）共同工作模式：当车辆需求功率较大时，发动机开启，与电动机一起提供能量驱动汽车。

3）发动机单独工作模式：当车辆在高速公路上巡航，并且所需功率不大时，发动机提供车辆所需的全部能量，电动机保持低速运转。这主要是因为电池的SOC已经很高了，车辆的功率需求阻止发动机关闭，或者是因为关闭发动机会降低效率。

4）功率分配模式：当发动机开启，车辆的需求功率较小并且电池的SOC较低时，发动机的部分功率会由发电机转化为电能，被用来给电池充电。

5）停车充电模式：当汽车停止时，发动机带动电动机发电，此时电动机被用作发电机为电池充电。

6）再生制动模式：电动机被用作发电机将汽车的动能转化为电能存储在蓄电池中。注意，再生制动时，原则上发动机应当照常运转，以便能更快地为蓄电池充满电（主驱动电动机处于发电状态），同时提供相应的力矩，即与总的电池输入功率相匹配。在这种情况下，发动机和电动机控制器应当能够很好地协调工作。

### 2.2.2 串联式混合

如图2-7所示，串联式混合动力电动汽车的结构比并联式混合动力电动汽车更简单，只由电动机提供所有的推进动力。当电池的荷电状态（SOC）下降到低于设定值时，车载发动机会驱动发电机对电池进行充电。除了发动机和发电机之外，推进系统与纯电动汽车相同。串联式混合动力电动汽车的优势有：发动机/发电机组位置的灵活性和传动系统的简洁性。但与此同时，由于其内在的结构特点，串联式混合动力电动汽车需要更多的推进组件（即发动机、发电机和电动机）。在发动机和机械传动之间不存在机械连接，可通过调整发

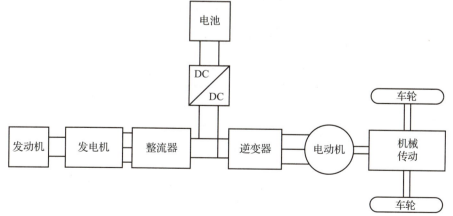

图2-7 串联式混合动力电动汽车的结构

动机速度和转矩使其工作在最大效率区。电动机必须根据车辆所需的最大功率设计。对于长途行程的应用，三个推进组件均需要根据最大功率进行设计。

**阅读材料：**

基于不同的工作条件，串联式混合动力电动汽车上的动力元件能够以不同的组合工作：

1）蓄电池单独工作：当蓄电池电量充足，并且车辆需求功率较小时，I/G 组关闭，车辆可由电池单独驱动。

2）共同工作：在大功率需求时，I/G 组开启并和蓄电池一起为电动机提供能量。

3）发动机单独工作：在高速公路上巡航，并且车辆需求功率中等时，I/G 组开启。蓄电池既不充电也不放电。这主要是因为蓄电池的荷电状态已经很高，车辆的功率需求阻止发动机关闭，或者关闭发动机会降低效率。

4）功率分配：当 I/G 组开启时，车辆需求功率小于其最优功率，并且电池的 SOC 较低时，I/G 组的部分功率被用来为蓄电池充电。

5）停车充电：车辆停止时，I/G 组为蓄电池充电。

6）再生制动：电动机被用作发电机，将车辆的动能转换为电能，并为电池充电。

### 2.2.3 混联式混合

基于串联和并联式结构的优势，制造商和研究人员已经开发出混联式混合动力电动汽车。这些混合动力电动汽车既可以由电动机单独驱动，又可以采用发动机共同来驱动。混联式混合动力电动汽车的结构如图 2-8 所示。在此结构中，内燃机和电动机的功率耦合驱动汽车运行在并联模式下，但是功率由发动机到发电机再到电动机的过程可以看作是串联的。

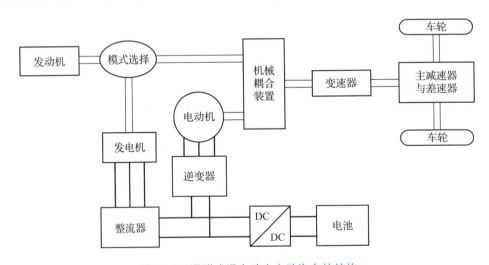

图 2-8　混联式混合动力电动汽车的结构

在设计"模式选择"设备时可以有很多选择。最简单的是采用离合器来选择哪一个轴连接到发动机，即要么连接主减速器要么连接发电机到发动机。另外一种选择是采用一种功率分流装置（例如行星齿轮组）将发动机的输出功率分流到传动轴和发电机。

电池可以靠发电机输出功率来充电。电动机也可以与发动机并联为前轮提供动力。控制单元负责驱动模式的选择。当需要短时间的瞬间功率时，发动机和电动机一起提供汽车所需的功率。

图2-9（英文图示，中文不显示）所示的丰田普锐斯汽车是典型的混联式混合动力电动汽车，其中除了小部分串联式结构外，主要为并联式混合结构。丰田普锐斯汽车在长时间的空挡运行期间，如红绿灯或者堵车时，电池一直保持在充电状态。据美国环境保护局的报道，丰田普锐斯汽车是2008年在美国销售的最省油的汽车。

阅读材料：

Prius是拉丁语，意指"领先一步"。当Prius首次发布时，它被评选为2002年度世界最佳设计客车。这是因为Prius作为第一辆混合动力车辆，有4~5人的座位外加随身行李放置的空间，是最经济环保的实用型车辆。此后，在2004年，第二代Prius赢得了有声望的Motor Trend Car年度奖以及2004年度世界最佳设计车辆的荣誉。

### ✵ 2.2.4 复联式混合

还有其他结构类型的混合动力电动汽车不能归类到上述三种类型中。图2-10所示是一个例子，它具有多个电动机和一个发动机，具有双轴四轮驱动能力。它与混联式混合动力电动汽车非常类似，然而主要的区别在于：复联式混合动力电动汽车中连接到功率分流或汇合装置的电动机允许双向功率流，而混联式混合动力的发电机只允许单向功率流。双向功率流动导致三种推进动力运行模式（由于存在发动机和两个电动机），这在混联式混合动力中是不可能的。另外一点不同的是通常混联式混合动力电动汽车靠发动机和/或电动机来驱动前轮，然而在复联式混合动力电动汽车中，前轮和后轮分别由混合动力总成系统和一个电动机来驱动。

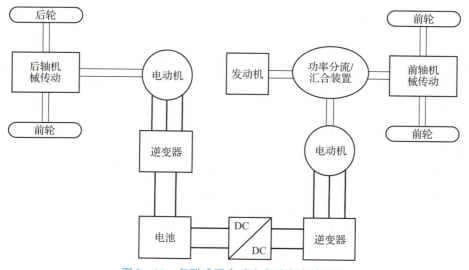

图2-10 复联式混合动力电动汽车的结构

在一般的运行模式中，来自发动机的功率分流为两部分，分别驱动前轮和电动机（作为发电机）对电池进行充电。当负载要求较低时，由电池向前轮电动机提供动力以驱动前轮,此时不需要使用发动机和后轮电动机。当车辆行驶在大负载(比如加速)时,由发动机和前轮电动机共同提供动力驱动前轮,同时后轮电动机驱动后轮。当处于再生模式时(制动或减速),前后轮电动机均成为发电机对电池进行充电。另一双轴复联式混合动力电动汽车与前者的区别在前后轮功能的互换,即图示的前后轮交换位置。此外,还有其他类型,比如,丰田的汉兰达汽车采用三个电动机和一个发动机,最大限度地提高了车辆的燃油经济性和动力性。然而,复联式混合动力与混联式类似,都具有相当高的复杂度和成本要求。

阅读材料:

丰田公司在 1997 年推出世界上首款量产化的现代混合动力电动汽车。2009 年 Prius 在全球范围内的销量超过了 100 万辆。Prius 利用行星齿轮机实现无级变速,因此在 Prius 系统中不需要传统的变速器。它的发动机和行星架相连,发电机和太阳轮相连。行星轮和电动机均与主减速器耦合。行星齿轮机同时充当功率/力矩分配装置。在正常的工作过程中,行星轮的转速由车速决定,而发电机的转速能够进行控制以确保发动机的转速维持在最佳效率区。$6.5 \text{ A} \cdot \text{h}$、$21 \text{ kW}$ 的锂氢蓄电池堆在汽车滑行时通过发电机充电,或在再生制动时通过驱动电动机发电模式充电。在低速行驶时,发动机关闭。

同样的技术也被应用在丰田 Camry HEV、Highlander HEV 和 Lexus HEV 上。然而不同的是,后两者均在后轮增加了第三个电动机。其驾驶性能如加速性和制动性,能够进一步提升。

## 2.3 插电式混合动力电动汽车

### 2.3.1 为什么需要插电式混合动力电动汽车

PHEV(Plugin Hybrid Electric Vehicle,插电式混合动力电动汽车),顾名思义,与 HEV 的不同之处在于,它允许从汽车引出一根电线插到家里或者其他地方墙壁的插座上,利用居民用电给汽车蓄电池充电。为了增加整个系统的灵活性和实用性,原则上,PHEV 能够利用发动机和/或蓄电池系统产生交流电,反哺公用电网。由于插电方式允许使用一定量的外部电力系统的能量来驱动汽车,因此相对于常规 HEV,PHEV 能够使用更大的电池。在 PHEV 上,大电池不是必需的,但毋庸置疑,能够获得更好的燃油经济性,当充满电时,增加了续航里程。在 HEV 上,当蓄电池需要充电时,由于内燃机总能够介入,因此从设计来看,使用更大的蓄电池不一定是最佳的选择。人们有时候认为,大电池在 PHEV 上是必需的,但实际情况可能并非如此。在汽车上,需要多大的电池取决于布置空间的大小。如果电池较小,那么 PHEV 的成本较低;反之,电池较大,成本就会很高,也需要花很长的时间利用电网充电。我们也应当注意,居民用电系统在为蓄电池系统充电时,其提供的电流大小有限制,因此有必要为插电方式设计保护装置。目前电网供能的成本比汽油的价格低得多,在一些可能的地方使用 PHEV 具有重要意义。

**阅读材料：**

PHEV 是一种可以从电网（或可再生能源）吸取并存储能量以驱动车辆的混合动力电动汽车。这个功能上的简单改变使得 PHEV 能够运用多源电力能源，包括可再生能源，如风能和太阳能，来取代石油。这种改变对于整个交通运输部门石油消耗、总排放量以及输电网络的性能和组成都有重大的影响。PHEV 被视为提高交通运输和固定能源部门短期可持续性的最有前途的方法之一。调查表明，PHEV 存在着相当大的市场。雷诺公司和戴姆勒－克莱斯勒公司已经生产制造了限量的 PHEV。通用汽车公司和福特汽车公司也开发并展出了 PHEV 概念车。

### 2.3.2 插电式混合动力电动汽车的结构

PHEV 在汽车上额外连接了一个插座，使得它能够方便地与墙壁上的电源插座相连。就转动车轮而言，当汽车与电源插座相连时，它的驱动电动机和内燃机就不再需要了。但是，汽车仍然需要一些辅助负载（通常在 12V 低压下工作）、空调（同样在低压下工作）、座位加热器以及车灯等。因此，在低压下传递这些载荷是恰当的。如果电池的快速充电是必需的，则应恰当运行内燃机，且驱动电动机被用作发电机，或利用一个独立的发电机来达到这一目的。基于所使用的原理，需要对齿轮传动系统进行改变。虽然在原理上，电力系统和 PHEV 系统之间整个过程的连接很简单，但是从图 2-11 所示的整车架构来看，需要考虑一些问题。

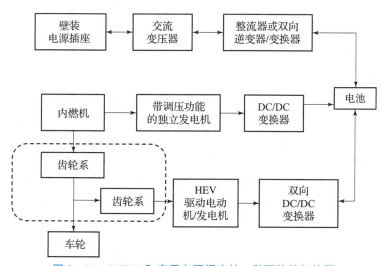

图 2-11 PHEV 和家用电源插座的一种可能的架构图

从图 2-11 中显然可以看出，为了给蓄电池充电，需要一条连接墙壁电源插座和蓄电池的线路，这条线路由隔离变压器和整流器或 DC/DC 变换器组成。它直接涉及整个系统的充电部分。图中最下面部分表示了充电过程既可以通过独立式发电机实现，也可以将驱动电动机用作发电机，最终实现充电。

当然，应当理解，在插电模式时，汽车是静止的且车轮保持不动。虽然图中所示的过程并没有直接涉及插电模式，但是整个能量管理系统必须协调插电模式和内燃机的工作，因为快速充电时，插电模式和内燃机（发电模式时）需要同时运行。最后应当注意，图中插电部分需要双向变换器。这考虑到，在未来当汽车具有足够的能量时，汽车上有效的电能管理使得它能将电能传输回电网。目前，这个问题还不是汽车工业急于考虑的。但是，当家里的电力设施失效时，这种可能性使我们能够使用汽车作为应急发电机来照明。

基本上，HEV 和 PHEV 之间唯一的区别正如图 2-11 最上面部分所示，在 PHEV 上使用了壁装电源插座。蓄电池的大小也有很大不同。另外，如上所述，插电系统必须与其他充电过程和整车系统的能量管理相适应。

阅读材料：

PHEV 有时也被称为增程式电动汽车，这是因为装有车载汽油或柴油使得它们走得更远，因为当车载电池能量耗尽时，这些车辆可以在延长的行驶距离中提供很高的燃料经济性。巨大的电池组可以存储更多的再生制动能量，并为延长行驶距离的发动机优化提供更大的灵活性。雪佛兰 Volt 汽车已配备了全尺寸的电动机，可以证明纯电动驱动能在各种驾驶条件下得以实现。

## 2.4 燃料电池电动汽车

### 燃料电池电动汽车的结构与相关课题

纯电动汽车的结构图在这里同样适用。从图 2-2 可以看出，高压源已经被标识为既可以是蓄电池也可以是燃料电池。因此，燃料电池电动汽车的基本组成元素与纯电动汽车一样。

燃料电池的一个问题是，它是一种单向设备，也就是说，它能输出能量，但与蓄电池或超级电容器不同，它不能回收能量。很显然，在汽车上它不能实现再生制动。这表明为了获得再生制动的能力，需要引入蓄电池或超级电容器。但储能电池或超级电容器的引入不仅仅为了再生制动，也为了燃料电池的正常启动。这对于串联式和并联式 HEV 非常重要。蓄电池或超级电容器被设计来满足启动过程中至少 30s 的大电流要求。另外，基于典型驾驶循环工况，要对汽车再生制动进行评价，并且蓄电池或超级电容器的尺寸必须足够大，以满足最差的工况要求。

燃料电池的第二个问题是单个电池电压的敏感性。它表征了燃料电池工作条件是否正常。如果电池电压不同，则表明出现了问题。燃料电池不能承受大的瞬变，因此蓄电池有助于减小燃料电池的尺寸，在动态过程中保护它不会剧变。

燃料电池，不是指单个电池而是指整个模块以及所有的外围设备，如压缩机、水分处理机构、加热系统等。这些设备使得整个系统的效率相对较低。

阅读材料：

制造商考虑如何为轻型车选择合适的燃料电池的标准是非常多的，但主要有以下几个：

1) 技术成本是最低的，与目前的内燃机成本应处于同一个数量级。
2) 与热能发动机具有相同程度的比质量和比容积。
3) 有足够低的工作温度以便在短时间内起动（1~2 min），但需要有足够的余热排放以保证冬天车厢内的温度。
4) 与传统汽车运行温度区间（-30℃~40℃）相匹配的技术。
5) 在含有各种杂质和污染物的空气中长时间运行，不会因为过于敏感而过早失效。

所有厂商根据这些标准选择了叫作"PEM"的技术。巴拉德 Power Systems（一个加拿大制造商）为他们现有的大部分原型车装配了 PEM 系统。然而，在燃料电池成为这项新技术的最主要组成部分的同时，所谓的"燃料"也成了人们争论的焦点。如果最终的能源是被大众认可的氢能源，而实际上氢气在目前的道路上并不能进行补给。因此，两种主要的方式在互相博弈。

1) 无论选择哪种一次能源，氢能源必须在厂内制备并以特定形态（压缩、液态、吸附）配送给使用者。
2) 汽车携带一种碳氢能源（碳氢化合物或乙醇），并在需要的时候，通过车载转换器将其转化为氢能源。

# 第 3 章
## 能量储存装置

"能量储存"定义为储存能量、向外传送能量（放电）和从外部接收能量（充电）的装置。现已提出几种应用于电动汽车（EV）和混合动力电动汽车（HEV）的能量储存类型。至今，这些能量储存主要包括化学蓄电池组、超级电容器组和超高速飞轮。燃料电池本质上是一类能量变换器。

对于汽车领域中所应用的能量储存有若干的技术条件，例如比能量、比功率、效率、维护要求、管理、成本、环境的适应性和友好性以及安全性。就电动汽车的应用而言，比能量是首要的技术条件，因为它约束了车辆的行程。另外，对于混合动力电动汽车的应用，则比能量的重要性较次，而比功率成为首要的技术条件，这是因为所有的能量来自能源，且为保证车辆性能，尤其是在加速、爬坡和再生制动期间的性能，需要足够的功率。当然，其他的技术条件在车辆驱动系统的开发中也应予以充分的考虑。

**阅读材料：**

混合能量储存装置是将两个或多个能量储存装置组合在一起，以使每一个能量储存装置都能显示其优点，并使其缺点可由其他的能量储存装置予以补偿。例如，化学蓄电池与超级电容器的混合组成可克服如同电化学蓄电池低比功率，以及超级电容器低比能量这样的难题，从而获得了高比能量和高比功率。本质上，混合能量储存装置由两个基本的能量储存装置组成：一个具有高比能量，而另一个具有高比功率。

## 3.1 电化学蓄电池组

电化学蓄电池组更一般地被称为"蓄电池组"，作为电化学装置，在充电时，它将电能变换为潜在的化学能；而在放电时，则将化学能变换为电能。一个蓄电池由几个叠在一起的单元电池组成。一个单元电池则是一个具有全部电化学特性的、独立且完备的单元。本质上，一个蓄电池单元由三个基本部件组成，两个电极（正极和负极）浸没在电解液中，如图 3-1 所示。

蓄电池制造业通常以库仑容量（A·h）表示蓄电池的规格，该容量定义为蓄电池在放电条件下，由全荷电状态到端电压降至终止电压时所获得的安培·小时数（安时数），如图 3-2 所示。应该注意，同样的蓄电池在不同的电流放电率下，通常具有不同的安时数。一般来说，如图 3-3 所示，在高电流放电率的情况下，容量将变得较小。蓄电池制造业通常以一给定的电流放电率所对应的安时数来表示蓄电池的规格，例如一个标记为 C5 放电率下 100（A·h）的蓄电池，是指在 5 h 电流放电率下具有 100（A·h）的容量［放电电流 = 100/5 = 20（A）］。

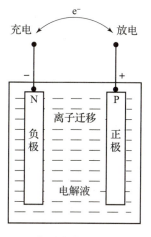

图 3-1　典型的电化学蓄电池单元

图 3-2　典型蓄电池的终止电压

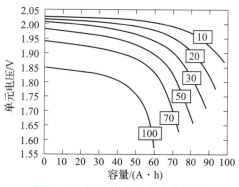

图 3-3　铅酸蓄电池的放电特性

## 3.2　电池特性参数

**1. 容量（C）**

电池容量是指在电池完全放完电之前，它能够提供的电荷量。电池容量的国际单位是库伦（C），常用单位为安时（A·h），其中 1（A·h）= 3 600C。例如，一个 20（A·h）的电池能够持续提供 1 A 的电流 20 h 或 2 A 的电流 10 h 的电荷量，理论上还可以提供 20 A 的电流 1 h。一般来说，电池的容量依赖于放电率。

电池的放电率可以表示为两种形式：C 放电率或 nC 放电率，nC 放电率时，经过 1/nh，电池放完电。例如 C/2 放电率时，电池能放电 2h；5C 放电率时，电池能放电 0.2h。对 2（A·h）容量的电池来说，C/5 放电率时，电流为 400 mA；5C 放电率时，电流为 10 A。

**2. 存储能量（E）**

电池中存储的能量取决于电池电压和存储的电荷量，其国际制单位是瓦时（W·h）。

假设电池电压为常数,则有 E = V × C,式中,V 是电压;C 是容量(A·h)。电池的容量随放电率改变而变化,相应地,放电电流会影响电压。因此,电池储存的能量不是恒定不变的,而是两个变量即电压和电池容量的函数。

### 3. 荷电状态(SOC)

电动汽车的一个关键参数就是电池的 SOC。SOC 用来测量电池剩余电量。一般地,SOC 被保持在 20%～95%。

关于电池电荷,人们经常错误地认为,当电池"没有电"时,电压从 12 V 降到 0 V(12 V 的电池)。实际上,电池的电压在 12.6 V 降到大约 10.5 V 时,SOC 从 100% 降到 0。一般建议,SOC 的值不要低于 40%,此时对应的电压为 11.9 V。所有电池都有 SOC - 电压曲线,它既可以从制造商的数据中查到,也可以通过实验得到。图 3 - 4 所示的是铅酸电池的 SOC - 电压曲线。对于锂离子电池来说,曲线可能会非常平坦,特别是当 SOC 在 40%～80% 变化时。

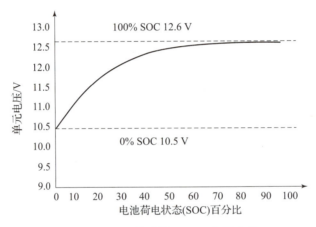

图 3 - 4　12V 电池的 SOC - 电压曲线

### 4. 放电深度(DOD)

放电深度(DOD)是电池所放电量占电池容量的百分比。

一般来说,电池的 DOD 不能过低,至少要放出 80% 的电才被看作深度放电。特别需要注意的是,电池电压不能降到 0V,否则电池将会永久性损坏。所以,电池中定义了截止电压,电池的端电压不能低于这个截止电压。电池电压为截止电压时,放电深度为 100%。

### 5. 比能量

比能量是电池单位质量能够存储的电能。它的国际制单位是瓦时每千克 [(W·h)/kg]。已知电池储存的能量和比能量,用能量除以比能量可以很容易得到电池的质量。此外,由于储存能量随放电率而变化,所以比能量不是一个固定值。表 3 - 1 是大部分能量源的比能量。

### 6. 能量密度

能量密度是电池每立方米能够存储的电能,用电池存储的能量除以电池的体积来计算,其国际制单位是瓦时每立方米 [(W·h)/m³]。

表 3-1　不同能量源的比能量

| 能量源 | 比能量/[(W·h)·kg$^{-1}$)] | 能量源 | 比能量/[(W·h)·kg$^{-1}$] |
| --- | --- | --- | --- |
| 汽油 | 12 500 | 镍氢电池 | 50 |
| 天然气 | 9 350 | 锂离子聚合物电池 | 200 |
| 甲醇 | 6 050 | 锂离子电池 | 120 |
| 氢气 | 33 000 | 飞轮（碳化纤维） | 30 |
| 碳 | 8 200 | 超级电容器 | 3.3 |
| 铅酸电池 | 35 | — | — |

**7. 比功率和功率密度**

比功率是电池每千克能提供的功率。它取决于电池的负载，所以是高速变化和无规律的，其国际制单位是瓦每千克（W/kg）。比功率表征的是电池提供功率的能力。比功率越高，电池的供能和吸收能量就越快。体积比功率又称为功率密度或体积功率密度，表明了电池每单位体积能提供的功率（能量传递的变化率）。如果电池有高的比能量和低的比功率，则意味着电池储存了很多能量，但是能量放出的速度很慢。Ragone 图可以用来描述某一电池比功率和比能量的关系。

**8. 深度循环次数和电池寿命**

EV/HEV 的电池可以经历几百次的低至 80% 深度的充放电循环。电池类型和设计不同，其深度充放电循环次数也不同。同时，使用模式也可以影响电池在失效前能够维持的深度循环次数。美国先进电池联盟（United States Advanced Battery Consortium，USABC）的中期目标是使 EV 电池的深度循环次数达到 600 次。因为深度循环次数影响电池寿命，所以这项指标非常重要。通常来说，在 EV 和 HEV 的控制策略中，应当尽量减少电池的深度放电次数，用以限制车辆的使用成本。

阅读材料：

安时（或电荷）效率

安时效率是电池放电期间的输出电荷量与电池恢复到之前电荷水平所需的电荷量之比。实际上，由于这两个值不会相等，则安时效率的最大极限值为 100%。一般安时效率的变化范围为 65%~90%，它取决于很多因素如电池类型、温度和电荷率。

## 3.3　蓄电池技术

适用的电动汽车和混合动力电动汽车的蓄电池由铅酸蓄电池、镍基蓄电池［如镍-铁、镍-镉、镍-金属氢化物（Ni-MH）蓄电池］和锂基蓄电池［如锂聚合物（Li-P）和锂离子（Li-I）蓄电池］构成。

### 3.3.1 铅酸蓄电池

一个多世纪以来，铅酸蓄电池已有成功的商业产品，且在汽车和其他应用领域中，至今仍然是广泛采用的电能源。它的优点在于：低成本、成熟的技术、相对的高功率容量。这些优点对其应用于混合动力电动汽车是有吸引力的，因为在混合动力电动汽车中高功率是首要考虑的技术条件。当铅酸蓄电池与其他较先进的对应物相比时，其有关材料（铅、铅氧化物、硫酸）的成本是相当低的。铅酸蓄电池也有若干缺点，如其能量密度低（主要是由于铅的高分子量）；温度特性差（当低于10℃时，其比功率和比能量显著降低，这一状况严格地限制了铅酸蓄电池在冷气候下的车辆牵引中的应用）。

高度腐蚀性的硫酸是对车内人员的安全隐患。通过自放电反应所释放的氢则是另一种潜在的危险，因为这一气体甚至在微量集聚态中都是极度易燃的。氢的排放也是密封式蓄电池应用中的一个问题。事实上，为了提供防止酸泄漏的可靠防护层，必须将蓄电池密封，从而在其外壳内截留所派生的气体。因此，蓄电池内的压力增加，在外壳和密封处可引起膨胀和结构性制约。铅具有毒性，因此电极上的铅是一个涉及环境的问题。在蓄电池制造期间，如果车辆失事（因开裂电解液流出）或在蓄电池寿命终止进行处理期间，都可以发生连续使用铅酸蓄电池所形成的铅的排放。

各种改进性能的铅酸蓄电池已开发应用于电动汽车和混合动力电动汽车，已制成具有快速充电能力、比能量超过40［（W·h）/kg］的改进型密封铅酸蓄电池。已开发的现代铅酸蓄电池补救了它的缺点。由于减少了不活泼物质，例如壳体、集电极和隔膜等，比能量已经提高，其寿命也已增加50%以上，但这是以成本升高为代价获得的。利用所设计的电化学过程吸收氢和氧寄生物的释放，从而使安全性问题得到改进。

阅读材料：

铅酸蓄电池曾经是电动汽车上应用最广泛的电池。设计铅酸蓄电池时已能够兼顾高功率、廉价、安全和可靠，且已有回收设施。然而，比能量低、低温工作性能差、循环寿命低等制约着铅酸蓄电池在电动汽车和混合动力汽车上的应用。

它有很长的历史，其应用可追溯到19世纪中期，目前已是非常成熟的技术。最早的一组铅酸蓄电池是1859年生产的。在20世纪80年代早期，铅酸蓄电池的年产量已经超过1亿。这类电池经久不衰的原因有以下几点：
- 相对较低的成本。
- 电池原料（铅、硫）获取容易。
- 制造工艺简单。
- 良好的机电特性。

### 3.3.2 镍基蓄电池

与铅相比，镍是较轻的金属，且有很好的合乎蓄电池应用的电化学特性。现有四种不同的镍基蓄电池技术：镍-铁、镍-锌、镍-镉和镍-氢（Ni-MH）蓄电池。

Ni – MH 蓄电池

自 1992 年以来，Ni – MH 蓄电池已进入市场，其特性类似于镍–镉蓄电池。两者之间原理上的差异在于吸收在金属氢化物中的氢的利用，该金属氢化物替代了镉，用作活性的负极材料。当与镍–镉蓄电池相比较时，因其占优的比能量，及其免除于毒性或致癌性的性能，Ni – MH 蓄电池正在取代镍–镉蓄电池。

目前，Ni – MH 蓄电池技术已制成额定电压为 1.2 V、比能量可达 65 [(W·h)/kg] 和比功率为 200 W/kg 的 Ni – MH 蓄电池。这类 Ni – MH 蓄电池的关键组成是贮氢合金，它被配制以获得在大量循环中稳定反应的物质。

至今 Ni – MH 蓄电池仍在开发之中，基于目前的技术，其优越性可概括如下：具有镍基蓄电池最高的比能量 [70~95(W·h)/kg]、最高的比功率（200~300 W/kg）、环境上的友好（无镉）、平坦的放电曲线（较小的电压降）和快速再充电能力。但是，这一蓄电池依然受到高初始成本的困扰，同时它可存在一种记忆效应，且可能在充电时发热。

Ni – MH 蓄电池已被认为是近期应用于电动汽车和混合动力电动汽车重要的选择。许多蓄电池制造商，如 GM Ovonic、GP、GS、Panasonic（松下）、SAFT、VARTA 和 YUASA 公司已经积极从事于这类蓄电池技术的开发，特别是应用于电动汽车和混合动力电动汽车的配置。1993 年以来，Ovonic 的 Ni – MH 蓄电池已装备在 Solectric GT Force 电动汽车上进行试验和示范运行。一组 19 kW·h 的蓄电池已能供给比能量大于 65 [(W·h)/kg]、车速达 134 km/h、14 s 内可从零车速加速到 80 km/h、在城市中行程范围为 206 km 的性能。丰田和本田公司均已分别在其混合动力电动汽车（Prius 和 Insight）上采用了 Ni – MH 蓄电池。

**阅读材料：**

与镍–镉蓄电池相同，镍–氢蓄电池也具有平稳放电特性。但镍–氢蓄电池容量明显高于镍–镉蓄电池，其比能量在 60~80 [(W·h)/kg]，其比功率可高达 250 W/kg。

近几年来，镍–氢蓄电池迅速进入市场。克莱斯勒公司的"Epic"小型货车就搭载镍–氢蓄电池组，续驶里程达到了 150 km。在商业化的丰田混合动力汽车上均使用镍–氢蓄电池。

镍–氢蓄电池的组成零部件均可回收，但相应的基础设施还未建立。镍–氢蓄电池具有比铅酸电池长得多的寿命，且具有安全、兼容性能好的优点。它的缺点主要有成本相对较高、自放电严重（与镍–镉蓄电池相比）、高温下充电能力差和单体效率低。未来镍–氢蓄电池将发展成为可充电动力电池的主体，可与其抗衡的只有锂离子电池。

### 3.3.3 锂基蓄电池

锂在所有金属中是最轻的，且从电化学观点上考察，它表征了令人非常感兴趣的特性。确实，它可具有很高的热力学电压，由此导致非常高的比能量和比功率。

Li – I 蓄电池

自 1991 年首次宣告 Li – I 蓄电池成果以来，其制造技术已有了空前的提高，现被认为是将来最有希望的可再充电的蓄电池。虽然依然处于发展阶段，Li – I 蓄电池已经在电动汽车和混合动力电动汽车的应用中获得了认可。

Li-I蓄电池采用氧化锂嵌入碳中形成的物质（LixC）为负极，替代金属锂；以氧化锂的过渡族金属嵌入氧化物（Li1-xMyOz）为正极，且应用有机溶液或固态聚合物为电解质。Li-I电池，具有额定电压为4 V、比能量为120 [(W·h)/kg]、能量密度为200 [(W·h)/L] 和比功率为260 W/kg的特性。可以预期，Li-I电池的发展将最终归结于锰基型Li-I电池，因为其成本低、原材料储量充裕，且锰基型材料对环境友好。

**阅读材料：**

20世纪70年代锂原电池（Lithium Primary Cell）被发明出来后，便掀起了研究二次锂离子电池（Secondary Lithium Cell）的热潮。锂离子电池的标称单体电压（Nominal Cell Voltage）为3.6 V，这是3块镍-氢或镍-镉单体电池的电压和。

锂离子电池具有高比能量、高比功率、高能量效率、高温工作性能好和低自放电率的特点。锂离子电池的零部件是可循环利用的。以上特点决定了锂离子电池十分适用于电动汽车和混合动力汽车，包括其他需要可充电电池的设备。

## 3.4 超大容量电容器和超级电容器

电容器是一种通过分离等量正负静电荷实现能量存储的设备。电容器的基本结构组成是两个称为极板的导体，极板被一种绝缘体电介质隔开。传统的电容器的功率密度非常高（为 1 012 W/m³），但能量密度非常低 [为 50 (W·h)/m³]。

这些被称为电解电容器的传统电容器作为中间储能元件，被广泛应用于电气线路中。传统电容器与电动汽车主能源存储设备相比，两者的时间常量处于完全不同的范围，前者要小很多。

除了像传统的电解质电容器那样用静电电荷存储能量之外，超级电容器中有能够使静电荷以离子的形式存储的电解质。超级电容器内部不发生任何电化学反应。超级电容器的电极由具有较大内部表面积的多孔炭制成，这有助于吸收离子，形成比传统电容器更高的电荷密度。由于离子移动速度比电子移动速度慢很多，因而超级电容器充电和放电的时间比电解质电容器的充电和放电的时间更长。

超级电容器的功率密度和能量密度分别是 $10^6$ W/m³ 和 $10^4$ [(W·h)/m³]，其能量密度比电池（为 $5×10^4$ ~ $25×10^4$ [(W·h)/m³]）能量密度低很多，但放电时间更短（1~10 s，电池为 $5×10^3$ s），循环寿命更长（为 $10^5$ 次，电池为 100~1 000 次）。

目前超级电容器的研究和发展目标为使其比功率和比能量分别达到 4 000 W/kg 和 15[(W·h)/kg]。尽管超级电容器能够为混合动力汽车提供充足的能源存储，但超级电容器成为汽车主能源的可能性还很小。另外，超级电容器比功率较高，非常适合作为中间能源传输设备。在电动汽车或者混合动力汽车上，将超级电容器同蓄电池或者燃料电池结合使用，可满足提供瞬时功率的需求，例如在加速和爬坡过程中的功率的需求。超级电容器可在再生制动过程中进行高效率的能量回收。

**阅读材料：**

由于电动汽车（EV）和混合动力电动汽车（HEV）频繁停车-起动运行，故其能量储存的放电和充电曲线呈现剧烈的变化，但其取自于能量储存装置的平均功率远低于在相对短的加速和爬坡期间所需的峰值功率。峰值功率与平均功率之比可超过 10∶1。在混合动力电动汽车设计中，能量储存装置的峰值功率容量比其能量容量更为重要，且通常约束了整车体积的减小。基于目前的蓄电池技术，蓄电池的设计必须在其比能量、比功率和循环寿命之间进行折中处置。就同时获得高量值的比能量、比功率和循环寿命的困难而言，必然给出关于 EV 和 HEV 能量储存系统的一些建议，即其应是一个能源和功率源混合组成的系统。能源多半是具有高比能量的蓄电池和燃料电池，而功率源则是具有高比功率的能量储存装置。功率源在较小的行驶需求量或再生制动期间可从能源处补充充电。获得广泛注意的功率源是超级电容器。

## 3.5 飞 轮

飞轮是一种以机械形式存储能量的能量供给单元。飞轮用旋转的轮状转子或者复合材料制成的圆盘来存储动能。汽车使用飞轮已有很长的一段历史，在目前所有的内燃机上，飞轮用来存储能量，以缓冲发动机动力传递过程中突然的冲击。然而，发动机飞轮所需存储的能量少，并且受车辆急加速需求的限制。目前人们正在研究不同容量飞轮的应用。飞轮作为动力辅助装置可以用在搭载标准内燃机的混合动力汽车上。另外，飞轮应用在电动汽车上时可取代化学电池作为主能量源，或者与电池一起使用。然而，在飞轮成为电动汽车或者混合动力汽车的能量源之前，需要突破的技术方面的问题是增加飞轮的比能量。目前使用的飞轮结构相当复杂，体积庞大并且很重。飞轮的安全性也是需要关注的问题。

飞轮的设计目标是最大限度地提高其能量密度。在飞轮中使用的材料必须具有重量轻、拉伸强度高的特点，而复合材料能很好地满足这样的条件。

飞轮作为能量源有一些优点，其中最重要的一个优点是比功率高。从理论上讲，飞轮的比功率已经可达到 5~10 kW/kg，在不超过安全应力的条件下可以轻松实现 2 kW/kg。飞轮之所以受到广泛关注，还在于其优良的机械性质。飞轮不会受到温度限制的影响。不用进行有毒的化学过程和没有废物的处理问题，使飞轮比化学电池更具环境友好性。飞轮储能可靠，且具有良好的可控性和可重复性的特点。通过测量转速，在任何时间都可精确地得知飞轮的荷电状态。从飞轮输入和输出的能量转化效率约为 98%，而电池为 75%~80%。在很少有维护需求的条件下，飞轮的使用寿命是电池的数倍。飞轮所充的电量只是电池所需充电量的一小部分，并且在飞轮充电站其充电时间可少于 10 分钟。飞轮可在很短的时间内吸收或释放很多的能量，这将有助于再生制动。

尽管飞轮有一些优点，但还有许多显著的缺点。飞轮储能系统的主要困难就是附加设备需要操作和容纳，额外部分会给飞轮在电动汽车和混合动力汽车上的应用带来很大困难，主要是增加的重量和成本所造成的巨大差异。

**阅读材料：**

为储能采用机械方式的飞轮并非一个新的概念。25 年前，Oerlikon 工程公司在瑞士制造了第一辆单独配置巨大飞轮的载客公共汽车。重达 1 500 kg、以 3 000 r/min 运转的飞轮，在每个公共汽车停车站由电力予以补充能量。传统的飞轮是一个巨大的、重达数百千克的钢制转子，它以每分钟数千转的转速旋转。相反地，改进的飞轮是一个重量为数十千克的轻型复合转子，其转速约为 10 000 r/min，被称为超高速飞轮。

超高速飞轮的概念看来是一个合理的途径，以满足应用于电动汽车和混合动力电动汽车的迫切的能量储存需求。换句话说，其高比能量、高比功率、长循环寿命、高能量效率、快速补充能量、免维护特配成本效应和环境的友好性令人瞩目。

## 3.6 燃料电池

近十年来，在车辆中，燃料电池的应用已是人们注意力的焦点所在。与化学蓄电池形成对比，燃料电池产生电能而不储存电能，并且只要维持燃料供给，它将继续运行。相比于配置蓄电池的电动汽车，配置燃料电池的车辆具有行程较长而无须过长的蓄电池充电时间的优点；相比于内燃机车辆，它具有高能量效率和低得多的排放的优点，因为其燃料中的自由能直接转换为电能，而不经历燃烧过程。

### 3.6.1 燃料电池的工作原理

燃料电池是一种原电池，借助于电化学过程，其内部燃料的化学能直接转换为电能。燃料和氧化剂持续且独立地供给电池的两个电极，并在电极处进行反应。电解液必须用以将离子从一个电极传导至另一个电极，如图 3-5 所示。燃料供给阳极或正极，在该电极处，依靠催化剂，电子从燃料中释放。在两电极间电位差作用下，电子经外电路流向阴极或负极，在阴极处，正离子和氧结合，产生反应物或废气。燃料电池中的化学反应类似于蓄电池中的化学反应。

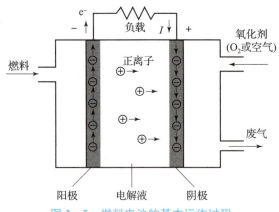

图 3-5 燃料电池的基本运作过程

阅读材料：

与电池相似，燃料电池是一种通过化学反应产生电能的电化学装置。电池和燃料电池最大的区别是后者只要为燃料电池提供燃料就能源源不断地产生电能，而前者的电能是从存储在储能装置的化学能中产生的，并且需要频繁充电。

燃料电池的基本结构（图 3-5）与电池类似，包括阳极和阴极。提供给燃料电池的燃料分别为氢和氧。燃料电池的原理与电解水的原理相反,即氢气和氧气相结合产生电,同时生成水。提供给燃料电池的氢燃料,每个分子上有两个氢原子,以化学键 $H_2$ 的形式存在。氢分子上有两个单独的核,每个核上有一个质子,两个质子共享两个电子。燃料电池在氢分子分解的过程中产生电能。

### 3.6.2 燃料电池技术

取决于燃料电池电解质的类型,可将燃料电池分类为六种:质子交换膜(PEM)或聚合物交换膜燃料电池(PEMFCs)、碱性燃料电池(AFCs)、磷酸燃料电池(PAFCs)、熔融碳酸盐燃料电池(MCFCs)、固态氧化物燃料电池(SOFCs)和直接甲醇燃料电池(DMFCs)。表 3-2 列出了这些燃料电池正常的运行温度及其电解质的状态。

表 3-2 各种燃料电池系统的运行数据

| 电池系统 | 运行温度/℃ | 电解质的状态 |
| --- | --- | --- |
| 聚合物交换膜燃料电池 | 60~100 | 固态 |
| 碱性燃料电池 | 100 | 液态 |
| 磷酸燃料电池 | 60~200 | 液态 |
| 熔融碳酸盐燃料电池 | 500~800 | 液态 |
| 固态氧化物燃料电池 | 1 000~1 200 | 固态 |
| 直接甲醇燃料电池 | 100 | 固态 |

**质子交换膜燃料电池**

聚合物交换膜燃料电池采用固态聚合物膜为电解质。该聚合物膜为全氟磺酸膜,也被称为 Nafion(美国杜邦公司),是酸性的,因此迁移的离子为氢离子($H^+$)或质子。聚合物交换膜燃料电池由纯氢和作为氧化剂的氧或空气一起供给燃料。

聚合物交换膜燃料电池中的催化剂是关键性的焦点所在。在早期实践中,为了燃料电池的特定运行,需要很可观的铂载量。在催化剂技术方面现已取得了巨大进展,使铂载量从 28 $mg/cm^2$ 减少到 0.2 $mg/cm^2$。由于燃料电池的低运行温度以及电解质酸性的本质,故应用的催化剂层需要贵金属。因氧的催化还原作用比氢的催化氧化作用更为困难,所以阴极是最关键的电极。

在聚合物交换膜燃料电池中,另一关键性问题是水的管理。为了燃料电池的特定运行,聚合物膜必须保持湿润。事实上,聚合物膜中离子的导电性需要湿度。若聚合物膜过于干燥,就没有足够的酸离子去承载质子;若聚合物膜过于湿润(被浸渍),则扩散层的细孔将被阻断,从而使反应气体不能扩展触及催化剂。

聚合物交换膜燃料电池中最后的关键是其毒化问题。铂催化剂极富活性,因而提供了优异的性能。该催化剂高度活性的制约在于其对一氧化碳和硫的生成物与氧相比有较高的亲和力。毒化效应强烈地约束了催化剂,并阻碍了扩展到其中的氢或氧。由一氧化碳引起的毒化是可逆的，但它增加了成本，且各个燃料电池需要单独处理。

**阅读材料：**

1960年，第一个聚合物交换膜燃料电池成功开发，并应用于美国载人空间项目中。目前，大部分研究燃料电池应用于汽车的技术来自像巴拉德这样的制造厂商，其产品运行于60℃~100℃，可提供0.35~0.6 W/cm²的功率密度。在其支持电动汽车和混合动力电动汽车的应用中，聚合物交换膜燃料电池具有一些确定的优点。首先，它可低温运行，因此对电动汽车和混合动力电动汽车而言，可期望有快速起动性能。其次，在所有可用的燃料电池类型之中，其功率密度最高。显然，功率密度越高，为满足功率需求所需安装的燃料电池的体积越小。再次，其固态电解质不变化、迁移或从燃料电池中气化。最后，在燃料电池中，因唯一的液体是水，故任何腐蚀的可能性本质上已被界定。然而，它也有某些缺点，例如需要昂贵的贵金属、高价的聚合物膜以及易于毒化催化剂和聚合物膜。

# 第 4 章
## 储能系统的管理

## 4.1 简　介

储能系统（ESS）在电动汽车、混合动力汽车和插电式混合动力汽车中发挥着重要的作用。这些汽车的性能很大程度上取决于储能系统。有几种不同类型的储能选择，可以用于不同的车辆应用。在过去十年中，镍金属氢化物电池曾在 HEV 中广泛应用。现在锂离子电池被认为是用在电动汽车和插电式混合动力汽车中的唯一可行方案。因为它的功率密度高、周期寿命长，超级电容也被研究应用在插电式混合动力汽车上。基于飞轮的混合动力汽车也曾被考察。包括高能锂离子电池和高功率超级电容的集成混合储能系统，可以为电动汽车和插电式混合动力汽车提供最好的解决方案。对电动汽车、混合动力汽车和插电式混合动力汽车储能系统的适当管理不仅能延长电池储能系统的寿命，还可以提高汽车整体的燃料效率。

阅读材料：

根据美国能源部插电式混合动力汽车会议总结报告（2006），电池保养成本被认为是阻碍插电式混合动力汽车向大众市场渗透的一个因素。特斯拉汽车公司只为他们的电动汽车电池提供 3 年的质保，超过 3 年用户要支付每年 300 美元的保养费。据估计，雪佛兰电池组的更换成本超过了 10 000 美元。在美国的"绿色国家"计划中，电动汽车和插电式混合动力汽车的电池有 10 年/15 万 mile（10 年或 15 万 mile，以较早发生者为准）的质保期，这是因为如果一辆插电式混合动力汽车电池有 10 年/15 万 mile 的质保，CARB 法规允许有 3 000 美元的奖励。同样，比保修成本更重要的是顾客对电池寿命的感知和对汽车转售价值（和剩余价值）的影响。

## 4.2 电池管理

在一系列单体电池被串联或并联起来传递大功率的系统中，都广泛应用电池管理系统（BMS）。在电动汽车、混合动力汽车或插电式混合动力汽车中，根据所用的电池类型，在一个电池组中有几百甚至几千个单体。监测和控制这些电池是至关重要的，以获得系统最佳性能，同时，维持车辆安全并且延长储能系统的寿命。

BMS 有几个不同层次的功能。在最简单的层次，BMS 要能够监测电池参数，如电压、电流、温度、荷电状态（SOC）和健康状态（SOH）。在下一个层次，BMS 要能够控制充电和放电，均衡单体，并维持电池健康。BMS 的其他功能还有热管理和安全保护措施，即在故障情况下能够隔离故障单体电池。

**阅读材料：**

能量管理能实现多个目标，它包含了基于负载需求的能量分配（表明瞬时功率需求）。在超过一些阈值（如电压、电流和 SOC 等）的时候，它给出了系统的保护措施。此外，由于动力源不受限，在满足各种约束条件的前提下，它提出了以油耗最小为目标的动力源最佳分配。因此，一个好的能量管理可以得到较好的燃油经济性和排放性能，也能提高零部件的使用寿命。例如，通过对电池 SOC 的合理控制，可以使电池更多地处于健康状态，从而减少电池的更换次数。更准确地说，功率管理的目标是从整个系统角度出发的，不仅仅着眼于单一的燃油经济性，或者从运行的角度来看，它能够使系统在整个寿命周期中的成本最低，维护更好，寿命也更长。

### 4.2.1 参数监测

要被监测的参数包括电池电压、电流和温度。我们首先研究电压监测。

在一个电池组中有两种电池电压测量：单体电压测量和电池组电压测量。对于电池组电压测量，由于电池组的高电压，不可能直接利用电压分割，在这种情况下适合使用隔离电压传感器。图 4-1 所示为一个为了测量电池组电压的隔离电压传感器，由 LEM 公司制造。

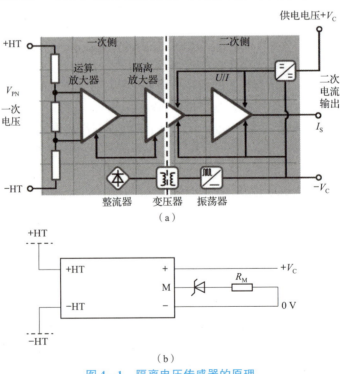

图 4-1 隔离电压传感器的原理
(a) 隔离电压传感器的原理；(b) 单电源供电的电压传感器结构

检测单体电池电压也是很重要的。当单体电池连成并联形式时，只需要测量所有并联单体中的一个单体电压。然而，由于有几百个单体串联，用一个微控制器测量所有单体的电压是不实际的。在实际中有两种方法：一种方法是把电池分成组（模块），然后一个模块内的电压用一个模块监控电路测量出来，送到中心的 BMS；另一种方法是利用"库技术（Banking Technology）"。

下面再看看温度监测。有三种可用的温度监测设备，即电阻温度检测器（RTD）、热敏电阻和热电偶。

电阻温度检测器包含一个贴在塑料薄膜上的铂薄膜。它的电阻随着温度改变，通常可以测量的温度高达850℃。它的电阻和温度之间呈高度的线性关系，通常在0℃时的电阻为100Ω。电阻温度检测器价格昂贵，因此多用在精确温度测量中，在电池组的温度监测中很少用。

热敏电阻由半导体材料或金属氧化物制成，其阻值随着温度的升高而降低，因此它们被称为负温度系数（NTC）传感器。热敏电阻在电池温度测量中很常用。图4-2是对数坐标下热敏电阻的阻值随温度变化曲线。

热敏电阻可以直接连接到微控制器（MCU）的 A/D 通道，但最好在热敏电阻和 MCU 之间加一个缓冲电路，如图4-3所示。在 MCU 内部要有一个数值表或自由方程，以便查询给定测量的温度（表4-1）。

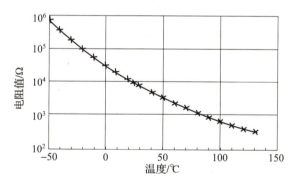

图4-2 热敏电阻的阻值随温度变化曲线

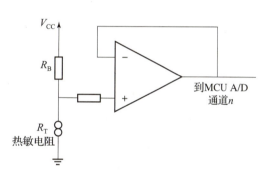

图4-3 温度测量电路

表4-1 给定测量的电池温度

| 电压/V | 4.963 | 4.927 | 4.863 | 4.755 | 4.586 | 4.336 | 3.996 | 3.571 | 3.333 | 3.085 |
| --- | --- | --- | --- | --- | --- | --- | --- | --- | --- | --- |
| 温度/℃ | -50 | -40 | -30 | -20 | -10 | 0 | 10 | 20 | 25 | 30 |
| 电压/V | 2.579 | 2.094 | 1.662 | 1.298 | 1.005 | 0.775 | 0.598 | 0.464 | 0.361 | 0.284 |
| 温度/℃ | 40 | 50 | 60 | 70 | 80 | 90 | 100 | 110 | 120 | 130 |

热电偶是基于这样的效应，即在两种不同金属的交界处会产生一个电压，该电压随着温度的升高而增加。由于它们是用金属制成的，所以可以测量的温度达到了几千摄氏度，但它们的稳定性和测量准确度不如电阻温度传感器。

最后，我们将研究电流监测。电流的测量是通过使用电流传感器实现的。有很多类型的电流传感器可以应用在电池组电流测量中。LEM DHAB S/25 型双通道电流传感器以及它的电路结构如图4-4所示。

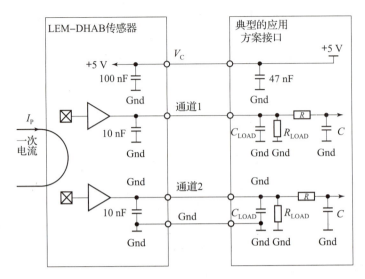

图4-4 LEM DHAB S/25型双通道电流传感器以及它的电路结构

这个电流传感器具有两个通道的放大器,一个额定值是200 A,另一个额定值是25 A。通道1的电流传感器输出刻度是10 mV/A,通道2的刻度是80 mV/A且有一个5 V单电源供电,在零电流时输出是2.5 V。对于通道1,0.5 V对应-200 A,4.5 V对应200 A。对于通道2,0.5 V对应-25 A,4.5 V对应25 A。电流传感器的放大器电路如图4-5所示。

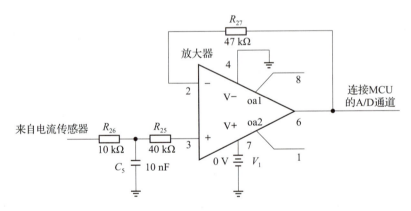

图4-5 电流传感器的放大器电路

**阅读材料:**

几乎所有的电池在闲置的时候都有内部漏电流(自身放电),通常情况下漏电流会随温度增加。对于这个电池组,如果漏电流是20 mA(包括电池漏电流以及与电池关联的外围电路的消耗,如BMS、电池监视电路和电池平衡电路),我们可以算出电池从100% SOC自己放电到30% SOC需要的时间。

$$40/0.02 = 2\,000 = 83(天)$$

这意味着当电池在闲置的情况下可以持续83天。应当注意,当电池储存在较高的温度或非常低的温度下时,电池的漏电会增加。

### 4.2.2 SOC 的计算

荷电状态（SOC）的计算是 BMS 的最重要的功能之一。通常，通过计数多少电流（或电子）进入或移出电池，从而计算出 SOC，即

$$SOC(new) = SOC(old) - I \times T_S / (A \cdot h)_{nominal} \qquad (4-1)$$

然而，这个计算受很多不确定因素的影响，具体如下：

1）测量准确度：电流传感器具有测量准确度和分辨率，随着时间的推移，误差会在 SOC 中累积。

2）放大器电路也有准确度，与电阻和供电电源的准确度有关。

3）MCU 计算的舍入误差。

4）MCU 的 A/D 分辨率。

5）MCU 可能不知道电池的初始 SOC。

6）使用上述方程不能把电池损耗算进 SOC 的计算中。

7）通过 SOC 算法不能把电池的自放电算进去。

8）由于 MCU 的离散采样，电流谐波会引起测量误差。

9）测量回路和放大器电路中的噪声。

10）电池老化会影响电池能够充进去多少能量。因此 SOC 的百分比可能无法真实地反映多少能量可用。

因此，必须研发其他方法来补充传统的 SOC 计算方法。一种流行的方法是用电池端电压来校准电池 SOC。在这种方法中，电池在不同的充电/放电电流和温度下被测试，找到端电压和 SOC 之间的关系。然后建立一个数值查找表，在测量电池电压、电流和温度的基础上找到相应的 SOC。这个 SOC 再与用积分方法计算到的 SOC 做比较，如果差异超过一定的限度，则需要注意并做出进一步的诊断。一种典型的电池 SOC 与端电压的对应关系如图 4-6 所示。这种方法不能考虑电池老化的影响。

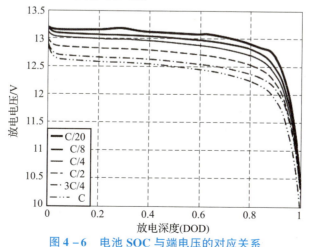

图 4-6 电池 SOC 与端电压的对应关系

第二种方法是当电池充满电时测试 SOC。一些电池不允许充满电，但现代锂离子电池每次都可以充满电且不损害电池寿命。

**阅读材料：**

最后，可以用先进的数学模型预测电池 SOC，比如卡尔曼滤波等。卡尔曼滤波器可以在相信传感器读数与相信可获得最可能状态估计的模式之间做出最佳平衡，关键是消除噪声并与良好的数学模型相结合。卡尔曼滤波器把测量噪声当作随机变量，并从系统中消除测量噪声。在卡尔曼滤波中，我们用下式对每个 $K$（状态）估计信号 $X$ 为

$$X_K = K_K Z_K + (1 - K_K) Z_{K-1}$$

式中，$Z_K$ 是具有误差的测量值；$K_K$ 是卡尔曼增益，对不同的增益要分别确定。

一个良好的数学模型是基于卡尔曼滤波器的 SOC 估计关键的一个部分。

### 4.2.3 故障和安全保护

图 4-7（a）中的电路可以在充电期间用来均衡电池组单位，并且在充电或放电期间隔离故障单体。每个单体都与两个晶体管相关联，这些晶体管是典型的低通电阻 MOSFET，具有毫欧等级的内阻。

在正常运行时，并联的晶体管关断，串联的电阻导通，如图 4-7（b）所示。在故障情况下，假设 $B_1$（图 4-7（c）中的 $B_1$）出现故障，与故障单位并联的晶体管 $T_{1P}$ 导通，与故障单位串联的晶体管 $T_{1S}$ 关断。

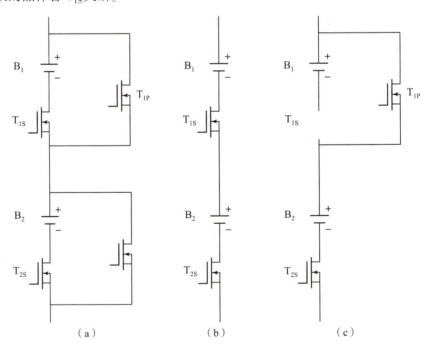

图 4-7　PHEV 中管理电池组的平衡和隔离电路
(a) 结构图；(b) 正常运行；(c) $B_1$ 出现故障或绕开

在充电期间，使用同一个电路可以进行均衡。当 $B_1$ 充满电时，$T_{1P}$ 导通，$T_{1S}$ 关断，所有的充电电流通过旁路晶体管 $T_{1P}$。这更适合充电电流恒定的情况，因为当一个单位从电池组

中去除时，总电池组电压就减小了一个单位电压，因此，充电电压要做相应的调整。

这种电路的优点是在均衡期间不消耗能量（晶体管损耗除外），并且在使用电池组期间可以隔离故障电池。缺点是在电流很大时，串联的晶体管损耗会很大。因此，这种设计不适合大功率应用。例如，如果 MOSFET 在 200A 时的电压是 0.2 V，导通内阻 $R_{DS\_ON} = 0.001\ \Omega$，价值 2 美元，则单个晶体管上的损耗将是 $200^2 \times 0.001 = 40$（W）。对于具有 100 串单体的电池组来说，损耗最高时将达到 4 kW。然而，当电流减小到 60 A 时，由晶体管引起的电池组损耗将仅有 360 W。然而，假设每个单位电压的额定值是 4 V，此时电池组只能供应 24 kW 的功率。

阅读材料：

最根本的问题是电池组中不同的电池将得到相同的充电电流并持续相同的时间长度（它们是串联的，否则不会这样），但各个电池具有不同的容量，且在开始时具有不同的残余电量，因此不同的电池几乎肯定需要稍微多些或少些的电流／充电时间。随着电池组长度的增加，问题会更严重。

### 4.2.4 充电管理

电池适当的充电和放电可以维持电池系统的健康状态。因此，不适当的充电和放电会影响电池寿命和容量。

电动汽车、混合动力汽车和插电式混合动力汽车中的电池在三种情况下被充电：插电式充电期间、可再生制动期间以及利用发电机功率充电期间。插电式充电通常是在较长的时间内以较低的充电速率进行的。但可再生制动会在很短的时间内以很高的电流进行。

插电式充电通常经过以下五个阶段：

1）诊断阶段。当汽车插上电时，BMS 和充电器会进行一系列测试来保证电池具有接受充电的能力。一个小电流（通常是 C/20）流入电池。这个阶段会维持几分钟，充电电流渐渐提高到第二阶段的阈值。

2）恒电流充电阶段。一旦电池通过诊断，电池就会以恒定电流充电，常规充电电流一般是 C/5，快速充电电流是 C/2 ~ 2C。

3）恒定电压或充电电流减小阶段。在恒电流充电阶段，一旦其中一节电池达到最大电压，充电电流将减小。在这个点，电池组或者以减小的电流充电，或者进入恒电压充电阶段。

4）均衡阶段。由于单体组中单体之间的不平衡，恒电压阶段将持续很长时间。在这个阶段，已达到阈值的电池的均衡电路启动。一旦所有的单体都达到预设的电压阈值，充电就停止了，充电器关闭。

5）维持阶段。一些电池需要一个维持阶段，在这期间，有很小的电流流进电池来弥补泄漏损耗。一些电池组设计利用这个小电流，使电池在寒冷的天气里保持温度。插电式充电的五个阶段，如图 4-8 所示。

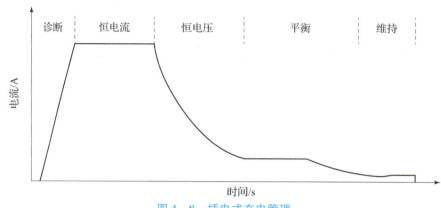

图 4-8 插电式充电管理

可再生制动期间的管理。插电式充电管理是相对比较直接的,而可再生制动期间的充电是非常复杂的。这是由于很大的电流流入电池以产生期望的制动转矩,也由于电池内部电阻产生大量的热。

## 4.3 电池单体均衡

在混合动力汽车、电动汽车或插电式混合动力汽车中,电池被连接成并联或串联形式来形成一个电池组。当电池被串联形成一个串时,这个串的可用能量取决于含有最小能量的电池。同样,当为电池组充电时,能够传输到电池组的能量取决于剩余能量最多的那个电池。

当用成百上千的电池单体连成串时,各个单体的容量和内阻有微小的差别。随着时间的推移,由于使用模式特别是运行温度的不同,这种差别会被放大。

因此在电池组运行期间,保持电池单体的均衡是非常重要的。有两大类可用的均衡方法:被动式均衡和主动式均衡。对于被动式平衡,能量高的电池单体通过电阻或晶体管放电,能量以热量形式耗散。对于主动式均衡,能量高的电池单体放电给能量低的电池单体。

对于被动式均衡,通常有电阻和晶体管或 IC 均衡电路。这两种方法在充电或闲置状态下都可以使用。

图 4-9 展示了 3 个单体电池串基于电阻的被动式均衡。电阻/晶体管与每个电池单体并联。当通过任何一个电池单体的电压低于设定电压时(本例中为 3.65 V),晶体管关闭,因此没有电流通过旁路电路,所有充电电流都通过电池组为电池组充电。一旦单体电压到达 3.65 V,晶体管闭合,通过电阻/晶体管的电流开始增加。在本例中,电压低于 3.65 V 的单体继续充电,但电压达到或超过 3.65 V 的单体被旁路并停止充电。当电池组中的所有电池单体电压都到达 3.65 V 时,充电过程就停止了。

这种均衡方法的优点是电路小而简单,因此成组可以很容易实现。同时电压可以非常精确,精确到几个毫伏。其缺点是:①均衡基本上是基于电压的均衡方法。即使每个电池单体的开路电压彼此相同,它们含有的能量可能也不同。②通过电阻/晶体管的能量以热能形式浪费了。这不仅降低了充电效率,也为电池组的热管理造成了困难。通常旁路电流的设计都不超过几个安培。

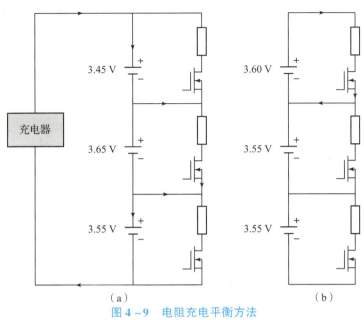

图 4-9 电阻充电平衡方法
(a) 充电时的平衡；(b) 闲置时的平衡

另一方面，主动式均衡可以非常有效，有两种主动式均衡：一种是传统的基于电容器或电感的电池均衡，另一种是基于 DC/DC 变换器的电池均衡。主动式均衡可以提供很高的效率，但会增加接线和控制算法的复杂度，而且如果把它建在电池组内会非常昂贵。

基于 DC/DC 变换器的单位均衡结合了 DC/DC 变换器和感性均衡方案的优点，如图 4-10

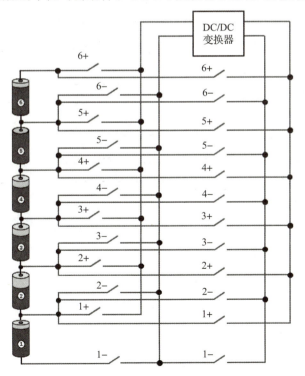

图 4-10 基于 DC/DC 变换器的均衡方法

所示。在这个电路中,通过选择开关,可以将 DC/DC 变换器的输入切换到任何一个单体,也可以将其输出切换到任何一个单体。在充电、放电或闲置期间,当 DC/DC 变换启动后,控制算法将搜索所有单体中电压最低的和电压最高的单体。一旦发现了电压最高的和电压最低的单体,DC/DC 变换器就被控制利用最高电压单体的能量向电压最低的电池单体充电,直到单体达到平均电压。这个过程将继续下去直到所有的单体都具有相同的电压。

阅读材料:

为了限制均衡过程中的热生成,当电池均衡电路开启时,充电电流应减小。因此,图 4-11 和图 4-12 分别阐述了充电控制器和均衡控制器的平衡控制过程。本例中,电池在 3.65 V 时被充满电(开路电压),并且在 4.0 V(浮动电压)时充电到 100%。在电池电压达到 3.65 V 时开启平衡。在均衡期间,当最大电压 $V{\max} = 3.65$ V 时充电电流被减小一个比例,在 $V{\max} = 4.2$ V 时减小到 1.65 A。

当一节电池单体的电压到达 3.65 V 时,充电器算法会启动均衡电路,同时,将充电电流减小到 1.65 A。然而,如果最大电池电压低于 3.65 V,则均衡电路被关闭,充电电流恢复。以 3.3~3.65 V、3.65~4.0 V 滞回,可避免电路进入不稳定状态。

均衡控制算法将增加晶体管的开启时间,因此更多的电流将通过旁路电路。

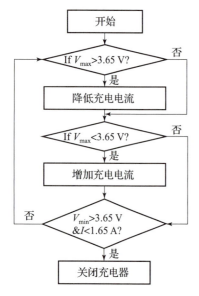

图 4-11 为电池平衡设计的充电器控制算法

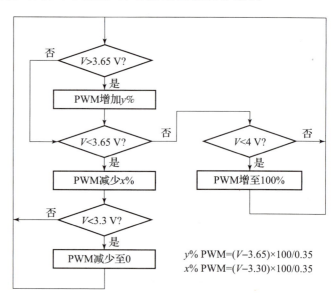

图 4-12 为电池平衡设计的均衡器控制算法

# 第 5 章
## 电驱动系统

电驱动系统是电动汽车（EV）和混合动力电动汽车（HEV）的心脏。这些系统由电动机、功率变换器和电子控制器构成。电动机将电能转换成机械能推动车辆，或反之将机械能转化为电能进行再生制动和（或）对车载储能装置充电。功率变换器用来对电动机提供特定的电压和电流。电子控制器根据驾车要求，通过对功率变换器提供控制信号来控制功率变换器，进而调整电动机的运行，以产生特定的转矩和转速。典型电驱动系统的功能模块框图如图 5-1 所示。

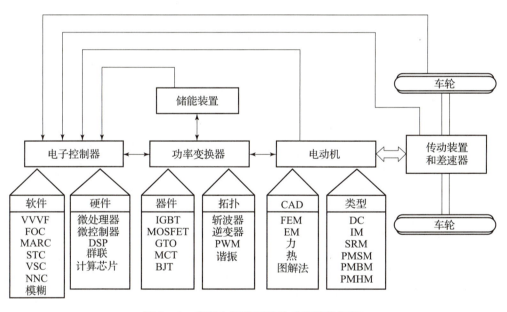

图 5-1 典型电驱动系统的功能模块框图

电动汽车的电驱动系统主要根据以下因素来选择：驾驶员对行驶性能的期望、车辆规定的性能参数以及车载能源的性能。驾驶员的期望值由包括加速性能、最高车速、爬坡能力、制动性能和行驶里程在内的行驶循环予以定义。含体积和重量在内的车辆性能约束取决于车型、车重和载重量。能源系统则与蓄电池、燃料电池、超级电容器、飞轮及各种混合型能源相关联。因此，电驱动系统的优选特性和组件选择过程必须在系统层面上实施，必须研究各子系统间的相互作用以及系统权衡中可能的影响。

**阅读材料：**

电子控制器可进一步分为三个功能单元：检测器、接口电路和处理器。检测器通过接口电路将所测量的物理量，如电流、电压、温度、速度、转矩和磁通转换为电信号。这些信号被处理成相应的电平后，输入处理器。处理器的输出信号通常被放大后，经由接口电路，驱动功率变换器的功率半导体器件。

## 5.1　电动机

### 5.1.1　电动机应用优势

我们知道电动机的机械转矩是由磁通量在通过一定电流的线圈中变化而产生的。在电动机中，磁性材料（铁）的尺寸影响磁通量的大小；组成电枢绕组的线圈（一般是铜制）的直径影响电流的大小。因此，电动机的尺寸很大程度上取决于我们所需的转矩特性。电动机的功率等于转矩乘以转速，因此对于一个给定的功率，如果转速越高，则电动机的尺寸越小。

不管是直流电动机还是交流电动机，作为电动机它们都具有以下特性：都可以在任意转速下输出转矩，特别是在静止状态起动时能够提供较大转矩。由于具有这个特性，直流电动机可以借助于合适的受控供电电压，交流电动机可以借助于变频器使车辆正常起步，从而不需要采用原内燃机车辆传动系统中的离合器。

电动机可以提供短时间过载特性，可以在加速或起步阶段提供超过额定转矩 2～4 倍的过载转矩。它有很大的热惯性，在工作中短时间内可提供的最大功率超过额定的连续输出功率值。额定连续输出功率与最大功率比值取决于电动机的尺寸及其冷却方式，在一般情况下，用于电驱动系统的电动机，其比率约为 1.3。

**阅读材料：**

直流电动机的转速有以下限定：
1）机械方面要防止线圈和整流环节烧结出现故障。
2）电气方面需要考虑为保护换向器而设置通过电流的极限。

实际公路车辆驱动系统中使用的电动机的单位功率低于 50～60 kW，并且在大部分时间，工作时的供电直流电压低于 200 V。

在上述条件下，可以制造出的一般直流电动机的转速上限为 5 000 r/min。由于没有集电极的限制，交流电动机可以达到比直流电动机更高的转速，能达到 10 000 r/min，此转速完全可以适用于传统公路车辆的功率需求。因此，交流电动机的比功率高于直流电动机。

### 5.1.2　电动机的分类

与电动机的工业应用不同，用于电动汽车的电动机通常要求频繁地起动和停车、高变化率的加速度/减速度、高转矩且低速爬坡、低转矩且高速行驶以及非常宽的运行速度范围。应用于电动汽车的驱动电动机可分为两大类，即有换向器电动机和无换向器电动机，如图 5-2 所示。

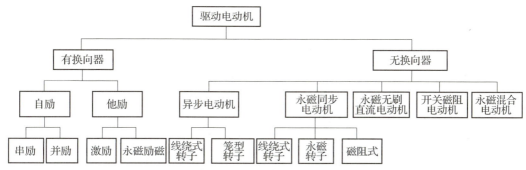

图 5-2 应用于电动汽车的驱动电动机的分类

**1. 直流电动机**

有换向器电动机主要指传统的直流电动机，包括串励、并励、激励和永磁（PM）励磁的直流电动机。直流电动机需要换向器和电刷以供电给电枢，因而使该类电动机可靠性降低，不适合免维护运行和高速运行。此外，线绕式励磁的直流电动机其功率密度低。然而，由于技术成熟和控制简单，直流电动机驱动一直在电驱动系统中有着突出的地位。

**2. 异步电动机**

最近，技术的发展已将无换向器电动机推进到一个应用的新阶段。与有换向器直流电动机相比，无换向器电动机的优点包括高效率、高功率密度、低运行成本、高可靠性以及免维护。因而，当今无换向器电动机更受人们青睐。

作为一种驱动电动汽车的无换向器电动机，异步电动机得到了广泛应用。这是因为异步电动机的低成本、高可靠性和免维护运行。但是，异步电动机的传统控制，如变压变频（VVVF），不能提供所期望的性能。随着电力电子和微机时代的到来，异步电动机的磁场定向控制（FOC）原理，即矢量控制原理已被用来克服由于异步电动机非线性带来的控制难度。然而，这些采用矢量控制的电动汽车用异步电动机在轻载和限定恒功率工作区域内运行时，仍遭遇低效率的问题。

**3. 永磁同步电动机**

采用永磁体替代传统同步电动机的励磁绕组，永磁同步电动机可排除传统的电刷、集电环以及励磁绕组的铜耗。实际上，这些永磁同步电动机（图 5-3）因其正弦交变电流的供电和无刷结构，也被称作永磁无刷交流电动机或正弦波永磁无刷电动机。由于这类电动机本质上是同步电动机，它们可在正弦交流电源或脉宽调制电源（PWM 电源）下运行，而无须电子换向。这种电动机通常结构简单、成本低廉，但输出功率相对较低。与异步电动机类似，对高性能要求的应用场合，这种永磁同步电动机通常也

图 5-3 利莱-森玛永磁同步电动机

使用矢量控制。因为其固有的高功率密度和高效率，在电动汽车应用领域中，永磁同步电动机已被认为具有与异步电动机相竞争的巨大潜力。

**阅读材料：**

当永磁体安置在转子表面时，因永磁材料的磁导率与空气磁导率相似，故这种电动机特性如同隐极同步电动机。通过把永磁体嵌入转子的磁路中，此凸极将导致一个附加磁阻转矩，从而使电动机在恒功率运行时具有较宽的转速范围。另外，当利用转子的凸极性时，通过舍去励磁绕组或永磁体，就可制成同步磁阻电动机。

### 4. 永磁无刷直流电动机（BLDC）

实际上，通过转换永磁直流电动机（有刷电动机）定子和转子的位置，就可得到永磁无刷直流电动机（BLDC）。应该注意，"直流"这一术语可能会引起误解，因为它并不涉及直流电动机。事实上，这种电动机由矩形波交变电流供电，因此也称为矩形波永磁无刷电动机。这类电动机最明显的优点是排除了电刷，其另一优点是因电流与磁通间的正交相互作用，能产生大转矩。此外，这种无刷结构使电枢绕组可有更大的横截面。由于其整个结构的热传导有了改善，电负荷的增加会导致更高的功率密度。与永磁同步电动机不同，这种永磁无刷直流电动机通常配有转轴位置检测器。

### 5. 开关磁阻电动机（SRMs）

开关磁阻电动机（SRMs）已被公认在电动汽车应用中具有很大的潜力。基本上，开关磁阻电动机是由单组定子可变磁阻步进电动机直接衍生而来。开关磁阻电动机用于电动汽车的明显优点是其结构简单、制造成本低廉、转矩 - 转速特性好。尽管结构简单，但这并不意味着开关磁阻电动机的设计和控制也简单。由于其极尖处的高度磁饱和，以及磁极和槽的边缘效应，开关磁阻电动机的设计和控制既困难又精细。传统上，开关磁阻电动机运行，借助于转轴位置检测器检测转子与定子的相对位置。这些检测器通常容易因机械振动而受损，并对温度和尘埃敏感。因此，位置检测器的存在降低了开关磁阻电动机的可靠性，并限制了一些应用。最近，美国得克萨斯农工大学的电力电子与电机驱动研究所开发出了无位置检测器技术，该技术可保证从零转速到最大转速的平稳运行。

**阅读材料：**

对纯电动汽车来说，永磁电动机方案是较好的选择，主要有以下原因：电动汽车使用中电动机的工作范围宽、紧凑性好、质量小和噪声水平安静。

另外，对于一般用途（ISG、混合动力和纯电动）来说，由于其成本因素成为决定性因素，开关磁阻电动机与同步或者异步电动机相比较，开关磁阻电动机是较适用的，这是因为开关磁阻电动机的生产成本较低，并且如果考虑到较低的控制电流，开关磁阻电机对功率电子元件的要求也相对较低。各类电动机的技术比较见表 5 - 1。

然而，如果要使用此项非常有前景的技术还需面临以下两个重要挑战：
1) 控制噪声和振动。
2) 减小转矩波动。

表 5-1　各类电动机的技术比较（功率 30 kW，电压 DC 200 V，转矩 150 N·m）

| 项目 | 直流电动机 | 异步电动机 | 永磁同步电动机 | 励磁同步电动机 | 开关磁阻电动机 |
|---|---|---|---|---|---|
| 最大效率 | 好 | 较差 | 较差 | 好 | 中等 |
| 平均效率 | 一般 | 好 | 较差 | 好 | 好 |
| 最大转速 | 较差 | 好 | 好 | 好 | 好 |
| 电路维修成本 | 较差 | 较差 | 一般 | 一般 | 好 |
| 电机成本 | 较差 | | 一般 | 一般 | 较差 |
| 转矩/转速容量 | 一般 | 一般 | 较差 | 较差 | 好 |

## 5.2　电气结构

电动汽车中最常见的电气结构是蓄电池与驱动器直接相连，如图 5-4 所示。转换器和电机电压取决于电池，所有标准（性能和成本）不能达到要求。

图 5-4　直接驱动系统

另一种方案是在电池与驱动器之间加装一个 DC/DC 电压缓冲转换器（图 5-5），其主要功能是变频器 + 电动机的工作电压选择可以不受电池的限制（根据半导体工作电压的最优化、无源电子部件和电动机的特性来选择），同时也可以为电池解耦（有源滤波，减少对电容元件的要求）。

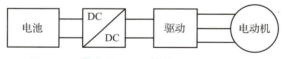

图 5-5　带有 DC/DC 转换器的电驱动系统

**阅读材料：**

在公路车辆上，使用电驱动电动机就意味着需要有车载电源的存在，即

1）在纯电动汽车上加装一个满足行驶需求的适当容量的电池。

2）在混合动力汽车上采用较小容量的电池，同时还需增程器（发动机和交流发电机组合）或者燃料电池。

上述简短说明使我们注意到大多数电动汽车会面临直流电与交流电的兼容性问题以及供电设备与用电设备之间的电压兼容性问题。公路车辆的这些兼容性问题的解决需要用到车载功率电子变换器，它的存在可以使我们消除上述操作中的不兼容问题。

## 5.3 功率电子变换器

### 5.3.1 功率电子元件

在纯电动汽车或者混合动力汽车上安装的静态逆变器是用来改变电功率表现形式的。其中，我们使用了功率半导体、二极管、晶闸管、绝缘栅双极型晶体管等。它们一般都在开或关的组合模式下，"换向"工作来降低能耗。

如果更加详细地研究功率半导体的工作原理，可以发现它们在"换向"工作时所起作用的不同，是这些部件的主要特征，我们可以根据以下来判断：

1）不可控部件，如二极管。

2）以晶闸管为代表的，只有在导通状态下才是可控部件。在任意时刻发送一个控制脉冲到触发器，这些半导体可以切换为导通状态，然而发截止指令到触发器时这些半导体并不能回到截止状态。若要重新回到截止状态，就要关掉电源或者消除负载的影响以将通过它们的电流截止，从而产生一个"自然的"电流换向。

3）当处于导通或者截止状态下均为可控部件。这种电流从截止到导通的变化是由电流脉冲发送到它们的控制电极引起的，从导通到截止的变化也是一样的。控制电极有以下几种：

① GTD 和其他 IGCT 触发器。

② IGBT 栅、MOS 场效应晶体管类型。

③ 双极型晶体管的基极。

在电动汽车中，最常用的半导体是二极管、IGBT 和 MOS，晶闸管只用在整流器中。

**阅读材料：**

在此工作模式下，半导体可以：

1）"导通"时相当于一个闭合的机械式开关，可以让电流通过，同时两端产生一个很小的电压降。

2）"截止"时相当于一个断开的机械式开关，两端电压稳定而电流几乎为零。

3）从"导通"状态非常快速地切换到"截止"状态，实际是电路中或者部件不同状态的变化，即上述的"换向"。

### 5.3.2 整流器

**1. 定义**

整流器是把交流电转换成直流电的能量转换装置。

**2. 简介**

有如下分类：

1）二极管整流器：这种转换器输出的直流电压与输入的交流电压有严格的函数关系。

2）晶闸管整流器：这种转换器可以连续改变输出终端的直流电压与输入端的交流电压间的关系，它是通过触发晶闸管的起始角进行调节的。

3）结合二极管与晶闸管的整流器。

4）晶闸管整流器集成模块，可以提高其性能并减小干扰。

5）由 IGBT 和二极管组合而成的 PWM 整流器，具有对输入控制源干扰较小的优点。

**3. 整流器在电动汽车上的应用**

在电动汽车上，整流器将公共电网或者与发动机相连的车载发电机提供的交流电转换为直流电，并储存在化学电池或者超级电容中。如果是由公共电网提供的电能，整流器系统可被视为单相结构的"充电器"。如果是由交流发电机提供的电能，整流器一般是三相模式。

### 5.3.3 斩波器

**1. 定义**

斩波器是将电压值固定的直流电，转换为电压值可变可调的直流电源的装置，输出电压不同于输入电压并且可以适应各接收器的所需电压（电动机、电池等）。

**2. 简介**

最简单的电子斩波器是由以下元器件组成的：

1）一个可控开关（如 IGBT、功率场效应晶体管、GTO 等）。

2）一个续流二极管。

3）无源部件、线圈和电容，这些用于提供斩波器的输入和输出电流滤波。它们的质量和体积在很大程度上取决于功率开关的操作频率。

4）控制装置。

**3. 斩波器在电动汽车上的应用**

斩波器在电动汽车上有两个必不可少的应用场合：

第一，它们在直流驱动电动机上是不可或缺的。

第二，它们需要将高压电调整为电池电压以适应电子辅助设备和 12V 工作电压（传感器、监测机构等）的使用。

实际上斩波器的使用可以使电动机电流保持在某个所需的数值，而且可确保电动机电压的逐步调整而不会有太大的损耗。使用斩波器可以调节电动机的转矩和转速，从而调节汽车的加速和制动。电动汽车制动过程包含了能量回收发电的功能。一般来说是电制动和机械制动联合工作的。当然，必须采取具体措施进行必要的控制和保护，例如，位于电池和斩波器之间的滤波器的使用就是为了确保电池和牵引电动机这两个电压源的解耦。

**阅读材料：**

实际上，我们不能将直流电动机与固定电压的电池直接相连，其中有以下两个原因：

1）这样做电动机的转矩和转速都将是固定的。

2）不管从电学的角度（过流）还是从机械的角度（过载）来看，这种电动机直接供电方式都是具有破坏性的。

但是如果将电流斩波器放在电源与直流电动机之间则可以解决上述两个问题，类似于在电源和电动机之间串联一个可变电阻，这样会给起动过程带来很大的改善。

###  5.3.4 逆变器

**1. 定义**

从直流电到交流电的转换器，称为逆变器。

**2. 逆变器在电动汽车上的应用**

在交流电动机驱动的电动汽车上，电动机是不能与电池组成的电源直接相连的。需要在电源和牵引电动机之间安装一个转换器（逆变器）来将直流电转换成交流电，以便能够对电动机在驱动和制动工况下的转矩和转速实施管理和控制。

有很多方法可以实现直流交流的转换，但公路车辆的特点和工业解决方案的合理性导致了人们更倾向于由六个双向开关结构组成的逆变器方案。这六个开关（由一个 IGBT 和二极管逆平行组合而成）根据标准 PWM 功能进行控制。这种类型的组合可以将电压源（电池）和采取电流控制方式的功率接收器（如异步电动机、同步绕线转子电动机、同步永磁电动机）相连。需要明确的是，在 PWM 逆变器中，输出电压是一系列不等宽的脉冲电压（矩形脉冲电压），但在一个周期内该波形的均值变化与正弦波等效。开关的断开和闭合通常都是由合适的电子控制设备实时给定的。

这种控制方法有两个重要的优势：

1）使输出的谐波电压具有较高的频率，有利于电压滤波。

2）可以改变输出电压的值。

# 第 6 章

## 电动汽车的充电系统

充电器的类型和充电设施的特性很大程度上依赖于车辆的类型及其用途。充电技术在提高电池性能方面起着关键作用。适当的电池充电技术能确保电池安全，增加系统可靠性。充电过程的主要目标是在不损坏电池的前提下，快速有效地充电。在电池充电时，要考虑到如下一些因素：
1）避免过度充电和不足充电。
2）快速充电不影响电池寿命。
3）保持良好品质的充电电流。

## 6.1 什么是电池的充电

车辆使用电池就是通过氧化/还原反应将存储在电极的化学能转化成电能。在充电时过程恰好相反。充电器施加比电池电压更高的电压和相反方向的电流。由充电器提供的电流能够被进行精确控制，以保证满足电池所要求的充电条件。

这需要一定数量的测量设备（包括测量电压、电流、温度的设备等）。这些测量设备受到充电器中电子控制装置的控制。最简单的系统只控制电池电压，只要电池电压不超过预设的阈值就保持恒定电流充电。电压超出上述的预设阈值时，电池端电压将保持恒定。在此之后，我们开始用一个较小的电流进行均衡充电。所有的电池制造商根据电池的工作情况推荐了特定的充电策略，以优化其产品的工作寿命。选择的充电策略是必须考虑电池后期维护要求的。在实践中，电池的优化管理就要求电池的制造商和车辆制造者紧密沟通以决定最佳的充电规范。

**阅读材料：**

充电程序的设定可以定义为以上提到的所有或部分控制并影响电池性能参数和使用寿命的总称。通过对充电进程的计算可以在实现整个电池组充电的安全性、有效性的同时对充电进程实时终止。实现由数以百计电池组成的高能电池组的电池充电需要考虑很多问题。因此为了控制这些性能参数，便需要有效精确可靠并安全的计算方法和备用的充电电路。在快进程充电时，由于高强度的电流涌入电池组产生了大量的热量，这时为了确保充电的安全性，便需要对其进行精确可靠的监控计算。为了完成这个复杂的任务，我们可以采用先进的控制技术，如模糊逻辑、监督控制和分散控制等。

## 6.2　不同类型的充电器

**1. 直接向电池充电的外部充电器**

这是适用于目前工业用动力电池的传统充电方法。工业上厂内车辆的电池组一般都是连接到这种类型的充电器上。

动力电池的传统充电方法是通过使用夹具或低压连接器将外部充电器与电池直接连接。在 20 世纪初，第一款电动汽车也正是采用了这种方法来实现充电的，并且直至今天仍然是厂内自用货车及其他工程车辆充电的首选。

**2. 车载充电器**

对于城市电动汽车，我们更希望用车载充电器，它可通过任意可以度量电量的电表和带功能保护的插座取电，如图 6 – 1 所示。

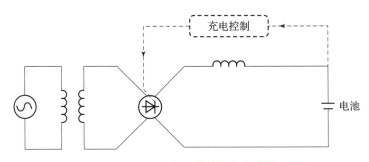

图 6 – 1　使用 50 Hz 变压器的车载充电器示意图

对于顾客来说，这种解决方案的便利性在很大程度上弥补了该方案增加了车辆重量和提高了购车成本的缺点。此外，该充电器与电池是高度兼容的。如果有了这类充电器，那么原有的电动车外部充电器将会被更大、更重的快速充电设备所取代。

这种类型的充电器受到的主要制约因素如下：

1）体积尺寸。
2）工作电网和电池之间的绝缘。
3）吸收电流的形态。
4）民用插座（已标准化处理的）。
5）民用插座墙上取电可用的最大功率。

在今天充电器都是开关元件控制类型的系统（PWM，脉冲宽度调制），如图 6 – 2 所示。目前电子充电器的组成部分有：

1）电网侧电流的调节器（整流器）。
2）功率振荡器。
3）高频变压器和整流器。

未来充电器的发展方向是功率增加、体积减小和成本降低。

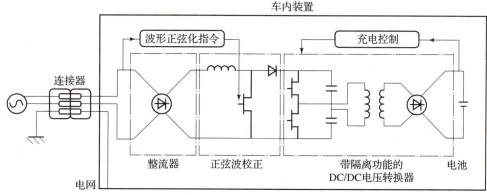

图 6-2 PWM 充电系统

### 3. 快速充电

快速充电可以在 20 min 内将电池最大存储能量的 80% 充入电池,这需要一个高功率的外部电力系统（20 kV·A 和 400 A）。

### 4. 车载快速充电

车载快速充电的物理限制如下:

1) 蓄电池允许的最大电流。
2) 不同容量下的快速充电电流的限制（在 50%~80%）。
3) 不同电池的类型的限制。
4) 通过连接器允许的最大电流的限制。

充电器所考虑的电路方面的因素有:50 Hz 变压器和高频变压器、三相电流、功率因数补偿。此外,车辆和充电站之间需要特定的连接协议。

**阅读材料:**

在电动汽车的数量超过内燃机汽车数量的那个年代,人们通过安装在车库外部的充电器直接完成充电。工业应用中的动力电池充电主要依靠连接到电网的外部充电器。充电设备和电池之间的连接是通过双插的特定连接器和两根软导线来完成的。除了两个高功率触头,连接器也包括用于保护电线的地线和为实现额外控制的附属设备的触头。

这种充电的方法最适合用于汽车车队和小型高尔夫球车。这个系统（图 6-3）简单而实用,且有很强的稳健性,比较适用于在工业电动车辆基础上发展起来的电动汽车开展的试验性应用。

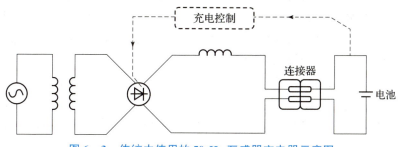

图 6-3 传统中使用的 50 Hz 互感器充电器示意图

### 5. 感应充电器

通过感应充电，车辆与充电器之间无须物理接触便能够将能量传递到车辆。能量是由可分离的一次线圈和二次线圈组成的变压器形成的磁场传输的。尽管可以通过电网工作频率（50 Hz 或者 60 Hz）的变压器进行能量的交换，但是使用的更普遍的是高频振荡电路，以便能够减小变压器线圈的体积。事实上，传递功率的大小与通过变压器气隙的电感（场强度）、转换介质和频率成正比关系。因此，我们经常会提高系统的工作频率和增加电磁场功率，以便能够减小线圈的体积。高频感应充电器的工作原理与前面已经说明的车载电子充电器相似，并且原理图也几乎相同。

图 6-4 可以分为两个部分：

1) 电网侧整流器，功率因数校正器和高频振荡器被安装在地面设备上。
2) 车辆和充电器之间的连接通过非接触式的变压器（这样也不会有接触电阻了）。
3) 高频整流器和充电检测系统被安装在车辆上。

值得注意的是，该图中需要的一个用于信息交换的协议和快速充电器的情况类似。

注：50 Hz 整流器供电的示意图仅作为示例给出。提供交流电的功能还可以通过其他各种方式（三相电流供电、无源滤波等）来实现。我们也可以使用其他类型的高频振荡器。

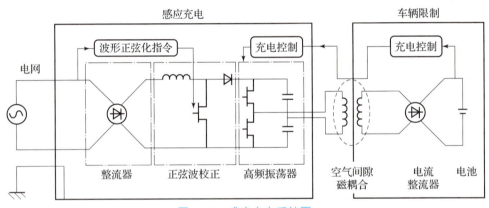

图 6-4　感应充电系统图

一个自动连接式感应充电案例如图 6-5 所示（英文图示，中文不显示。）

### 6. 无线充电

无线充电涉及在更远的距离进行功率和能量的传递。它与感应充电不同，后者包括一个一次绕组和二次绕组靠得很近的变压器。尽管感应充电能够消除直接的电气接触，但仍需要插座、电线以及感应耦合器的物理接触。插座和电缆的磨损和破损也会造成危险。

无线充电则可以将插座和电线一并去掉。在这种方案中，驾驶员可以将车拉到一个专门设计的停车场内，汽车的电池自动充电，无须任何插头和电线，如图 6-6 所示。这种方案为电动汽车电池充电提供了一种最安全的方法。

为实现无线能量传递，已经进行了各种实验。其中最有应用前景的技术是使用电磁谐振，如图 6-7 所示。在这种设置中，有一对天线，其中一天线放在停车场作为发射装置，另一个天线放在车内作为接收装置。两个天线被设计成在可控频率内谐振。极限值为功率传输水平和频率，后者取决于两天线之间大的间隔。

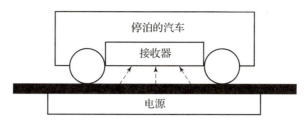

图 6-6 在停车地板上对 PHEV/EV 进行无线充电

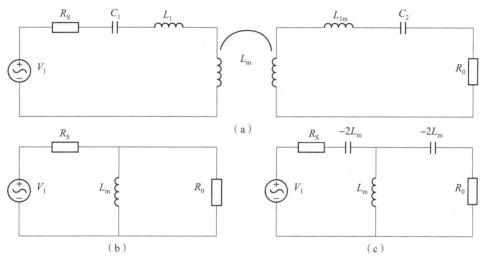

图 6-7 基于电磁谐振的无线充电电路
(a) 电路; (b) 谐振条件 1 下的等效电路; (c) 谐振频率条件 2 下的等效电路

## 6.3 充电效率

与所有的自然现象一样,充放电过程不能达到 100% 的效率。因为该化学过程是不完全可逆的,并且电池具有内部阻抗会耗散损失一部分的能量。因此,我们从下面两种效率进行讨论。

1) 电池的电效率。这是由电池放电释放的能量和在充电过程中,恢复电池的初始状态,由充电器提供给电池的能量之比。这里的能量值用瓦("电压与电流"的乘积)的积分给出,一般是在电池充电和放电时,在电池桩头测得。这个值比电池法拉第效率低,某些铅酸电池这个值为 70%,而在最佳条件下使用的一些采用了新技术的电池可达到 95%。

2) 电池充电系统的效率。它是通过测量由所述电池放电所能释放的能量和为恢复电池的初始充电状态而用充电器充电过程中电网所提供的总能量之比。这个系数考虑到"电池 + 充电器"系统中所有的相关损失。充电器的效率非常依赖于所采用的技术和它们的充电策略。因此,这是总效率中的关键因素。

**阅读材料:**

法拉第效率:它等于放电过程中电池提供的电量和充电过程中充至开始放电前的初始状态所需的电量之比。制造商一般会标明这个系数。新的锂离子电池、镍-氢电池该值可以接近于 1。而铅酸电池和开式镍镉电池会稍微低一些，其需要较长的过载充电过程。

## 6.4 充电的安全问题

**1. 标准**

电动汽车跨越了两个领域。在行驶的时候它是汽车，必须遵守汽车行业的所有规范；当充电时，它也作为电气设备，必须遵守相应的法规和标准。它不像家庭设备那么简单，因为它需要经受恶劣的环境考验，并且必须满足比家庭设备更严格的标准。20 世纪 90 年代相关人员就对充电过程中有关电气安全的问题展开了广泛讨论，并制定了一系列充电设备的具体标准。

这些标准成功地形成了共同的文本，可以为遍及全球各地的各类电网在实践中采用。这是一系列国际交流活动的结果。实际上，各国在接入电网及其保护方法上是有很大不同的。

**2. 氢气排放**

法规要求，在正常充电的情况下电池不得排出氢气。

**3. 各种充电用的插座**

16A 和 32A 民用插座已经标准化。

**4. 标准电源插头**

在正常充电时，车辆上的插头与民用 16A 插座对接，也可以与特定的终端快速充电设备对接。在车辆工程中，集成是一个重要方面。这些插头已经被开发出来和标准化了。

**5. 公共场所充电站**

例如，在法国有许多可用的充电点（图 6 – 8 和图 6 – 9 英文图示，中文不显示），例如地下充电点，在居民区充电，通过标准插头取电。在公共场所建立充电站面临的困难如下：

1）充电成本分析。
2）安装成本。
3）税务上的费用。
4）由于税务而引起的其他困难。

**阅读材料：**

区分不同充电模式的标准

这个标准中，四种直接充电（使用连接器）的模式被定义。充电可以在家里，在公司车间或在大街上完成。这种定义是有实际意义的，比如，在美国国内的民用电压只有 110 V，但电动车辆具有更高的性能和要求较高的车载能源（满足美国的电动续驶里程需要，车载电池要有 30 kW·h 的能量）。而在法国，电动汽车其包含的电池容量较小（只有 11 kW·h），电网的电压反而较高（有 230 V）。

## 6.5 电池的充电方式

总体上说，充电是将能量返还给电池的过程，也就是能量恢复。不同的化学物质可能需要完全不同的充电方式，这点是很重要的。其他一些影响选择充电方式的因素有电池容量、充电时间等。这里将会提到最普遍使用的技术。

### 6.5.1 恒压充电

当一个恒定电压输入电池组时，这便是恒压充电。这个恒压电压是由制造商提供的一个预置值。这种充电方式的充电过程大多会伴随有一个限流电路，尤其是在刚开始充电的阶段，电池相比于其自身电池容量能够很容易地获得高比率的电流。限流值主要取决于电池容量。这种充电方式通常用于铅酸电池，也可用于锂离子电池。在充电的过程中，尤其是在充电的第一阶段，使用限流器可以避免充电过程中电池过热现象。

### 6.5.2 恒流充电

恒流充电方式，即对电池进行恒定电流充电。适用于这种充电方式的电池在充电时温度较低而且伴随有独立的纹波电流，在相关书籍中将这种充电方式缩写为CC。该充电方式利用控制工程技术改变电池电压以用于充电，比如用电流控制模式来维持电流的恒定。分割型比率电流是利用CC充电方式来实现不同比率的电流，这项技术在不同的充电状态下是基于SOC、充电时间、充电电压或三者综合一起考虑的。因此，这便能够更加准确有效地平衡荷电状态，同时也能够防止电池的过电压充电。

### 6.5.3 锥电流充电

这种充电方式适用于不受限的电流源电路。它通过变压器提供相比于电池电压的一个较高的输出电压来实现充电，同时该电路中应串入一个电阻对充电电池进行限流。同样二极管也可以接入电路用以保证单向能量的流入。这种充电方式使得电流开始时以满载比率流入充电电路并随着电池的充电过程而递减。这种充电技术仅适用于密封铅酸（SLA）电池。

### 6.5.4 脉冲充电

这种充电方法应用短时电流或电压脉冲技术进行充电，同时电流或电压的平均值可以通过改变脉冲宽度来进行控制。脉冲充电方式有两个显著优势：①它能够减少充电时间；②这项技术可以大幅度提高电池的寿命周期。两个脉冲信号之间的间隔称为时间间隙，它在脉冲充电进程中起着重要作用。在这段时间间隙里，电池内部会发生化学反应并维持一定的稳定性。由于这种充电方式可以高效地利用电流和电压，所以它可以减少在电极处发生非预期化学反应的可能性，例如气体的形成和结晶。这两种化学反应是缩短电池寿命周期的重要因素。

### 6.5.5 反射充电

在充电过程中会有一些气泡出现在电极上,尤其是在快速充电过程中这些气泡会变大。这种现象称为"打嗝效应",该效应可以通过应用较短的放电脉冲或负脉冲来实现。例如可以在相比于电池充电时间较短的时间内使电池短路用以限流。这段时间通常是充电休止期内脉冲时间的2~3倍。这种充电方式可以使去极化的电池加快稳化过程,从而加快整个充电过程。此技术也被称为"打嗝充电"或"负脉冲充电"。

### 6.5.6 浮压充电

对于一些能源设备来说,当充电进程完成且电池完全充电时,需要电池长时间保持100%的荷电状态以备多次使用。不间断电源(UPS)便是这样一个能源供应元件,电池可在其能源供应下始终保持满电状态。然而由于电池的自放电特性,一段时间内电池会自行放电,比如,它们每月可能会耗电20%或30%。为了补偿电池的自放电,需要持久地向电池施加恒定电压。该恒定电压值是基于电池的化学稳定性和环境温度确定的,并将其称为"浮动电压"。锂离子和锂聚合物电池不建议使用这项技术,而且每天频繁使用的EV/PHEV也不需要使用该技术。

阅读材料1:

当要根据电池型号进行充电时,那么就要选择一个电压预置值。例如,锂离子电池的合理电压值是4.200 V±50 mV,所以整个电池组的当前值等于串联电池的数目乘以该电压值。由于过电压会损坏电池而欠电压会导致部分充电从而逐渐降低电池的使用寿命,所以设定一个准确的预设点是必要的。这样一来,充电电路便要接入控制器以补偿由于时间推移而引起充电源和负载的变化。这个充电电路根据输入和输出的电压比设定一个简单的降压、升压或降/升压的拓扑结构。当电池达到预设电压值时,此时电池处于待机模式以准备后续使用。这段待机时间不会很长而且这个数值是由制造商来建议限定的。

阅读材料2:

有时为了提高废旧电池的利用率,CC充电方式由于有着高比率电流和低耗时的优点也可用于延长废旧电池的使用寿命,但这种充电过程需要严谨的程序设定和谨慎的处理。镍-镉和镍-氢电池可用CC充电方式进行充电,但镍氢电池很容易由于过度充电而损坏,因此在充电期间它们应进行精确的实时监测。

## 6.6 充电的终止方式

在充电过程中,决定何时终止充电是很重要的,主要原因有两个:一是避免欠充电,即确保电池完全充电,而不是只充入一部分,这样可以保证电池容量的全部利用;二是避免过充电，特别是在高能量密度的锂基电池的情况下，这是非常危险的。如果充电不能及时终止，那么电池的过充电会导致电池的过度放气。尤其是在液体电解质电池中，过度放出的气体会增加每个电池的体积，而这种情况是刚性电池组所不能够承受的。还有一个问题是电池的过热，尤其是锂基电池。由于锂是一种化学性质非常活跃的材料，并极易在空气中与氧气结合发生反应，所以它很容易引燃从而引发整个电池组的爆炸，而这个化学反应发生的唯一条件便是足够的热量。

不同终止标准的选择决定了不同的终止方式。充电进程中对终止充电形式的选择取决于不同的因素，如能源供应设备和电池的使用环境。常规终止方式如下。

### 6.6.1 时间

设置电池的充电时间可以作为其中的一个最简单的方法。它主要用作快速充电或者为特定型号电池常规充电的后备充电。这种方法既简单又节约成本，但由于电池容量会随着使用次数的增加和时间的推移而减少，所以需要重新设置充电时间。这样一来，便可以避免旧电池由于过度充电产生的老化问题。

### 6.6.2 电压

正如之前所提到的，电压可作为一个终止充电的因素，即当电池电压达到一个特定值时可以终止充电进程。但此方法也存在一些不精确性，由于精确的开路电压是在电池充电后断电的那段时间获得的，发生在电池内部的化学反应需要一段时间来稳定，在稳定的那段时间内可以得到精确的开路电压。尽管这种充电方式存在不精确性，但这种充电方式已经广泛使用了。此外，该技术通常与恒流技术一起使用，这样可以避免电池过热。

### 6.6.3 电压降（dV/dT）

当含有镍镉化学元素的电池进行恒流充电时，电池电压会达到满充电状态点，在这之后电压会逐渐下降。这是由于氧气积聚在电池内部，电压降这一变化是显著的，所以电压与时间的导数可以用来测量是否过充电。当导数为负值时说明电池已经过了满充电状态而且温度会开始上升。在这一状态点之后的充电方式可以切换到涓流充电、浮压充电，或彻底终止充电。

### 6.6.4 电流

如果在充电的最后几个阶段采用恒压的充电方式，那么当电池达到满充电状态时，电流会开始减小。预设电流值可以设定为如 $C/10$ 率，这样当充电电流低于该值时充电进程将会终止。

### 6.6.5 温度

一般情况下，在充电过程中当电池温度上升到一定程度时，如果温度额外升高，那么说明电池已经过充电了。同时，温度传感器的使用大大增加了该系统的成本。然而，对于一些像镍氢的化学作用，不建议使用电压降的方式，这是因为电压降在电池达到满充电状态点后不是很显著，不能将其作为参考依据。这样一来，温度的升高便可作为衡量电池过充电的优良指标。

**阅读材料：**

充电的程序设定

正如之前提到的，铅酸电池虽然已经拥有了成熟的技术和基础设施，但它仍然面临300～400个循环这种较差的使用寿命。由于它具有成本低和良好实用性的优点，目前仍然有很多关于它的研究，希望借此提高它的使用寿命。这种化学进程有一个统一的系统设定，如图6-10所示。

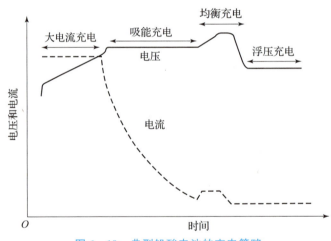

图6-10 典型铅酸电池的充电策略

根据应用，它包括三个或四个不同的阶段。

其中第一阶段有一个预设的恒流值施加到充电电池组中，这样可以加快充电进程。由于电池电压在此阶段随着荷电状态的升高而增大，所以这一阶段也被称为"大电流充电"的阶段。当达到预设的最大电压值时，便终止第一阶段。这些预设值都依据生产厂家提供的数据表。第二阶段称为"吸能充电"阶段，即向电池组施加一个恒定电压。在此阶段原本的大电流值会逐渐减小直到电池达到预设的 $C$ 倍率值，同时由于各个电池互不平衡的化学特性，每个电池虽然大致会充上一定电量，但其充电量是不等的。因此在这一阶段中会有一个相比于恒定电压较高的电压施加到电池组以平衡其内部的各个电池。这一阶段便被称为"均衡充电"阶段。同样，这种均衡状态也可以用之前提到的其他技术来实现。经过预设的充电时间后，充电器为了使电池保持在一个合适的备用待机状态，会向电池施加一个较低的恒压值。这就是所谓的"浮压充电"阶段，同时这一阶段也可以根据实际的应用程序进行省略。

# 参 考 文 献

[1] [美] 爱塞尼,等. 现代电动汽车、混合动力电动汽车和燃料电池车:基本原理、理论和设计 [M]. 倪光正,倪培宏,熊素铭,等译. 北京:机械工业出版社,2010.

[2] [美] 侯赛因. 纯电动及混合动力汽车设计基础 [M]. 林程,译. 北京:机械工业出版社,2012.

[3] [美] 米春亭,等. 混合动力电动汽车原理及应用前景 [M]. 赵志国,等译. 北京:机械工业出版社,2014.

[4] [法] 约瑟夫·贝雷塔. 电动汽车及其驱动技术 [M]. 赵克刚,译. 北京:机械工业出版社,2015.

[5] [美] 威廉森. 插电式混合动力与纯电动汽车的能量管理策略 [M]. 王典,译. 北京:机械工业出版社,2016.

[6] [美] 米春亭,张希. 车辆能量管理:建模、控制与优化 [M]. 北京:机械工业出版社,2013.

[7] [英] 约翰·哈代. 电动汽车实用技术 [M]. 徐永,等译. 北京:机械工业出版社,2013.

[8] Mehrdad Ehsani Write, Modern Electric, Hybrid Electric and Fuel Cell Electric Vehicles Fundamentals, Theory and Design [M]. Boca Raton:CRC Press,2009.

[9] Lqbal Husain Write. Electric and Hybrid Vehicles Design Fundamentals [M]. Boca Raton:CRC Press,2010.

[10] Chris Mi Write. Hybrid Electric Vehicles:Principles and Applications with Practical Perspectives [M]. HoboKen:Wiley. 2011.

[11] Joseph Beretta Write. Automotive Electricity:Electric Drives [M]. HoboKen:Wiley,2010.

[12] Sheldon S. Williamson Write. Energy Management Strategies for Electric and Plug–in Hybrid Electric Vehicles [M]. Berlin:Springer,2013.

[13] Xi Zhang,Chris Mi Write. Vehicle Power Management:Modeling,Control and Optimization [M]. Berlin:Springer,2011.

[14] Mr John Hardy Write. ICE Free:Electric vehicle technology for builders and converters [M]. New York:Tovey Books,2012.